The Fluent Mundo

J. S. Leonard

C. E. Wharton

The Fluent Mundo

WALLACE STEVENS
AND THE STRUCTURE
OF REALITY

THE UNIVERSITY OF GEORGIA PRESS
ATHENS

Paperback edition, 2016
© 1988 by the University of Georgia Press
Athens, Georgia 30602
www.ugapress.org
All rights reserved
Designed by Betty P. McDaniel
Set in Trump Mediaeval

Most University of Georgia Press titles are
available from popular e-book vendors.

Printed digitally

The Library of Congress has cataloged
the hardcover edition of this book as follows:
Leonard, J. S. (James S.)
   The fluent mundo : Wallace Stevens and the
structure of reality / J. S. Leonard, C. E. Wharton.
xiv, 208 p. ; 23 cm.
Bibliography: p. 193–200.
Includes index.
ISBN 0-8203-0971-0 (alk. paper)
   1. Stevens, Wallace, 1879–1955—Criticism and
interpretation.   I. Wharton, C. E. (Christine E.)   II. Title.
PS3537.T4753 Z6748 1988
  811'.52   87-19151

Paperback ISBN 978-0-8203-3982-5

For J. W. L.

... We seek
Nothing beyond reality. Within it,

Everything ...
—WALLACE STEVENS

Contents

LIST OF ABBREVIATIONS viii

PREFACE ix

CHAPTER I
A New Knowledge of Reality 1

CHAPTER II
The Vocabulary of Romanticism 38

CHAPTER III
The ABC of Being 59

CHAPTER IV
The Phenomena of Perception 83

CHAPTER V
Sun and Symbol 103

CHAPTER VI
The Marriage of the Rest 140

NOTES 167

LIST OF WORKS CITED 193

INDEX 201

Abbreviations

Works by Stevens are cited in the text as follows:

CP	*The Collected Poems of Wallace Stevens.* New York: Knopf, 1954.
Letters	*Letters of Wallace Stevens.* Edited by Holly Stevens. New York: Knopf, 1966.
NA	*The Necessary Angel: Essays on Reality and the Imagination.* New York: Knopf, 1951.
OP	*Opus Posthumous.* Edited by Samuel French Morse. New York: Knopf, 1957.
Palm	*The Palm at the End of the Mind: Selected Poems and a Play by Wallace Stevens.* Edited by Holly Stevens. New York: Vintage, 1972.
Souvenirs	*Souvenirs and Prophecies: The Young Wallace Stevens.* By Holly Stevens. New York: Knopf, 1977.

Quotations from these works are reprinted by permission of Alfred A. Knopf, Inc.

Preface

Our subtitle, "Wallace Stevens and the Structure of Reality," will surely disquiet readers widely familiar with Stevens criticism. The route to the poetry via imagination/reality is well-worn, to say the least. But as current critical theory (and Stevens' poetics) insists, the more clichéd an idea becomes, the more it needs to be reconsidered. Our examination of Stevens' poetry is not intended to establish preferential adherence to either imagination or reality, or to encourage, given conventional usages of the terms, an acceptance of his testimony favoring their "interpendence" (NA, 27). We propose not so much to resolve the standard issue surrounding the duality as to consider the casting (and recasting) of the question itself. In other words, we will interrogate the critical vocabulary of imagination/reality—determining the degree to which the terms stand up under close scrutiny and at what point they collapse beneath the weight of a given critical approach and the evidence of the poetry.

Samuel Johnson says in his "Preface to Shakespeare" that a "great part of the labour of every writer is only the destruction of those that went before him. . . . The chief desire of him that comments an authour, is to show how much other commentators have corrupted and obscured him" (7:99). And in the Socratic tradition of dialogical pursuit of ideas, this is as it should be. Ours is a contentious book. Pursuit of Stevens' elusive terminology necessitates, along the way, some criticism of nearly every major study of his poetry. We first investigate various forms of the general supposition (prime advocates: Roy Harvey Pearce, Helen Regueiro) that Stevens' later poetry denies the value of imagination for the sake of an unobscured view of the "things themselves." Then, turning to the dialectically opposite, we weigh the argument(s) for Stevens-as-Romantic (leading proponents: Joseph Riddel, Harold Bloom, James Baird, Helen Vendler). In the wake of the opposition of these extremes, we explore a significant third critical development, heavily dependent on twentieth-century Continental philosophy: that in the later poetry Stevens wants to effect a difficult ontological revelation/experience associated with his use of the word "being" (principal spokesmen: J. Hillis Miller, Thomas J. Hines, Richard Macksey). Finally, we address criticism that regards Stevens' work as explicitly Husserlian or Heideggerian (chief perpetrators: Hines, Macksey, Glauco Cambon, Paul Bové). Demarcation of the limits (in terms of the poetry and relevant philosophical material) of these critical approaches does not deny their value: adequate appreciation includes a survey of boundaries. But since the critics with whom we deal are already eloquent in behalf of their own methods and conceptions, our final emphasis falls more on limitations than on strengths.

These dismantlings of critical structure clear the space for a perspective on Stevens somewhat different from, but in company with, those of recent books confirming his place in modernist thought and art. Among such books are *Wallace Stevens: The Poetics of Modernism*, edited by Albert Gelpi; Glen MacLeod's *Wallace Stevens and Company: The Harmonium Years, 1913–1923*; Peter Brazeau's *Parts of a World: Wallace Stevens Remembered*; and Milton Bates' *Wallace Stevens: A Mythology of Self*. Our explications develop out of, and attempt to circumscribe, Stevens' philosophic/aesthetic/poetic relation to Nietzsche and Cassirer—two Continental thinkers whose differences have tended to obscure regions of similarity.

Stevens' interest in Nietzschean philosophy has been acknowledged by previous criticism, but we delineate a Nietzschean influence more direct and pervasive than has been recognized, showing that Nietzsche's imagery permeates Stevens' poetry and certain Nietzschean assumptions are fundamental to main themes, or figurations, in the poetry from beginning to end—not just for the period (early 1940s) sometimes identified as Stevens' Nietzschean phase. Following Stevens, we rediscover Nietzsche (particularly the later and increasingly flamboyant Nietzsche of *The Gay Science* and *Thus Spoke Zarathustra*) as poetic precursor even more than philosophical influence. Stevens pictures Nietzsche (in "Imagination as Value") "walk[ing] in the Alps in the caresses of reality" (*NA*, 150) but also speaks (in "A Collect of Philosophy") of Nietzsche's "poetic way of writing" (*OP*, 184) and remarks that "the formidable poetry of Nietzsche . . . ultimately leaves us with the formidable poetry of Nietzsche and little more" (*OP*, 187). Without arguing this last point, we trace Stevens' poetic incorporation/transformation of such Nietzschean tropes as the "three metamorphoses of the spirit"—for Stevens a powerfully suggestive figure of the essentiality of change.

Cassirer, our second (but not less important) point of comparison, is the twentieth-century thinker who, we maintain, most profoundly and comprehensively articulates the complicated tenets that enable Stevens to see the history of belief and culture as a history of the "imagination"—an understanding intrinsic to Stevens' pivotal notion of the "supreme fiction." As a result, Cassirer's "phenomenological" philosophy of symbolic forms offers a valuable counterpoint to Husserlian or Heideggerian interpretive instruments.

The Nietzschean/Cassirerian reading of Stevens reflects the nature of the book's joint authorship, which unites a literary background with a philosophical. But within the literary-critical context, we advocate perspectives in which the philosophical, however central, remains an illuminating element and the poetry the centrally illuminated. We have also tried to represent all periods of Stevens' poetry—from "Sunday Morning" and "Peter Quince at the Clavier" to "Of Mere Being" and

"As You Leave the Room"—with greatest attention to the major poems, especially "Notes toward a Supreme Fiction," "An Ordinary Evening in New Haven," and "The Rock." If, in the last analysis, we rely more on the late poetry than the early, this recognizes both that our most relevant interlocutors concern themselves primarily with the later period (and should be met on their own terms) and that in the later poetry Stevens' philosophical vision becomes sharpest and most consistent. However, we would (and do) contend that in clearly important ways the Stevens of the later writings is the Stevens of the earlier—a stance which takes issue with the underlying assumption shared by Miller, Hines, Pearce, Regueiro, and others that the later work reveals a poetics fundamentally different from the earlier.

This contention directs us in a generally nonchronological path through the poetry, as to both the strict sequence of the poems themselves and the historical/biographical context of contemporaneous events. Biographical chronology finds its value in exposing correlational aspects between Stevens' poetizing and the detailed circumstances of time, place, etc.; but the Stevens we want to flesh out is the essential Stevens-as-author-figure, who, though inevitably a "fiction" (in Stevens' positive sense of the word), will display a coherence and consistency within which seemingly disparate poems can be seen as a "body of poetry." Our inquiry coalesces around the progression of critical notions outlined above and, in keeping with our understanding of Stevens' consistency, draws from all periods of his writings. However, when earliness, lateness, or coincidence with some other poem or comment seems significant, we indicate the date or period (as appropriate).

Despite our philosophic interest, we do not intend this to be a comprehensive analysis of philosophical influences and affinities in Stevens—of which genre Frank Doggett's *Stevens' Poetry of Thought*, though twenty years old, is still the standard example. We rather conspicuously do not deal with Santayana, with whom Stevens was personally acquainted, and say little about William James, who, like Santayana, was a teacher at Harvard when Stevens was there. There is no question that, as we do indicate, Stevens was interested in James' notion of the "will to believe" or that his view of the relation of aesthetics to religion has something in common with Santayana's. But these are matters that have been worked over thoroughly by others, and our abiographical strategy makes them inessential to this present study (although parenthetical references are made to the recent comparisons of Stevens and James in Margaret Peterson's *Wallace Stevens and the Idealist Tradition* and David La Guardia's *Advance on Chaos: The Sanctifying Imagination of Wallace Stevens*). Ours is a specific philosophical and literary perspective which, ultimately relegating even the uniquely Stevensian imagination/reality "complex" to the "marginal" status Stevens apparently intended, shows the "body of poetry" in the light of what he referred to as his "central theme" (*Letters*, 820): the fictional/experiential sufficiency of the "supreme fiction."

While avoiding the rigorously chronological, we find it useful to trace the way a phrase, thought, or image seems to linger in Stevens' mind for many years—as with the central phrase "supreme fiction," which occurs rather casually in "A High-Toned Old Christian Woman" in 1922, then resurfaces twenty years later in "Notes toward a Supreme Fiction" as the basis for a more definite and much more extensive elaboration. Likewise, the figuration of the "palm" appears in "A High-Toned Old Christian Woman," returns in 1945 as the emblem of description in "Description without Place," and makes a final appearance as habitat for the "gold-feathered bird" in "Of Mere Being" (1955). We find the course of such particulars to be the chronology most relevant to Stevens' poetry, revealing a Stevens whose philosophical point of view, inextricably intertwined with the images that embody it, follows in a continuous fashion throughout.

Our appreciation to the Citadel Development Foundation for its continued funding of our Stevens research, to the Henry E. Huntington Library for a Huntington Library

Fellowship in support of our use of the Huntington's Wallace Stevens Collection, to the Southern Regional Education Board for travel grants to examine Stevens materials at other libraries, and to the following libraries and their staffs for their cooperation in making Stevens materials available to us: Huntington Library, San Marino, California; Daniel Library, The Citadel; Rockefeller and John Hay Libraries, Brown University; Watkinson Library, Trinity College; Baker Memorial Library, Dartmouth College; Special Collections and Rare Books, University of Massachusetts at Amherst; Houghton Library, Harvard University; Beinecke Rare Book and Manuscript Library, Yale University; Princeton University Library. We acknowledge, with appreciation, permission from Alfred A. Knopf, Inc., to quote from the works of Wallace Stevens, permission from the Henry E. Huntington Library to quote from and refer to unpublished materials in the Huntington's Wallace Stevens Collection, and permission from *Texas Studies in Literature and Language* to use (in altered form) material drawn from our article "Wallace Stevens as Phenomenologist," 26 (1984): 331–61.

We are, of course, indebted to Stevens scholarship generally for providing a rich context for discovery and debate. We owe a special debt of gratitude to the following colleagues and friends: the late Peter Brazeau for valuable suggestions, Mark Spilka and B. J. Leggett for their counsel and considerable support, James Schevill and Albert Cook for their comments, Henry W. Johnstone, Jr. for his Socratic example, Frank Doggett and Dorothy Emerson for their encouragement and insightful responses to our manuscript, Betsy Postow, Alistair Duckworth, and the late Jay J. Kim for their interest and encouragement, George Meenaghan for helping us through administrative tangles, and Malcolm Call, Nancy Holmes, and Ellen Harris for their considerate and skillful assistance in editorial matters. And finally, we wish to thank our colleagues at The Citadel, especially E. F. J. Tucker, for their interest and support during the course of our work on Stevens.

The Fluent Mundo

CHAPTER I

A New Knowledge of Reality

"We keep coming back and coming back / To the real: to the hotel instead of the hymns / That fall upon it out of the wind" (*CP*, 471). Lines like these set the tone for much Stevens criticism of the past two decades. The critic, like Stevens' protagonist, seeks the "poem of pure reality" (*CP*, 471). The poetic interplay—a dialectic of the imaged and the real—is not resolved in the language of the poem but dissolved, simply, by an "eye made clear of uncertainty, with the sight / Of simple seeing, without reflection" (*CP*, 471). If we follow this view, imagination, at most, takes on "a nocturnal shine" (*CP*, 473). The reflected light of the imagination is devalued in favor of direct intuitive perception.

This "decreative" approach reacts against early studies—William Van O'Connor's *The Shaping Spirit* (1950) and Robert Pack's *Wallace Stevens: An Approach to His Poetry and Thought* (1958), for example—that see Stevens as a celebrant of poetic imagination, the poet exalting poetic acts, and to later books by Riddel and Doggett that explore philosophical and poetical assumptions defining the creative/aesthetic dimension in Stevens' thought. Setting the opposing standard, *The Act of the Mind* (1965), essays edited by Pearce and Miller, and Pearce's *The Continuity of American Poetry* (1961) find Stevens an ingenious skeptic of the imagination's validity—a prophet of postmodernism, writing at the limits of language, exposing, with metaphorical ironies, the inadequacy of metaphorical imagination: "The great cat must stand potent in the sun" (*CP*, 473). Poetic language is turned back by the opacity of the external and the ferocity of the subconscious internal. The extreme of this view, developed in Regueiro's *The Limits of Imagination* (1976), sees the imagination wholly discredited in the later poetry: Stevens, to overcome subjective obscurations, performs various mental and linguistic gymnastics that thwart the imagination's insidious chromatisms, making possible a momentary revelation of "the things themselves." The poet-as-critic becomes a de-creative creator inscribing an anti-poetic poetry.

Stevens' own essay "The Relations between Poetry and Painting" supplies the central terminology for decreative criticism:

Simone Weil in *La Pesanteur et la Grâce* has a chapter on what she calls decreation. She says that decreation is making pass from the created to the uncreated, but that destruction is making pass from the created to nothingness. Modern reality is a reality of decreation, in which our revelations are not the revelations of belief, but the precious portents of our own powers. The greatest truth we could hope to discover, in whatever field we discovered it, is that man's truth is the final resolution of everything. (*NA*, 174–75)

This passage, Stevens' only reference to decreation, seems to convey a double message: decreation makes "pass . . . to the uncreated," yet in doing so, it reveals "man's truth [as] the final resolution. . . ." If we stress its last lines, the passage hardly marks a shift toward the real-as-such. But as attached to "uncreated," decreation appears to advocate a counter-creativity, the destruction of poetic structures for the sake of simple disclosure; and this appearance has directed "decreationist" interpretations.

Relying on the latter set of associations, Pearce offers a seminal analysis of decreative processes:

The sum total of all poems—or, as Stevens was to declare in *The Auroras of Autumn* and "The Rock," of all creative acts—is decreation, and makes pass to the reality on which such creative acts are operative. Thus the poet as decreator apprehends reality as it has been before (if "before" can be used in a dialectical and not a temporal sense) it could be overcome and transformed by the poet as creator. (*Continuity of American Poetry*, 412)

Here decreation, a passing beyond the created, opens onto a reality described in a hybridization of Kantian and Hegelian categories: the Kantian "thing-in-itself" taken as dialectically (by which Pearce seems to mean logically) prior. Pearce puts this understanding to work, distinguishing Stevens' early poetry from the later: "The late vision differs from the early in this: that at the end Stevens wants to conceive of confronting and knowing reality directly, not as it might be mediated by the formal elegancies of an ultimate composer of words. Poetic form is made to negate itself and to point to an ultimate vision beyond poems, to poetry as ultimate and inclusive poem" (*Continuity of American Poetry*, 382). By the last formulation Stevens, as decreator, becomes a kind of inverse transcendentalist: "Where Emerson was driven in the end to postulate a nature beyond nature, a supernatural, Stevens would postulate a reality within reality, an intranatural, or an infranatural" (413). This furthers the view that the object of decreation is, like the Kantian "thing-in-itself," both extraphenomenal and, except in a most general sense, extralinguistic; mirroring the elusive transcendental, decreative reality establishes itself beyond phenomenal experience and beyond the language used in shaping that experience.

Intimations of a "nature beyond nature" are plentiful in Emerson's transcendentalism—in *Nature* or in "The Over-Soul," for instance; but to postulate a "decreative" corollary independent of the language of the perceiver, independent of the poet's perceptions, forgets the complexity of Stevens' decreative hypothesis, bypassing the conclusion that decreation leads us to the "portents of our own powers."[1] In other words, while Pearce, drawn to Weil's "uncreated" as the essential incomplicate, emphasizes that decreation "makes pass to the reality on which . . . creative acts are operative," Stevens' own intricacies of thought indicate that the "reality of decreation" is making pass to that which is operational in moments of creation—a realization Stevens particularly identifies with his present era. To Weil's contention that, in contrast to destruction, "decreation is a making pass . . . to the uncreated," Stevens adds that decreation discloses the centrality of the human. The terms read consistently—the double message resolves—when "uncreated" denotes "our own powers," and not an independent (extrahuman) reality.

Frank Kermode, focusing on Weil's use of the term "decreation," argues that it

> depends upon an act of renunciation, considered as a creative act like that of God. "God could create only by hiding himself. Otherwise there would be nothing but himself." She means that decreation, for men, implies the deliberate repudiation (not simply the destruction) of the naturally human and so naturally false "set" of the world: "we participate in the creation of the world by decreating ourselves." (*Continuities*, 75–76)

Kermode's explication, recognizing an interdependency between decreation and creativity, at the same time subverts the creator. Extending Weil's tenet that artistry must be concealed, the creator hidden by his creation, he infers a denial of the "naturally human and so naturally false 'set' of the world." Kermode's language plays off the "stiff and stubborn, man-locked set" of Stevens' poem "Angel Surrounded by Paysans" (*CP*, 496–97). In that poem, the "angel of reality" proclaims:

> . . . I am the necessary angel of earth,
> Since, in my sight, you see the earth again,
>
> Cleared of its stiff and stubborn, man-locked set,
> And, in my hearing, you hear its tragic drone
>
> Rise liquidly in liquid lingerings,
> Like watery words awash . . .

The angelic figure ushers us beyond recalcitrant, landlocked images so that we experience the fluidity of the earth's own speech. The surface of the poem seems to repudiate the human and privilege a nonhuman truth/reality. And certain of Stevens' prose comments encourage this reading, though not without complication: "The angel is the angel of reality. This is clear only if the reader is of the idea that we live in a world of the imagination, in which reality and contact with it are the great blessings. For nine readers out of ten, the necessary angel will appear to be the angel of the imagination and for nine days out of ten that is true, although it is the tenth day that counts" (*Letters*, 753).

Without denying that "we live in a world of the imagination," Stevens affirms that contact with reality is "the great blessing" of life. But as with the controversial question of decreation, the significance here of Stevens' figurations—the "angel," the "great blessing"—depends on the eccentric coordinates and compass of "reality." He says elsewhere about "Angel Surrounded": "The point of the poem is that there must be in the world about us things that solace us quite as fully as any heavenly visitation could" (*Letters*, 661). Reality, as conveyed by the angel, is the earthly, the close-at-hand, necessarily appropriated by poetry which fulfills the role recommended in section V of "The Man with the Blue Guitar": to "take the place / Of empty heaven and its hymns" (*CP*, 167). The angel, agent of vision personifying the refreshment that our glimpse of reality may provide, distinguishes itself from the reality it brings into view; yet the decreative process—an essential clearing away—takes place in the "sight" and "hearing" of the angel. Existing through the sensibility of a being created by imagination, the experience which is the "great blessing" is, "like meanings said / / By repetitions of half-meanings," not unmediated or extrahuman. Although the angel is the angel of reality, not of imagination, it functions as surrogate of an imagination which transcends egocentrism.[2] Weil, discussing decreation, draws attention to the parallelism between God-as-creator and man-as-creator; Stevens modifies the comparison by asserting that disclosures are no longer those of "belief."[3] As creative/decreative center, the angel figures an ascendant form of our own vision, simultaneously displacing the "stubborn, man-locked set" of ordinary vision and its metaphysical accomplice, the all-pervasive vision of the Absolute. The angel of reality shows us a world without "concealed creator" (*CP*, 296).

Eleanor Cook, in "The Decreations of Wallace Stevens," maintains that "he is turning [Weil's] term to his own uses, in a decreation of her decreation, or a borrowing back of religious terms for secular usage" (46). Weighing the metaphysical implications of Stevens' usage, she defines his redefinition of the word: "Decreation in Stevens' essay is seeing the *schema* of the world move from a *schema* of something that is created—a world issued, say, by divine fiat from the Logos—to a *schema* of something that is uncreated" (46). Though it follows Stevens' emphasis more closely to say decreation exposes the schematizing process (thus, the schematizer),[4] the broader recognition that decreation deconstructs theocentric assumptions underscores the relatedness of "decreation," "the uncreated," and "our own powers." In religious terms, passage from created to uncreated takes us from God's works to the Creator;[5] but if, as in Stevens' "modern reality . . . of decreation," the idea of God is itself decreated (as by "the idea of God is the ultimate poetic idea" [*OP*, 193]), what remains is our own improvisational sensibility. Imagination becomes the ultimate uncreated—thus Stevens' conclusion: man's truth is the final resolution of everything.

Stevens' resolution, relying on imaginative generation, projects past the obsolete and discordant. He writes in "The Noble Rider and the Sound of Words": "All the great things have been denied and we live in an intricacy of new and local mythologies, political, economic, poetic, which are asserted with an ever-enlarging incoherence" (*NA*, 17). Formerly vigorous, now faded, mythical imaginings that once "sufficed," as Stevens says in "Of Modern Poetry" (*CP*, 239–40), having been decreated, are so far replaced only by fragmented, pedestrian mythologies. This is the decreative tenor of modern reality.

A New Knowledge of Reality

Riddel says about "Of Modern Poetry" that it describes "a world from which the old gods have disappeared—or have, as Stevens says elsewhere and everywhere, become fictions" ("Metaphoric Staging," 309). But Riddel's negative association of fictionality itself with the outmoded evades Stevens' premise that the gods were fictions all along.[6] This is not to deemphasize their original relation to reality; as conditions shifted, however, that relation was dissipated. Stevens assumes that "imagination loses vitality as it ceases to adhere to what is real" (*NA*, 6); and on this basis, "it is always at the end of an era. What happens is that it is always attaching itself to a new reality, and adhering to it. It is not that there is a new imagination but that there is a new reality" (*NA*, 22). This notion of a new reality signals that Stevens' "reality" is of a curious sort—such that he can say, "There are fictions that are extensions of reality" (*Letters*, 430).[7] The opening lines of "Of Modern Poetry" describe a Stevensian decreation/creation:

> The poem of the mind in the act of finding
> What will suffice. It has not always had
> To find: the scene was set; it repeated what
> Was in the script.
>   Then the theatre was changed
> To something else. Its past was a souvenir.
>   (*CP*, 239)

"What will suffice" is an originative contemporary fiction. There was a time, Stevens postulates, when our truths—the fictions of the age (in conjunction with the "realities" of the age)—seemed pre-established; that time is past. The difficult task of "modern poetry" is to compose fictions sufficient for a "decreative era."

In a recent essay Pearce takes into account the inevitable relation of decreation to creation: "What is reduced/negated is not the world, reality (for that is by definition impossible), but rather the imagination itself. Such a reduction/negation is, however, only temporary, a way on to a further stage;

for as I have said, quoting Stevens, in the course of projecting the decreative process, the imagination discovers 'the precious portents of its own powers'" ("Toward Decreation," 289). This emendation recognizes what Pearce had previously overlooked—namely, the second half of Stevens' formulation about modern decreative reality. Yet the revision retains the supposition that the decreative denies the imagination—a misconception furthered by misquotation: Stevens' "the precious portents of our own powers" becomes "its own powers." Pearce's reading still rests on the putative antagonism between imagination and reality, incongruent with Stevens' notion of their "interdependence" (*NA*, 27)—the necessary intimacy on which, for Stevens, the cycle of decreation and creation depends.

Stevens' poem "So-and-So Reclining on Her Couch" (*CP*, 295–96) describes an artwork—a painting or sculpture—for which "The arrangement contains the desire of / The artist." Regueiro says about the poem: "The sculpture is an intentional structure, created in an act of consciousness, not of reality. It is not reality that the artist reveals in his creation, but himself" (*The Limits of Imagination*, 186). As Stevens suggests in the "Adagia": "The subjects of one's poems are the symbols of one's self or of one of one's selves" (*OP*, 164). That is, if poetry has a mimetic function, it reflects the fluent (affluent) world of the poet rather than an objective external. Like painting or sculpture, poems, too, are intentional structures, and this particular poem, taking intentionality as its subject, effects a double turning: artwork to artist, poem to poet. The poem retains a measure of its own likeness in the described work of art. That work, too, has a subject, of whom the poem says, "She is half who made her"; she is "Born . . . at twenty-one, / Without lineage or language." These lines show that we should consider her not as an imitation of an actual woman but as a newly created object. She has no history, as things of the real world do. And she has no language to speak except that given by her creator; her form itself, as gesture of the artist, is that language.

The poem's delineation of the art object is an art-critical description which isolates the form as artifice. It is the poet, in this case, who makes the relation between artist and work visible. But the persona's shifting "projections" also reveal a rift between his vision and the art object. And this breach regarding the artwork transforms into a self-critical awareness with respect to all art as the persona's thoughts, leaving the work, turn inward to some "unpainted," "unsculpted" shape of landscape. In what could be thought of as a poet's reversal on *trompe-l'oeil* painting, the poem's last six lines open a schism between what appear as art (the created) and nature (the seemingly uncreated).[8]

> ... one confides in what has no
> Concealed creator. One walks easily
>
> The unpainted shore, accepts the world
> As anything but sculpture. ...

The world in which we confide is a world which seems to be simply what it is, with no assumption of concealed teleology; it is "anything but sculpture." We feel at home on "the unpainted shore." For Regueiro the lines imply that although the artist finds himself (and his experience) in his creation, he is cut off from the external reality which lies behind it. He is, in her words, "denied access" to reality: "Precisely because he is present in it, because it is an image of himself, it lacks the reality of what has not been intentionally created" (186). But the effect of the inverted *trompe-l'oeil* is to incorporate the schism into the work. The inwardness of the persona, experiencing a tension between "art" and "nature," establishes their difference in its own terms, such that the poem, opening onto the "unpainted shore," becomes as if more than blind sculpture or "arrangement" without self-realization.

Having scrutinized the art form and having drawn us to the expanse of its opposite (nature), Stevens' fictive form takes possession of both. Painted and unpainted take shape, as such, in our elaborations.

> ... To get at the thing
> Without gestures is to get at it as
> Idea. She floats in the contention, the flux
>
> Between the thing as idea and
> The idea as thing....

The idea "without gestures" is ideality in a rarefied Platonic sense; the artwork, by contrast, lends particularity to the abstraction—thus "floats in the contention." But we could also say that the artist's gesture is an act by which idea becomes object; his task is to render "idea as thing." The persona, as viewer (or critic), reverses the process. Following the clue of the artist's gestures, he responds to (without extracting) the abstract quality of the thing-as-idea. Northrop Frye writes: "The maxim that art should conceal art is based on the sense that in the greatest art we have no sense of manipulating, posing or dominating over nature, but rather of emancipating it" ("The Realistic Oriole," 172). But Stevens' convolution emancipates art by forcing an illusionary confrontation between "concealment" and "nonconcealment." The forms of art, if we are to "confide" in them and walk easily on their shore, must inscribe their own provocative dimensionalities. The poem intimates that its lines do not desire an unmediated reality but, in Henry James' phrase, the "air of reality" (*Theory of Fiction*, 35). Stevens puts the point this way: "To study and understand the fictive world is the function of the poet" (*OP*, 167); and as for the real world, "Poetry increases the feeling for reality" (*OP*, 162).

Cassirer writes, "Art is not the mere reproduction of a ready-made, given reality.... It is not an imitation but a discovery of reality" (*Essay on Man*, 143). "Notes toward a Supreme Fiction" assumes that "to impose is not / To discover" (*CP*, 403); and yet such discovery involves more than immediate perception.[9] The reality which interests Stevens—that to which "we keep coming back and coming back"—is neither the undiscoverable "thing-in-itself" nor the empirically "given." It is, at least in part, "A definition with an illustration, not / Too exactly labelled" (CP, 443)—a signification discovered through the synthesizing gesture of the artist. Stevens pursues this line in "Notes":

> ... To discover an order as of
> A season, to discover summer and know it,
>
> To discover winter and know it well, to find,
> Not to impose, not to have reasoned at all,
> Out of nothing to have come on major weather,
>
> It is possible, possible, possible. It must
> Be possible. ...
>
> (CP, 403-4)

To "discover" an order in the world ("as of a season," itself not fact but a form of comprehension) is to find a significance that is not "ready-made" (either by nature or through the *Logos*)—that can be said to exist only when apprehended. Yet "finding" such "major weather"—a poetic order—is not at all the imposition of a "reasoned" order. Ratiocination, from its distance, becomes propagandistic—imposes/presupposes; the poetical discovers/refreshes.

Stevens says that "to confront fact in its total bleakness is for any poet a completely baffling experience. Reality is not the thing but the aspect of the thing" (NA, 95). The poet discovers not the "things themselves" but their consequence; "discovered" reality is, as Cassirer tells us, a compelling, complicate realization:

Aesthetic experience is incomparably richer [than sense perception]. It is pregnant with infinite possibilities which remain unrealized in ordinary sense experience. In the work of the artist these possibilities become actualities; they are brought into the open and take on a definite shape. The revelation of this inexhaustibility of the aspects of things is one of the great privileges and one of the deepest charms of art. (*Essay on Man*, 145)[10]

For Stevens, "fact destitute of any imaginative aspect whatever" is irrelevant to "poetic truth" (NA, 60); "The subject-matter of poetry is not [the] 'collection of solid, static objects extended in space' but the life that is lived in the scene that it composes; and so reality is not that external scene but the life that is lived in it. Reality is things as they are" (*NA*, 25).

This last formulation is more than tautological. As we have already seen (by his reference to a "new reality"), reality, in Stevens' usage, changes: it is things as they are now (as opposed to things as they once were, things as they will be, things as they ought to be).[11] He says in "Two or Three Ideas": "That the revelation of reality has a character or quality peculiar to this time or that or, what is intended to be the same thing, that it is affected by states of mind, is elementary" (*OP*, 214). And he writes to Victor Hammer in 1948: "Food for the imagination in this country . . . is what it is in any country: reality. It is true that reality over here is different from the reality to which you are accustomed. It is also true that it not only changes from place to place, but from time to time and that in every place and at every time the imagination makes its way by reason of it" (*Letters*, 577). Reality, so described, is always present and at the same time elusive: it alters with place or era. These transformations rely on the complexity of the "real." As if in illustration, his 1944 poem "The Bed of Old John Zeller" points out the need "to accept the structure / Of things as the structure of ideas" (*CP*, 327).

For Stevens the structure of reality confounds our usual categories of objective, subjective, and intersubjective. By this, the poetry accomplishes something of what Merleau-Ponty, speaking of Cézanne, claims for painting: "Essence and existence, imaginary and real, visible and invisible—a painting mixes up all our categories in laying out its oneiric universe of carnal essences, of effective likenesses, of mute meanings" ("Eye and Mind," 263).[12] Stevens' "The Figure of the Youth as Virile Poet" advocates a similarly acute anti-rationality: "There are so many things which, as they are, and without any intervention of the imagination, seem to be imaginative objects that it is no doubt true that absolute fact includes everything that the imagination includes. This is our intimidating thesis" (NA, 60–61). Even when more compromising, Stevens' uses of "imagined" and "real," unlike the sharply delimited usages of decreationist criticism, escape the reductiveness of "reasoned" order: the imagination ("the sum of our faculties" [NA, 61]) "makes its way by reason of" a reality already infused with the subjective/intersubjective. Section III of "Description without Place" (CP, 341–42) offers:

> Things are as they seemed to Calvin or to Anne
> Of England, to Pablo Neruda in Ceylon,
>
> To Nietzsche in Basel, to Lenin by a lake.
> But the integrations of the past are like
>
> A *Museo Olympico*, so much
> So little, our affair, which is the affair
>
> Of the possible: seemings that are to be,
> Seemings that it is possible may be.

Calvin, Anne, Neruda, Nietzsche, and Lenin were innovators of the real; things became as they made them in their "seemings"—their "integrations." Aspects of these transformations persist in the disposition of the present—as materials for some new possibility by which the present can become our own, shaped by contemporary innovations.

Stevens says in "The Noble Rider and the Sound of Words":

There is, in fact, a world of poetry indistinguishable from the world in which we live, or, I ought to say, no doubt, from the world in which we shall come to live, since what makes the poet the potent figure that he is, or was, or ought to be, is that he creates the world to which we turn incessantly and without knowing it and that he gives to life the supreme fictions without which we are unable to conceive of it. (NA, 31)

Here again he finds the subjective/intersubjective inseparable from what is commonly thought of as objective. Poets—along with philosophers, politicians (or political thinkers), theologians—effect the reality of the age, and beyond, through fictions that affect the truth of the way we feel: "thought / Beating in the heart" (*CP*, 382). In the "generations of thought" (*OP*, 103) one fiction, or matrix of fictions, displaces another; the outmoded, once seen as such, dis-integrates, making way for the viable and what will be seen, for a time, as the veritable. In the informal language of the "Adagia," "A dead romantic is a falsification" (*OP*, 160); and writing to Henry Church in 1942, "The first step toward a supreme fiction would be to get rid of all existing fictions. A thing stands out in clear air better than it does in soot" (*Letters*, 431)—an exposition related less to recent anti-poetics than to Samuel Johnson's dictum that "the first care of the builder of a new system, is to demolish the fabricks which are standing" (7:99).[13]

If in Stevens' view past fictions must be substantially cleared for the sake of the more relevant, it is also true that in order to achieve the most relevant—most "central"—reality, even our most current fictions must be cleared or consolidated for the sake of that one which can comprise our newly present reality. In this remaining fiction, "the real" will be discovered—a reality which in the creative cycle will become a base for future fictions:

> ... It must be that in time
> The real will from its crude compoundings come,
>
> Seeming, at first, a beast disgorged, unlike,
> Warmed by a desperate milk. To find the real,
> To be stripped of every fiction except one,
>
> The fiction of an absolute—Angel,
> Be silent in your luminous cloud and hear
> The luminous melody of proper sound.
>
> (*CP*, 404)

"Reality" is revealed as fictional, but not because it falsifies: the structure of the "real" is bound up with the figural structurings of thought. This process of discovery penetrates beyond the chaos of discordant fictions/realities, the cacophony of unharmonious sound, to that center at which the "luminous melody of proper sound" emerges against a background of silence. The fictional form progresses from "crude compoundings" to a mellifluent rapport. This is the innovated transcendence in which imagination has come to be seen as part of the reality discovered—leaving us floating, we might say, like "So-and-So Reclining on Her Couch," "in the contention, the flux, // Between the thing as idea and / The idea as thing."

In "Bouquet of Roses in Sunlight" (*CP*, 430–31), "this effect [the colors of the roses] is a consequence of the way / We feel and, therefore, is not real, except / In our sense of it," and "Our sense of these things changes and they change." This again is reality's complication. The quality of the perceiver's attention merges with sunlight and the seeming factuality of the roses, and from the complex interaction a correspondingly complex experience of reality arises: "black reds, / Pink yellows, orange whites."[14] Though the poem tells us, paradoxically, that the roses appear "far beyond the rhetorician's touch," this too is only a seeming. The idiosyncracies of one's rhetorical touch inhere in the perception, producing the multiplied effects of the way "we are two that use these roses as we are."

Of the imagination Stevens says in "The Figure of the Youth as Virile Poet":

Like light, it adds nothing, except itself. What light requires a day to do, and by day I mean a kind of Biblical revolution of time, the imagination does in the twinkling of an eye. It colors, increases, brings to a beginning and end, invents languages, crushes men and, for that matter, gods in its hands, it says to women more than it is possible to say, it rescues all of us from what we have called absolute fact and while it does these things, and more, it makes sure that

> ... *la mandoline jase,*
> *Parmi les frissons de brise.*
> (*NA*, 61–62;
> ellipsis is Stevens')

But if, in this sense, "imagination is the only genius" (*OP*, 179),[15] yet "reality is the spirit's true center" (*OP*, 177).

Though not the "thing itself," reality, as a varying mixture of the objective and subjective/intersubjective, subsisting in the present, is not reduced to a function of the moment's imagination; at its barest, "the real is only the base. But it is the base" (*OP*, 160). This fundamental aspect of reality appears in section VI of "An Ordinary Evening in New Haven" (*CP*, 469):

> Reality is the beginning not the end,
> Naked Alpha, not the hierophant Omega,
> Of dense investiture, with luminous vassals.
>
> It is the infant A standing on infant legs,
> Not twisted, stooping, polymathic Z.

The poem identifies reality as the source, or starting point: "the beginning not the end"—"naked Alpha"; while "the hierophant Omega," that is, human reality seen in its fuller complexity, possesses "luminous vassals" which have not accrued to Alpha's naïve self. Although the nakedness of Alpha might seem to represent reality as "thing-in-itself," the status of Alpha-as-beginning inexorably relates it to its end.[16] In the progression from Alpha to Omega the beginning is already appropriated by the reality of its end, just as the nature of the beginning destines the configuration of the end. Unlike the decreationist notion of the "thing itself," the reality of naked Alpha is a signification in relation to Omega—an infant participant in the development of new interpretations. Omega's luminous vassals assemble from imaginative illumination which "adds nothing, except itself . . . brings to a beginning and end." Stevens, metaphorizing the shapes of the letters, has us notice the configurative kinship between A and Z: Z is a "twisted, stooping" version of the same three bars that shape the body and "infant legs" of A. The cycle from Alpha to Omega (or from A to Z) images the creative/decreative cycle: the possibility inherent in the naked Alpha becomes a world confirmed—clothed with innovative interpretation (Omega)—then, as maturity degenerates into obsolescence, re-turns to Alpha. "Basic" reality without the timely attendants which the "genial" imagination provides is a prelude from which Omega will arise, but just as surely, no developed conception of reality will continue to suffice. Thus, "Alpha continues to begin. / Omega is refreshed at every end."

The cycle renews itself in the "poem of pure reality" suggested by section IX of "An Ordinary Evening" (*CP*, 471–72):

> We keep coming back and coming back
> To the real: to the hotel instead of the hymns
> That fall upon it out of the wind. We seek
>
> The poem of pure reality, untouched
> By trope or deviation, straight to the word,
> Straight to the transfixing object, to the object
>
> At the exactest point at which it is itself,
> Transfixing by being purely what it is,
> A view of New Haven, say, through the certain eye,
>
> The eye made clear of uncertainty, with the sight
> Of simple seeing, without reflection. . . .

Using this passage, Michel Benamou draws a comparison between Stevens and Mallarmé: "For exactly opposite purposes Stevens and Mallarmé sought a poetry 'untouched by trope or deviation': Mallarmé because he despaired of transposing the world materially into words, Stevens because he hoped to return to the real—'straight to the object. . . . At the exactest point at which it is itself'" (*Wallace Stevens and the Symbolist Imagination*, xv). For Benamou, Stevens' "real" is, again, the "thing itself." But Stevens' compounding—straight to the word/object—forces the question: at what point is the object precisely itself? The lines, for a moment, let us believe that the point is "naked Alpha" (as opposed to the "thing itself"); as the poem continues, however, we learn that it is Omega, the hierophant, the priest who initiates us into the mystery. Although the poem speaks of a desire for "the object," it is the object seen "through the certain eye"—"certain" not by afterthought but by a comprehension accompanying the act of perception ("sight and insight" [*CP*, 473]). Benamou maintains: "Mallarmé seeks a land of the mind beyond reality; Stevens a land beyond the mind, as part of reality" ("Wallace Stevens and the Symbolist Imagination," 92); but as the remainder of section IX makes clear, the mind is very much a part of that "hierophant" experience of reality of which the poem speaks:

> ... We seek
> Nothing beyond reality. Within it,
>
> Everything, the spirit's alchemicana
> Included, the spirit that goes roundabout
> And through included, not merely the visible,
>
> The solid, but the movable, the moment,
> The coming on of feasts and the habits of saints,
> The pattern of the heavens and high, night air.

These lines disclose the broadest structure (and Stevens' broadest usage) of reality. In this most comprehensive definition the contemplated "real" takes in the imagination's present genius ("the spirit's alchemicana") as well as the subjective/intersubjective background ("the spirit that goes roundabout / And through"); it is the expansive, inclusive concept of the real described in "Notes":

> ... the things
> That in each other are included, the whole,
> The complicate ...
>
> (*CP*, 403)

Dislocating this fuller context, however, one easily finds in the poem indication that imagination inevitably distorts: the "poem of pure reality, untouched / By trope or deviation." Vendler, believing that Stevens, as he enters the later stages of his poetic career, distrusts imagination, argues: "Rebelliously, the imagination continues its chromatisms, but by now Stevens is living in distrust of its variegation, and senses a possible madness resulting from a wholesale and licentious imaginative dispensation, where anything is beautiful if you say it is, and oak leaves are hands, if the poet chooses to make that metaphor about them" (*On Extended Wings*, 147).

Though there is little evidence in Stevens' published (or unpublished) letters, or in the accounts of his acquaintances,[17] to support the claim that he felt his sanity was tenuous, Vendler is not alone in considering the imagination as a source of distortion. Regueiro, for instance, believes that the later Stevens recognizes "that the imagination transforms and destroys the real, leaving in its place painted strawberries and constructed pineapples" (*The Limits of Imagination*, 11). The imagination, in spite of, or even because of, its constructive function, becomes a destructive or degenerative agent. Regueiro, with particular attention to "Metaphor as Degeneration," sees the result of imaginative processes—represented (metonymically) by metaphor—as an emptying out of meaning: "Instead of finding in metaphor a generation of reality, the poet sees 'metaphor as degeneration' (*CP*, 444), always altering the object and undermining the possible experience" (179). Similarly, Hyatt Waggoner reads the poem as literally asserting that "metaphors do *not* tell the truth" (*American Poets*, 440), and Hines suggests that "the poet announces in 'Metaphor as Degeneration' the demise of metaphor" (*Later Poetry*, 248). Stevens says in that poem:

> It is certain that the river
>
> Is not Swatara. The swarthy water
> That flows round the earth and through the skies,
> Twisting among the universal spaces,
>
> Is not Swatara. It is being.
> That is the flock-flecked river, the water,
> The blown sheen—or is it air?
>
> How, then, is metaphor degeneration,
> When Swatara becomes this undulant river
> And the river becomes the landless, waterless ocean?
>
> (*CP*, 444)

To maintain that the poem finally portrays metaphor "as degeneration" misses the irony of the extravagant rhetorical question that finishes the passage. By way of the experimental "metaphor as degeneration," Stevens activates its opposite. The poem traces the way the actual (the river), by incorporation into the metaphorizing structure of thought, becomes a symbol for a deeper sense of the nature of things. Redirecting the poem's orientation toward its title, the lines intimate that, since an ordinary river like the Swatara through metaphor becomes the river of "being," which "flows round the earth and through the skies," then metaphor is decidedly not degeneration but a maturation from "infant A" to "polymathic Z"—"naked Alpha" to "hierophant Omega." As if to specify the complications of his language, Stevens tells us, "Originality is an accentuation, through sensibility, of differences perceived" (*Souvenirs*, 38), while in "Three Academic Pieces" (from roughly the same period as "Metaphor as Degeneration"), after defining metaphor as "the creation of resemblance by the imagination" (*NA*, 72), he says,

> Poetry is a satisfying of the desire for resemblance.... Its singularity is that in the act of satisfying the desire for resemblance it touches the sense of reality, it enhances the sense of reality, heightens it, intensifies it. If resemblance is described as a partial similarity between two dissimilar things, it complements and reinforces that which the two dissimilar things have in common. It makes it brilliant. (*NA*, 77)

Here resemblance and difference cohabit the partially similar; metaphorizing circulates the similar and dissimilar. If metaphor produces this reinforcing and intensifying, yet differentiating, resemblance which "touches the sense of reality," how, then, is metaphor degeneration?

Regueiro's Stevens sees poetry's tropological character as the chief obstacle in the poet's search for reality. Exemplifying the unsettling double edge of discourse: "to express things, to light the obscure world of reality, the metaphor must usurp the 'thingness' of the object, casting it into a shape that is not its own" (*The Limits of Imagination*, 180). This is to say that metaphor, while illuminating reality, skews it, becomes fictional in the derogatory sense of falsehood. She extracts from "Poem Written at Morning" (*CP*, 219): "The painting of metaphor is ultimately a faking of reality, not a valid means of experiencing it" (183). In the poem's opening lines:

> A sunny day's complete Poussiniana
> Divide it from itself. It is this or that
> And it is not.
>   By metaphor you paint
> A thing. Thus, the pineapple was a leather fruit,
> A fruit for pewter, thorned and palmed and blue,
> To be served by men of ice.

For Regueiro, "Through the metaphor the object is posed into 'this' or 'that'—always into something that violates its 'thingness'" (183). But is it as a negative—a question of posturing—that the poem muses: "By metaphor you paint / A thing"? And within this setting, what does it mean to say that the day is "divided" from itself? Two possibilities unfold from the phrase "sunny day's complete Poussiniana." The "Poussiniana" could be the works of seventeenth-century French painter Nicolas Poussin,[18] whose metaphorical seeing would be the prelude to painting a picture; the day would be quite literally converted into a work of art and so, by the addition of the artist's vision, would no longer be itself. Equally, "Poussiniana" relates to "*poussin*," the French word for chick; the sun in its yellow, morning newness appears before us as a newborn chick, just emerged from the egg of its nocturnal concealment; our metaphorical seeing "paints" the morning, dividing it from itself. Still, for Stevens are such metaphorical conversions gain or loss? He writes in "Three Academic Pieces": "The mind begets in resemblance as the painter begets in representation; that is to say, as the painter makes his world within a world; or as the musician begets in music" (*NA*, 76).[19] It is *this* "world within a world," not the seemingly uncompounded fact-world, which, ironically, expresses the non-divisive inclusiveness of experience. The subsequent lines of the poem reveal the effect of such artistry:

> The senses paint
> By metaphor. The juice was fragranter
> Than wettest cinnamon. It was cribled pears
> Dripping a morning sap.

The metaphorical seeing paints the pineapple so that scent, taste, and touch are added to sight; the poem's metaphors are ultimately generative; our experience of the pineapple is deepened and expanded, brought closer.[20] The poem concludes:

> The truth must be
> That you do not see, you experience, you feel,
> That the buxom eye brings merely its element
> To the total thing, a shapeless giant forced
> Upward.
> Green were the curls upon that head.

"The total thing," be it morning or pineapple, is a "shapeless giant" to which the mind gives shape. The mind "beget[s] in resemblance," giving birth to the day as if the sun were a newly hatched chick and playfully turning the pineapple's actually lifeless leaves into "green curls": a surprising, amusing, and, in this way, satisfying instance—"provoking a laughter, an agreement, by surprise" (*CP*, 248)—of Stevens' pervasive association of the color green with the vigorously/fictively real. "A sunny day's complete Poussiniana / Divide it from itself" with fresh transformations which, by metaphor, render ("paint") an experience that takes us beyond the hypothetically atropical.

Such experience finds its zenith—"green's green apogee"—in "the fertile thing that can attain no more" in section II of "Credences of Summer" (*CP*, 373). Here the morning's potentiality has developed into the full realization of noonday. The lines make reference to "the very thing" and to "evasion" by metaphor, a conjunction highly suggestive for those concerned with the "decreative" in Stevens' later poetry. Yet if we look at these in context, they lose their seemingly anti-metaphoric character. The section begins:

> Postpone the anatomy of summer, as
> The physical pine, the metaphysical pine.
> Let's see the very thing and nothing else.
> Let's see it with the hottest fire of sight.
> Burn everything not part of it to ash.

Although the third line proposes that we "see the very thing and nothing else," the first two lines have specified that we are not to "anatomize" summer by breaking it into "physical" and "metaphysical"—that is, empirical and theoretical/theological, or, from these, the "thing-in-itself" and "consciousness," or ordinary language's "reality" and "imagination." The "very thing" we are to see is "summer," which is not the "thing itself,"[21] nor a literal season, but a seasonable complex of thought and feeling much like the "great noon" which compels Nietzsche's Zarathustra to proclaim: "Gone is the hesitant gloom of my spring! Gone the malice of my snowflakes in June! Summer have I become entirely, and summer noon!" (*Thus Spoke Zarathustra*, 210). Like Zarathustra, the poet wants to experience summer "with the hottest fire of sight":

> Trace the gold sun about the whitened sky
> Without evasion by a single metaphor.
> Look at it in its essential barrenness
> And say this, this is the centre that I seek.

These succeeding lines ask for no "evasion" by metaphor. But "summer" itself in the poem is metaphorical. The "whitened sky" on a vibrantly sunny summer day expresses the perfection (mythically associated with whiteness) shaped by the day—an expression which by its own sonorous and conceptual intricacies is refracted toward its origin in what "The Rock" refers to as "the whitest eye" (*CP*, 527).[22] The denunciation of "evasion" is not a literal call for the elimination of figures of speech from poetry. Instead it metaphorically reiterates the desire to experience summer in its fullest intensity. Stevens' play on "single metaphor" underscores/undercuts the monotony of either metaphysical or physical rhetoric, and his emphasis on "essential barrenness" shuns indirection (and, again, "deviation") or peripheral considerations ("Burn everything not part of it to ash")—which, of course, include malconceived metaphors.[23] In the section's final lines the informing role of imagination becomes abundantly clear as the perfected present moment, for which summer serves as symbol, is placed in a context within which its significance can be fully appreciated:

> Fix it in an eternal foliage
>
> And fill the foliage with arrested peace,
> Joy of such permanence, right ignorance
> Of change still possible. Exile desire
> For what is not. This is the barrenness
> Of the fertile thing that can attain no more.

Proposing that we "exile desire" for metaphorical evasion (either concealed metaphysical origin or physical thing-as-it-is), the poet requires a human world we can confide in, which will "solace us quite as fully as any heavenly visitation could."

In the first section (*CP*, 372) of "Credences" we have learned that

> This is the last day of a certain year
> Beyond which there is nothing left of time.

In this "final" moment, past and future are dispelled, and we dwell in a spacious present: "It comes to this and the imagination's life." It is left for the imagination to situate this moment in "an eternal foliage" infused with an "arrested peace, / Joy of such permanence," arising from consciously imposed "right ignorance / Of change still possible." In such deliberate "ignorance," "what is" is wholly accepted, as we choose to "Exile desire / For what is not." The "barrenness" is not that of things themselves but of "the fertile thing" (like the pineapple in "Poem Written at Morning") which grows out of the relatedness of perception and perceived—suggested by the "fathers," "mothers," and "young broods" of section I and the "marriage-hymns" of section III (*CP*, 373).

But if summer means for Stevens "mostly marriage-hymns"—imaginative integrations—what of the poem of "winter"? According to Pack, "The difference between winter and summer is a difference in visible order, and it can be said, speaking symbolically, that the longing for winter is a desire for fact and the longing for summer is the desire for the relationships into which fact may enter" (*Wallace Stevens*, 134). This is roughly consonant with what we see of summer in "Credences"; as for winter, Stevens writes in "Man and Bottle" (*CP*, 238–39):

> The mind is the great poem of winter, the man,
> Who, to find what will suffice,
> Destroys romantic tenements
> Of rose and ice.

The destruction of "romantic tenements" (as Stevens plays on the sounds and forms of "winter," "wind," "mind") does seem close to "a desire for fact"; yet the poem's last lines (recovering: "The mind is the great poem of winter") project a need for more than factuality:

> The poem lashes more fiercely than the wind,
> As the mind, to find what will suffice, destroys
> Romantic tenements of rose and ice.

The "bottle" of the title represents an ordering concept much like the "jar" in "Anecdote of the Jar" (*CP*, 76), and the poem surely prescribes the breaking of that "bottle"; but there is also the indication that a new sufficing concept will take its place. The violence, which, in spite of reference to "destruction," appears as decreative, is again a means to another construction of "tenements."

In contrast to this wintry violence (against what may be the romantic rose fixed in ice), "The Poems of Our Climate" (*CP*, 193–94) opens with a serene description:

> Clear water in a brilliant bowl,
> Pink and white carnations. The light
> In the room more like a snowy air,
> Reflecting snow. A newly-fallen snow
> At the end of winter when afternoons return.

These lines circumscribe a time (of clarity and the freshness of pinks and whites) in which the mind is at rest, seemingly released from the machinations of the imagination; "romantic tenements" have been leveled. And yet the imagined simplicity, if it were actual, would not, finally, be enough: "one desires / So much more than that":

> Say even that this complete simplicity
> Stripped one of all one's torments, concealed
> The evilly compounded, vital I
> And made it fresh in a world of white,
> A world of clear water, brilliant-edged,
> Still one would want more, one would need more,
> More than a world of white and snowy scents.[24]

If winter images the decreative, in the cycle of creation/decreation there will always follow, as in "Esthétique du Mal," "the yes of the realist spoken because he must / Say yes" (*CP*, 320)—an affirmation of compositions dormant/germinal in the scene. The "I" may be "evilly compounded," as by the Fall of mankind away from a mythical simplicity of original, unselfconscious innocence, but a world without its elaborations is untenable:

> There would still remain the never-resting mind,
> So that one would want to escape, come back,
> To what had been so long composed.[25]

In the later poem "The Plain Sense of Things" (*CP*, 502–3), Stevens extends his argument with: "the absence of the imagination had / Itself to be imagined." Vendler claims for these lines: "'A necessary function of the imagination,' we might represent Stevens as saying, 'is to imagine its own absence'" ("Qualified Assertions," 166); and Regueiro asserts: "Stevens at the end of his career ... attempts to return to 'the plain sense of things' through the very language, the very self-consciousness that separate [poetry] from that world" (*The Limits of Imagination*, 12). Here, then, if the thing desired is, as Vendler and Regueiro contend, the "thing itself," the poem should exude a plain "sufficiency" as the culmination of the poet's pendulum swing toward factuality. But their readings have inverted the sense of Stevens' lines by holding that the imagination, most significantly, cancels itself by conceiving its own absence; while the poem suggests that the imagination's absence must, indeed, be imagined and, from this, that the imagination, however thinly, defines even the image of its absence. And rather than sufficiency, what we see at this negative antipode are some of the bleakest images of poverty in Stevens' poetry—images reminiscent of the desolation of Eliot's "The Hollow Men" and *The Waste Land*—as the poem continues:

> ... The great pond,
> The plain sense of it, without reflections, leaves,
> Mud, water like dirty glass, expressing silence
>
> Of a sort, silence of a rat come out to see,
> The great pond and its waste of the lilies.

Regueiro finds in the poem "acceptance of an imagination that has consciously turned against itself" and "the imagination's realization that in questioning its capacity to transform and reconstruct reality it is capable of perceiving reality in its 'plainness' and its 'thingness'" (210); but instead of an appropriation of the "things themselves," the poem describes only a diminished sense of the real:

> The great structure has become a minor house.
> No turban walks across the lessened floors.

Here "structure" represents a certain structural relation between thought and object—a relation which has been but is now absent. The "house" is an impoverished variation; the "turban"—an imaginative element—is present only as an absence. The absence is manifest in the nouns: "structure," a loftier term of Latinate origin, reduced to "house," the commonplace term of Germanic origin; and more acutely, in the modifying adjectives: the structure described as "great," the house "minor" (as with Stevens' musical "minors"), and its floors "lessened." The poem offers a sense of the world at the point of imaginative exhaustion, when "romantic tenements" are no longer valid:

> A fantastic effort has failed, a repetition
> In a repetitiousness of men and flies.

And while imagination may now seem "Inanimate in an inert savoir," the sense is that of temporary dormancy, or, more accurately, diminution, rather than permanent abdication. After all, a "savoir," which is itself a way of knowing, does remain, even though "inert." And though spare, even this scene is not barest "fact": "all this / Had to be imagined as an inevitable knowledge"—again, inevitably, imagined. As "Ozymandias" insists in "Notes," "A fictive covering / Weaves always glistening from the heart and mind" (*CP*, 396). It is not, in the "plain sense," the end of the imagination but *"as if /* We had come to an end of the imagination."

"An Ordinary Evening in New Haven" affords an extended example of the "poem of winter." Vendler describes it as "the poem of an old man living in the lack and the blank" and as, "humanly speaking, the saddest of all Stevens' poems" (*On Extended Wings*, 269). Stevens says about the poem: "Here my interest is to try to get as close to the ordinary, the commonplace and the ugly as it is possible for a poet to get. It is not a question of grim reality but of plain reality. The object is of course to purge oneself of anything false" (*Letters*, 636). This reads as a reference to section XIV (*CP*, 475), in which "Professor Eucalyptus of New Haven" looks for

> God in the object itself, without much choice.
> It is a choice of the commodious adjective
> For what he sees, it comes in the end to that:

> The description that makes it divinity, still speech
> As it touches the point of reverberation—not grim
> Reality but reality grimly seen
>
> And spoken in paradisal parlance new
> And in any case never grim, the human grim
> That is part of the indifference of the eye
>
> Indifferent to what it sees. The tink-tonk
> Of the rain in the spout is not a substitute.
> It is of the essence not yet well perceived.

The desire to "get . . . close to the ordinary" may parallel (the dry?) Eucalyptus' interest in nothing beyond the "object." Yet as if both by way of and despite ("without much choice") his concentration, what constitutes the end of the search is not the "object itself" but "the description that makes it divinity" (as, later in the poem, it is "exterior made / Interior: breathless things broodingly abreath" [*CP*, 481]). This, as Stevens says, "is not in any sense a turning away from the ideas of Credences of Summer: it is a development of those ideas" (*Letters*, 637). It is "a thought revolved" (*CP*, 184) around the conclusions of "Credences," again displaying the interdependency of summer and winter phases.[26] The passage leaves no doubt that imagination, as in "Credences," is to "fix" the object "in an eternal foliage," transmuted here into "the commodious adjective." The object is brought into nearness by the outward gesture which resonates in the inward aspect of speech—"still speech [recognizing the doubly-intended "still"] / As it touches the point of reverberation." Not the noun (the object) but the adjective ("the description that makes it divinity") "touches the point of reverberation" at which inner and outer coalesce (and "Real and unreal are two in one" [*CP*, 485]). If Professor Eucalyptus is to find God (or what satisfies the mind) "in the object itself," his discovery must be by means of the sacralizing modifier. The projection sought is again "the fertile thing" which, in the more comprehensive perception—the "paradisal parlance" of his speech—will yield the "paradisal" fruit of a regional harmony between the "Professor" and his "New Haven." If such new speech gathers reality (not grim but grimly [seriously] seen) to itself, it is out of desire for a significance inaccessible to the indifferent eye—the inverse of of the "sight indifferent to the eye" which composes description in "Description without Place" (*CP*, 343). And the bare sound of the rain, though "of the essence," will not be, without translation, the essence of that significance. In section XV we find reference to a "heaviness" which we, like light and imagination, adding "nothing, except" themselves,

> . . . lighten by light will,
> By the hand of desire, faint, sensitive, the soft
> Touch and trouble of the touch of the actual hand.
> (*CP*, 476)

Here, out of desire, a certain touch becomes an image of the significant integration, as, in section XXVI, "the inamorata . . . // Touches, as one hand touches another hand."

Section XXX (*CP*, 487–88) of "An Ordinary Evening" begins:

> The last leaf that is going to fall has fallen.
> The robins are là-bas, the squirrels, in tree-caves,
> Huddle together in the knowledge of squirrels

—much like the opening of "The Plain Sense of Things": "After the leaves have fallen, we return / To a plain sense of things." Again the images belong to "winter": "The wind has blown the silence of summer away"; but, as in summer, there is a degree of absorption in the moment:

> The barrenness that appears is an exposing.
> It is not part of what is absent, a halt
> For farewells, a sad hanging on for remembrances

—lines which recall the exhortation in "Credences" to "Exile desire / For what is not." The plain reality of "The Plain Sense" is matched here by an even more obviously decreative reality:

A New Knowledge of Reality

> The glass of the air becomes an element—
> It was something imagined that has been washed away.
> A clearness has returned. It stands restored.

The casual reader might take these lines to mean that the imagination itself has been "washed away," but closer examination shows that what has been banished is a particular idea: "the glass of the air"—extending a figuration found in "Notes" (*CP*, 383).

> ... Adam
> In Eden was the father of Descartes
> And Eve made air the mirror of herself,
>
> Of her sons and of her daughters. They found themselves
> In heaven as in a glass; a second earth.

The "washing away" of this mirroring image returns the supernal to ourselves, restoring the "clearness" of an immanence. And section XXX continues

> It is not an empty clearness, a bottomless sight.
> It is a visibility of thought,
> In which hundreds of eyes, in one mind, see at once.

In this clarity the transparence of thought becomes visibility. The divisive substitution of "object" for "aspect" has been overcome; what was seen as meta-physical, we now see clearly ("reflectively") as an image of "ourselves." What remains is not a "bottomless sight," a seeing without horizons; and this clearness is not "empty": it is filled with a multiplicity of relational perspectives—as if the whole matrix which is consciousness-as-self-consciousness were directly sighted.

Stevens asks in "The Auroras of Autumn" (*CP*, 417):

> Is there an imagination that sits enthroned
> As grim as it is benevolent, the just
> And the unjust, which in the midst of summer stops
>
> To imagine winter? ...

This continues the motif of "winter" and "summer" seasons of the mind, with winter, as in "The Plain Sense of Things," evidence of a dismantling imagination. The thought is similar to that in "The Figure of the Youth as Virile Poet": "Suppose the poet discovered and had the power thereafter at will and by intelligence to reconstruct us by his transformations. He would also have the power to destroy us" (*NA*, 45). Imaging the strangeness of this creative/decreative potence, "Poetry Is a Destructive Force" (*CP*, 192–93) emphasizes some central (not factual) sense of things:

> That's what misery is,
> Nothing to have at heart.
> It is to have or nothing.
>
> It is a thing to have,
> A lion, an ox in his breast,
> To feel it breathing there.

Within the ambiguities of the poem's lines/lions, "It is to have or nothing" indicates the peculiar potential of an imaginative thing/act as a "thing to have." The realization is given shape in the relation between lion and ox. The underside of the prolifically imaginative is, as Borroff says, that "the imagination, for Stevens, is a destructive force in that it is constantly saying farewell to its ideas, abandoning its integrations of a present become the past" ("Wallace Stevens," 16). Such destruction could leave "nothing . . . at heart." The protagonist, who, punningly, "is like a man / In the body of a violent beast" (lionlike and oxlike), is vulnerable to destruction of the oxlike integration he has (or is) "at heart":

> The lion sleeps in the sun.
> Its nose is on its paws.
> It can kill a man

—the "man" here representing both literal protagonist and abstract version of himself that the satisfying, yet tenuous, integration embodies.[27]

In section II of "It Must Be Abstract" in "Notes" (*CP*, 381–82), what imagination decreates is specifically an outdated, overly cognitive compartmentalization—the "naming" of "the truth," a process that Stevens terms "the celestial ennui of apartments." As winter is the preparation for summer,[28] the destruction of such tenements "sends us back to the first idea," the root of metaphors which have become opaque:

> ... and yet so poisonous
>
> Are the ravishments of truth, so fatal to
> The truth itself, the first idea becomes
> The hermit in a poet's metaphors,
>
> Who comes and goes and comes and goes all day.

Cambon tells us in regard to Stevens' poetry: "If metaphor (and, by implication, all of poetry, all of knowledge) is a mere evasion, a 'shrinking from' being, it has no value. If it merely duplicates being, it likewise has no value. The only way out seems to lie in discarding 'metaphor' and confessing our impotence vis-à-vis the purity of being, which is ultimately inexpressible" (*The Inclusive Flame*, 84). But the poetry discloses that at the lowest ebb the "first idea" still inhabits the "poet's metaphors"; metaphor becomes a hermitage for the "central" truth: "The monastic man is an artist" (*CP*, 382). Again and again, what is discovered through the poetry is less a matter of "discarding" metaphor than of examining it, producing the "visibility of thought" described in "An Ordinary Evening." Cassirer says, "The nature and meaning of metaphor is what we must start with if we want to find, on the one hand, the unity of the verbal and the mythical worlds and, on the other, their difference" (*Language and Myth*, 84). Stevens, at the beginning of "Notes," rejecting figurational conventions for the sun, redefines the point toward which verbal and mythical converge: the "muddy centre," the "myth before the myth began" (*CP*, 383)—the metaphorical beneath the conventional, the central fiction of the pre-mythical and the starting point for invention of new fictions, since

> ... not to have is the beginning of desire.
> To have what is not is its ancient cycle.
> It is desire at the end of winter, when
>
> It observes the effortless weather turning blue
> And sees the myosotis on its bush.
> Being virile, it hears the calendar hymn.
>
> It knows that what it has is what is not
> And throws it away like a thing of another time,
> As morning throws off stale moonlight and shabby sleep.
>
> (CP, 382)

This is the expressed decreation of Stevens' poetry: to discard "what is not" (the obsolete/insufficient) in favor of "what is" (the vital image that rejuvenates belief). The clarity of the new day sheds "stale" and "shabby" remnants of night. "A thing of another time" cannot suffice: "the calendar hymn" of the changing seasons of belief figures the imagination's essential decreative/creative activity.

Of this cycle, Alan Perlis finds:

> Language provides an illusion of natural process while the ideas that it embodies attempt, with a futility that Stevens frankly acknowledges, to overcome natural process through transformation.... [I]t is in fact precisely from the tormented center, the "subtle" and ultimately inscrutable center, of the object-in-itself, object-perceived conflict that the poems secrete as vital, yet futile transformations of the object world itself. (*Wallace Stevens*, 16)

Stevens, as Perlis indicates, sees the breach between object and aspect as a source of poetry, proposing in "Notes":

> From this the poem springs: that we live in a place
> That is not our own and, much more, not ourselves.
>
> (CP, 383)

But the center of this conflict is not the primal "muddy centre," nor is it the "centre that [we] seek" (CP, 373); it is a schism that creates desire. And though the seasonal metamorphoses suffice only temporarily, this does not presuppose futility. The gravitational center, as in "Credences," is a fictive absolute—what draws the eye as we "Trace the gold sun about the whitened sky" and "Look at it in its essential barrenness / ... the barrenness / Of the fertile thing that can attain no more"; its issue is "Joy of such permanence, right ignorance / Of change still possible." And the sun—as the locus of integration, center of the solar system, life-source, source of the light which "adds nothing," the inconceivably visible, that which makes visible, the invisible original of lunar light, symbol of summer, mark of high noon, what has been the physical/metaphysical center—is something that exists as it exists for us because it is "believed," as Stevens often says and as the title "Credences of Summer" implies.

Perhaps Stevens' most satisfactory image of the visible integration is the "rock" of "Credences" (*CP*, 375):

> It is the rock of summer, the extreme,
> A mountain luminous half way in bloom
> And then half way in the extremest light
> Of sapphires flashing from the central sky,
> As if twelve princes sat before a king.

This opulence, set apart from the "stale moonlight and shabby sleep" of "unreal" (not now real) fictions, figures the spectral opposite of the poverty bred by lack of imagination in "The Plain Sense of Things." In such opulence the sky becomes "central"—something to have at heart.[29] To assume antagonism between imagination and reality (as Stevens uses these) is to halve (and not have) the rock, and Stevens makes clear that "the rock cannot be broken. It is the truth." This innovative "truth" does not compromise reality; it carries the real to a luminous extreme where the mind, de-centered from the givenness of things or the given meaning of a concealed creator, finds its own centrality—a gemlike comprehension:

> It rises from land and sea and covers them.
> It is a mountain half way green and then,
> The other immeasurable half, such rock
> As placid air becomes. . . .

The image of the rock exposes that "visibility of thought" which greets the "object" within the experience of the signification:

> It is the visible rock, the audible,
> The brilliant mercy of a sure repose,
> On this present ground, the vividest repose,
> Things certain sustaining us in certainty.

The truth of the figuration depends upon "this present ground," the current reality. And what sustains the perceiver's repose is the metaphorized natural-as-symbol, apotheosized by "the description that makes it divinity."

For Stevens, "reality," even as most minor, "is the footing from which we leap after what we do not have and on which everything depends" (*Letters*, 600); as he writes in "Forms of the Rock in a Night-Hymn" (section III of "The Rock"; *CP*, 528),

> The rock is the gray particular of man's life,
> The stone from which he rises, up—and—ho,
> The step to the bleaker depths of his descents . . .

In this improvisation on the "rock," though the particular is already an adjectivally modified "gray particular," its gray particularity is, like the infant A, a bare beginning. Imaging the Stevensian/Cassirerian "discovery of reality," the section continues:

> . . . through man's eye, their silent rhapsodist,
>
> Turquoise the rock, at odious evening bright
> With redness that sticks fast to evil dreams;
> The difficult rightness of half-risen day.

In the clear seeing of this re-vised image, turquoise integration transposing gray particular, the rock's composure—reality's fertile green and imagination's "amorist" blue (*CP*, 172)—"is the habitation of the whole." It is

> The starting point of the human and the end,
> That in which space itself is contained, the gate
> To the enclosure, day, the things illumined
>
> By day, night and that which night illumines.[30]

Here the compassing fiction of the turquoise rock (not the seeming bedrock of the "objective real") becomes an integration which exhibits the texture and pleasure of experience; rather than metaphor-as-evasion, once again metaphor makes visible. As in the "Adagia," reality's conventional sense (and philosophic extension into the hyperobjective "thing-in-itself") "is a cliché from which we escape by metaphor. It is only *au pays de la métaphore qu'on est poète*" (*OP*, 179).

CHAPTER II

The Vocabulary of Romanticism

The more we pursue elusive "reality" in the poetry, the more we find it filled with things of the mind—almost as if Stevens shared the bent of the pre-Romantic Edward Young: "How independent of the world is he, who can daily find new acquaintance, that at once entertain, and improve him, . . . the minute but fruitful creation of his own mind" ("Conjectures on Original Composition," 222). Stevens' attraction to Romantic vocabulary is conspicuous both in his poetry and in the subtitle—*Essays on Reality and the Imagination*—of his only book of essays; and within the volume, the title "Imagination as Value" is similarly suggestive. Yet that essay extends a direct, unambiguous, even enthusiastic, repudiation of the "romantic":

The imagination is one of the great human powers. The romantic belittles it. The imagination is the liberty of the mind. The romantic is a failure to make use of that liberty. It is to the imagination what sentimentality is to feeling. It is a failure of the imagination precisely as sentimentality is a failure of feeling. The imagination is the only genius. It is intrepid and eager and the extreme of its achievement lies in abstraction. The achievement of the romantic, on the contrary, lies in minor wish-fulfillments and it is incapable of abstraction. (*NA*, 138–39)

It would seem that such blunt denial definitively dissociates Stevens from Romanticism; but in other instances, consonant with his love of complication, he recognizes a more positive side of the "romantic." Specifying in "A Poet That Matters" that "the romantic in the pejorative sense merely connotes obsolescence" (*OP*, 251), he continues: "The romantic in its other sense, meaning always the living and at the same time the imaginative, the youthful, the delicate and a variety of things which it is not necessary to try to particularize at the moment, constitutes the vital element in poetry. It is absurd to wince at being called a romantic poet. Unless one is that, one is not a poet at all" (*OP*, 251–52).

Collectively, these remarks invite the charge of inconsistency leveled by Bloom—"Stevens was at once curiously shy and passionately defensive in regard to the Romantic" ("*Notes*: A Commentary," 82) (though shy/defensive falls short of the energetic affirmation in "A Poet That Matters")—and Peterson's related indictment that the cited passages "give evidence of nothing more than the defensiveness with which Stevens advocates a theory of imagination which, in spite of its modernist elements, is largely indistinguishable from its romantic predecessors" (*Stevens and the Idealist Tradition*, 13).[1] But Riddel comes closer to sorting out Stevens' usages by delineating "two kinds of romanticism": "the one an 'obsolescence' because it imputes to the world a vitality of transcendent origins; the other something 'living' because it incorporates ('hybridizes'), in a kind of symbiosis, fact and feeling" (*The Clairvoyant Eye*, 26). Still, the distinction Stevens assumes is more decisive, and at the same time more involved, than Riddel's "two kinds of romanticism": Stevens' approach rejects Romanticism as literary and philosophical "relic" (*OP*, 251) while welcoming the imagination's improvisations. As Romanticism, "the romantic . . . is a failure of the imagination" (and not only because it "imputes . . . transcendent origins"); as the imaginative (beyond "symbiosis [of] fact and feeling"), it becomes "the vital element in poetry." In aesthetic terms, this element is a constant; in the alternate context of Stevens' broad category of romantic-as-imaginative, "it must change": the "romantic" in any era is in concert with an imagination which initiates "repetitions" of creation/decreation. A letter to Hi Simons in 1940 localizes this cyclic fluctuation: "At the moment, the world in general is passing from the fatalism stage to an indifferent stage: a stage in which the primary sense is a sense of helplessness. But, as the world is a good deal more vigorous than most of the individuals in it, what the world looks forward to is a new romanticism, a new belief" (*Letters*, 350).

"Sailing after Lunch" (*CP*, 120–21), from *Ideas of Order*, evidences these necessary revolutions within the romantical. Stevens' protagonist, describing himself as "A most inappropriate man / In a most unpropitious place," complains,

> My old boat goes round on a crutch
> And doesn't get under way

—suggesting the ineffectualness of convention, and more specifically, the degree to which nineteenth-century forms are out of sync with the twentieth. The disparity between going "round on a crutch" and the "merely going round" of "Notes" (*CP*, 405) indicates that the energetically romantic, which continually discovers a newness in existence, "throws off stale moonlight." In the appeal that follows, the "romantic," though fervently desired, can neither remain nor return. The vital alternative exposes the subtlety of "merely going round":[2]

> Mon Dieu, hear the poet's prayer.
> The romantic should be here.
> The romantic should be there.
> It ought to be everywhere.
> But the romantic must never remain,
>
> Mon Dieu, and must never again return.

The "prayer" retains the creative/decreative movement in which the romantic-as-innovation repeatedly replaces itself—with the added implication that the Romantic is irretrievable.

"Two or Three Ideas" calls attention to "the difficulties of the imagination in a truth-loving time" (congruent with "modern reality is a reality of decreation"): "The whole effort of the imagination is toward the production of the romantic. When, therefore, the romantic is in abeyance, when it is discredited, it remains true that there is always an unknown romantic and that the imagination will not be forever denied" (*OP*, 215). "Unknown romantic" underscores that here, unequivocally, "the romantic" does not mean Romanticism; it refers to a new experience/knowledge of reality ushering in a fresh tropological era, displacing past constructs. Stevens' own commentary on "Sailing after Lunch" differentiates between the two:

While it should make its own point, and while I am against explanations, the thing is an abridgment of at least a temporary theory of poetry. When people speak of the romantic, they do so in what the French commonly call a *pejorative* sense. But poetry is essentially romantic, only the romantic of poetry must be something constantly new and, therefore, just the opposite of what is spoken of as the romantic. Without this new romantic, one gets nowhere; with it, the most casual things take on transcendence, and the poet rushes brightly, and so on. What one is always doing is keeping the romantic pure: eliminating from it what people speak of as the romantic. (*Letters*, 277)

"What people speak of as the romantic" is plainly Romanticism proper. And while a "new romantic" is needed, it opposes evasive nostalgia for Romanticism (or Romantic traditions): the "pure romantic" captures/creates the contemporary. Again, the poet's difficulty, the difficulty of inspiration, includes the business of overcoming the outdated: transforming or discarding tradition according to his purpose, he cleanses the "dirty sail" of a flagging poetic inheritance. The sailboat must be light, in order that, to the fullest extent of his senses and imagination, he can be a man of his own time and place, "a pupil / Of the gorgeous wheel"—the wheel of fortune, or, less literally (or is it more?), the turning earth.

"This heavy historical sail," the poem reveals, "Is wholly the vapidest fake." In contrast, the new integration (here, again, associated with "summer") lets one give

> That slight transcendence to the dirty sail,
> By light, the way one feels, sharp white,
> And then rush brightly through the summer air.[3]

And as Riddel implies, referring to obsolete "transcendent origins," Stevens' "slight transcendence" in both poem and letter is not metaphysical transcendence. Poetry is a "transcendent analogue" (*NA*, 130) of one's experience. This "transcendence," as Frye notes, is a "going beyond sense experience but not beyond the mental organization of that experience" ("Stevens and the Variation Form," 410); the "analogue" is continuous with a reality in which we "dwell in an analogy" (*NA*, 129).[4]

These explications support a version of Baird's claim that "Stevens began with the contention that the romantic is the end of all true poetry" (*The Dome and the Rock*, 35), provided that "the romantic" is taken in its more general sense—which excludes Baird's conclusion that "the full estate of English romanticism would seem to be the first realm of the possible and the satisfying for Stevens" (36). Stevens extensively explores and tests the vocabulary of the English Romantics, especially on the question of imagination versus reality; but it is worth remembering both his designation of imagination/reality as "marginal to [his] central theme" and his insistence that "while, of course, I come down from the past, the past is my own and not something marked Coleridge, Wordsworth, etc. . . . My reality-imagination complex is entirely my own even though I see it in others" (*Letters*, 792).[5] Stevens is, as Benamou has seen, a "subtle double-deal[er] in the rhetoric of Romanticism" (*Stevens and the Symbolist Imagination*, 38); or in Bové's "destructive" terminology, "Stevens . . . employs the form of romantic quest against itself, not merely to destroy it by describing its 'inadequacy' to the Modern world, but to reveal what it obscures, what, as a form, it 'intends to say' and could not" (*Destructive Poetics*, 89). Stevens' poetic elaborations within what seems to be the province of English Romanticism tend toward parody, redefining and transposing terms or refuting basic assumptions of the originals. He counters Shelley's Platonic "Spirit of Beauty" with the lines, in "Peter Quince at the Clavier,"

> Beauty is momentary in the mind—
> The fitful tracing of a portal;
> But in the flesh it is immortal.
> (CP, 91)

The "idiot minstrelsy" of the "bethous" of "Notes" (CP, 394) openly satirizes Shelley's "Be thou me" from "Ode to the West Wind." He responds to Keats' "Ah, happy, happy boughs, that cannot shed / Your leaves, nor ever bid the spring adieu" from "Ode on a Grecian Urn" with the questions "Is there no change of death in paradise? / Does ripe fruit never fall?" and the enigmatic "Death is the mother of beauty" from sections V and VI of "Sunday Morning" (CP, 68–69). And "The Idea of Order at Key West" (CP, 128–30) revises "The Solitary Reaper," converting the wistful emotiveness of Wordsworth's "Will no one tell me what she sings?" to an epistemological meditation on the song's capacity to order the scene:

> Ramon Fernandez, tell me, if you know,
> Why, when the singing ended and we turned
> Toward the town, tell why the glassy lights,
> The lights in the fishing boats at anchor there,
> As the night descended, tilting in the air,
> Mastered the night and portioned out the sea,
> Fixing emblazoned zones and fiery poles,
> Arranging, deepening, enchanting night.

Although the motif is by no means anti-Romantic (the contest between mind and nature being of considerable interest to the Romantics, especially Coleridge), the specific contrast with Wordsworth's less theoretical treatment adds definition to Stevens' theme. "Key West" enlarges Wordsworth's closing emphasis on memory ("The music in my heart I bore, / Long after it was heard no more") into a speculation on the meaning of the experience:

> Oh! Blessed rage for order, pale Ramon,
> The maker's rage to order words of the sea.

Stevens' disparagement of Romanticism itself, coupled with an elevation of feeling and imagination, signals an alteration of the categories. At this point, the vocabulary of Romanticism fails both Stevens and his readers. While he continues in prose comments to try to make headway with reference to the battered opposition of imagination/reality, his poetry has already transposed the duality;[6] as we have seen (in "Notes," "An Ordinary Evening," and elsewhere), "reality" achieves an inclusiveness that mitigates its conflict with imagination. The Romantic dichotomy, as such, is transcended; the poet pursues "the poem of the composition of the whole" (*CP*, 442) on (if not in) his own terms. As for the character of the transcendence (the "new romantic"), Stevens further orients himself by way of his approach to two contemporaries whose works (by Stevens' interpretation) represent divergent aspects of "romantic" inclination: Williams and Eliot.[7]

Stevens, labeling Williams a "romantic poet" (*OP*, 254), finds Williams' poetry "slightly sentimentalized" (*OP*, 255), but in that it undercuts poetic/aesthetic feeling by taking refuge in the "real." He says about this complication: "To a man with a sentimental side the anti-poetic is that truth, that reality to which all of us are forever fleeing" (*OP*, 255)—a perspective comprehending I. A. Richards' "The man who, in reaction to the commoner naïve forms of sentimentality, prides himself upon his hard-headedness and hard-heartedness, his hard-boiledness generally ... is only displaying a more sophisticated form of sentimentality" (*Practical Criticism*, 253). And conversely, Williams thinks that Stevens "seldom comes down on a statement of fact. It is always, 'thirteen ways of looking at a blackbird,' which cannot but weaken any attack" ("Wallace

Stevens," 236). In other words, both poets divide Williams' "anti-poetics" from Stevens' attraction to imaginative variation—the "fictional."

Williams' poetic theory is empiricist: in the last analysis, there are "no ideas but in things" (*Paterson*, vi), and our access to those things is sensuous. As with Wordsworth, though tending toward a different end, Williams turns sense impressions into a poetry concerned with direct experience of his environment. Stevens understands him as "a writer to whom writing is the grinding of a glass, the polishing of a lens by means of which he hopes to be able to see clearly" (*OP*, 258). Williams' poetry is a vehicle encouraging concentration on the world-as-it-is but doing so through personal accounts of experience. For Stevens, on the other hand,

> ... Things as they are
> Are changed upon the blue guitar
>
> (*CP*, 165)

—through a strength of "mind" eclipsing the personalized ("A strong mind in a weak neighborhood" [*CP*, 474]);[8] this interest abjures both Williams' brand of sentimentality and (to the extent to which the distinction is appropriate) that often associated with Romantic idealism.[9]

If, in certain respects, Williams' poetry lies close to the personal expressiveness of Wordsworth's, the nature of Stevens' objection to Williams/Wordsworth automatically allies him more closely with Eliot and, among Wordsworth's contemporaries, with Keats' obstinate impersonalness (opposing Romantic sentimentality)—though Stevens overcomes the idealist turn of Keats' Romantic enthusiasm.[10] Like Stevens (and unlike Wordsworth and Williams), Keats inclines toward abstract speculation—as if in anticipation of the Stevensian "abstraction blooded" (*CP*, 385) and "new romanticism." Critics who, with Bloom and Baird, mark Stevens as a literary descendent of Wordsworth tend to construe his poetry as a history of the poet's development. But Stevens' "mundo" is an invented world "revolving ... in crystal" (*CP*, 407), for which the conception, confoundingly, sustains the irrationality of the aesthetical—a convolution not incompatible with Keats' doctrine of "negative capability": a talent for enjoying "uncertainties, Mysteries, doubts" (*Selected Poems and Letters*, 261) without a specifically emotional resolution.[11] This attention to impersonalness and the vitally new puts Stevens in league with Eliot's "Poetry is not a turning loose of emotion, but an escape from emotion; it is not the expression of personality, but an escape from personality" (*The Sacred Wood*, 58). Eliot (aptly stamped by Bates as "a notorious anti-romantic" [*Wallace Stevens*, 169]) proposes that "the more perfect the artist, the more completely separate in him will be the man who suffers and the mind which creates; the more perfectly will the mind digest and transmute the passions which are its material" (54). And in his celebrated rejection of Wordsworth's approach to poetry: "The business of the poet is not to find new emotions, but to use the ordinary ones and, in working them up into poetry, to express feelings which are not in actual emotions at all. And emotions which he has never experienced will serve his turn as well as those familiar to him. Consequently, we must believe that 'emotion recollected in tranquillity' is an inexact formula" (58).

Those characterizing Stevens as Romantic often miscast Eliot as his opposite. Baird's "One does not expect to find Stevens and Eliot at any point in accord" (*The Dome and the Rock*, 194) overlooks that, for instance, Stevens' "Poetry is not personal" (*OP*, 159) almost exactly reproduces Eliot's "The emotion of art is impersonal" (*The Sacred Wood*, 59). Riddel supposes that "Stevens and poetry had weathered three decades of Eliot's broadsides against romanticism, and had gone about its business creating a new secular (and humanistic) poetry out of the vestiges of a routed Romantic style" ("The Contours of Stevens Criticism," 262). Yet Stevens tells us that Romanticism "belittles" the imagination (*NA*, 138), and that "it is natural for us to identify the imagination with those that extend its abnormality. It is like identifying liberty with those that abuse it" (*NA*, 153)—in the same vein as Eliot's "Romanticism is a short cut to the strangeness without the reality, and it leads its disciples only back upon themselves" (*The Sacred Wood*, 31). Pearce traces an "insistent opposition: the egocentric as against the theocentric, man without history as against history without man, the antinomian as against the orthodox, personality as against culture, the Adamic as against the mythic.... In modern times the great figures in the opposition have been Stevens and Eliot" (*Continuity of American Poetry*, 423). But for Stevens, agreeing with Eliot's emphasis on the poet's relation to tradition, "poetry is the scholar's art" (*OP*, 167). While Bloom reads Stevens' "The Creations of Sound" and "Esthétique du Mal" as direct attacks on Eliot (*Poems of Our Climate*, 151–52 and 226–28), this interpretation is turned on its head when Stevens thinks of "the romantic" in the positive sense and the poet who comes to his mind is Eliot: "It is in the sense of living intensity, living singularity that it is the vital element in poetry. The most brilliant instance of the romantic in this sense is Mr. Eliot, who incessantly revives the past and creates the future" (*OP*, 252).[12]

Stevens' recurrent references to poetry and the poet tempt the reader to accept literally and autobiographically the dictum from "The Man with the Blue Guitar" that "poetry is the subject of the poem" (*CP*, 176)—turning the poem into, in A. Walton Litz' phrase, "an ars poetica of stunning complexity" (*Introspective Voyager*, 235). However, as we have begun to see, while the surface of Stevens' poetic subject is often the activity of writing, the improvisations disclose the effort of "the essential poem at the centre of things"—"the huge, high harmony" (*CP*, 440) of the fictional integration. It is

> ... the poem of the whole,
> The poem of the composition of the whole,
> The composition of blue sea and of green
>
> (*CP*, 442)

—component colors of the "turquoise rock." The Introduction to *The Necessary Angel* makes the point:

> The theory of poetry, as a subject of study, was something with respect to which I had nothing but the most ardent ambitions. It seemed to me to be one of the great subjects of study. I do not mean one more *Ars Poetica* having to do, say, with the techniques of poetry and perhaps with its history. I mean poetry itself, the naked poem, the imagination manifesting itself in its domination of words. (*NA*, vii–viii)

Frye refers to Stevens as "a poet for whom the theory and the practice of poetry were inseparable," maintaining that "Stevens is of particular interest and value to the critical theorist because he sees so clearly that the only ideas the poet can deal with are those directly involved with, and implied by, his own writing: that, in short, 'Poetry is the subject of the poem'" ("The Realistic Oriole," 161). Like the "decreationist" approach (in other respects its opposite number), the view of Stevens-as-Romantic, reading the poetry as autobiography, believes that, as Litz puts it, "The real tradition in Stevens' art is his own poetic progress" (*Introspective Voyager*, 51).[13] Or as Bloom says with reference to "An Ordinary Evening": "'The never-ending meditation' is not 'experience' but rather the process of Stevens' writing" (*Poems of Our Climate*, 311). But Stevens leaves no doubt that by "the poet," he means "any man of imagination" (Edelstein, *Wallace Stevens*, 29); and in the "Adagia" he writes, "Poetry is a poetic conception, however expressed. A poem is poetry expressed in words" (*OP*, 163).

From this vantage point, the task of writing poetry is seen as ostensible subject—a constantly recurring symbol for the general process of integrative thinking. This subtlety makes a discrimination which rethinks Coleridge's idealist differentiation between primary and secondary imagination. Though Marius Bewley's notion that "Coleridgean imagination has become the theme of Stevens' poetry as a whole in a way it never became the theme of Coleridge's poetry as a whole" (*The Com-*

plex Fate, 184) both skews and overstates the case (considering Stevens' negative view of idealism and recognition of the peripheral relation of imagination/reality to his "central theme"), there is a sense in which an analogy between "primary" and "secondary" (expressly poetic) imagination interests Stevens.[14] As Coleridge describes it, primary imagination is the act of mind by which we invent both world and self ("as a repetition in the finite mind of the eternal act of creation in the infinite I AM [*Biographia Literaria*, 1:202]);[15] and it is in an analogously broad sense that Stevens discusses imagination/creation (the "central poem"). In Stevens' work, poetry, as product and process, becomes a synecdoche for creativity in general—a figuration found in section XXVIII of "An Ordinary Evening":

> This endlessly elaborating poem
> Displays the theory of poetry,
> As the life of poetry. A more severe,
>
> More harassing master would extemporize
> Subtler, more urgent proof that the theory
> Of poetry is the theory of life,
>
> As it is, in the intricate evasions of as,
> In things seen and unseen, created from nothingness,
> The heavens, the hells, the worlds, the longed-for lands.
>   (*CP*, 486)

The initial hypothesis of the passage—"the theory of poetry, / As the life of poetry"—conforms to what Lucy Beckett calls "that constant preoccupation with poetry itself and what it may achieve, that self-consciousness, that some have seen as Stevens' great fault" (*Wallace Stevens*, 173). But the preoccupation of the passage is not with this preliminary. Instead the emphasis falls on the subtler revision by "a more severe, // More harassing master" who would find "the theory of poetry" to be "the theory of life."[16] A letter of December 1940 (though preceding "An Ordinary Evening" by nine years) clarifies Stevens' intent: "To most people poetry means certain specimens of it, but these specimens are merely parts of a great whole. I am not thinking of the body of poetic literature, because that whole body is merely a group of specimens. I am thinking of the poetic side of life, of the abstraction and the theory" (*Letters*, 383). In this way,

> One poem proves another and the whole,
> For the clairvoyant men that need no proof:
> The lover, the believer and the poet.
>
> (*CP*, 441)[17]

"The poetic side of life" is "the central poem" (*CP*, 441): "It is something seen and known in lesser poems" (*CP*, 440). The poet's activity instances that more comprehensive generative capability/clairvoyance assumed by the "higher human being" in Nietzsche's *Gay Science*:

The higher human being ... calls his own nature *contemplative* and overlooks that he himself is really the poet who keeps creating this life.... As a poet, he certainly has *vis contemplativa* and the ability to look back upon his work, but at the same time also and above all *vis creativa*.... We who think and feel at the same time are those who really continually *fashion* something that had not been there before: the whole eternally growing world of valuations, colors, accents, perspectives, scales, affirmations, and negations.... Whatever has *value* in our world now does not have value in itself, according to its nature—nature is always value-less, but has been *given* value at some time, as a present—and it was *we* who gave and bestowed it. Only we have created the world *that concerns man!* (241–42)

Stevens conjures a counterpart of Nietzsche's "higher human being" in the person of the "impossible possible philosophers' man" of "Asides on the Oboe":

> The man who has had the time to think enough,
> The central man, the human globe, responsive
> As a mirror with a voice, the man of glass,
> Who in a million diamonds sums us up.
>
> (*CP*, 250)

While momentarily bridging the gap between poetic and philosophic, such far-reaching metaphoricity indicates the primacy of poetic discovery and its "unofficial view" (*NA*, 40)—since philosophy, too, depends on central insight of an ultimately poetical sort.[18] The "impossible possible philosophers' man," being "impossible," has only hypothetical existence; but his image, as an aspect of humanity, is a satisfaction:

> He is the transparence of the place in which
> He is and in his poems we find peace.
> (*CP*, 251)

And "Examination of the Hero in a Time of War" offers an intensified Nietzschean vision of the contemplative/creative in which the comparative "higher human being" becomes the superlative "highest man":

> To meditate the highest man, not
> The highest supposed in him and over,
> Creates, in the blissfuller perceptions,
> What unisons create in music.[19]

> The highest man with nothing higher
> Than himself, his self, the self that embraces
> The self of the hero, the solar single.
> (*CP*, 280)

Illustrating the maxim that "the theory / Of poetry is the theory of life," section XXIX (*CP*, 486–87) of "An Ordinary Evening" schematizes the "poetic side of life." Two seemingly discrete scenes are described: "In the land of the lemon trees, yellow and yellow were / Yellow-blue, yellow-green, pungent with citron-sap," while

> In the land of the elm trees, wandering mariners
> Looked on big women, whose ruddy-ripe images
> Wreathed round and round the round wreath of autumn.[20]

Yet in the poem's narrative progress, the overlapping language dissolves, and the adjectival alternatives re-place, the illusory boundaries of what we would ordinarily think of as the actual:

> When the mariners came to the land of the lemon trees,
> At last, in that blond atmosphere, bronzed hard,
> They said, "We are back once more in the land of the elm trees
>
> But folded over, turned round." It was the same,
> Except for the adjectives, an alteration
> Of words that was a change of nature, more
>
> Than the difference that clouds make over a town.
> The countrymen were changed and each constant thing.
> Their dark-colored words had redescribed the citrons.

The fable, displaying Stevens' contention (from "Description without Place") that "the word is the making of the world" (*CP*, 345), further extends "An Ordinary Evening"'s explanation of "the commodious adjective." The "poetic" change of "adjectives" signifies the changing "sense of things" by which a more primary intuition recreates the experience. This correlative function of poetry's particulars subsumes the narrowly poetic into the arena of the "primary" and "central," so that any given poem establishes

> Variations in the tones of a single sound,
> The last, or sounds so single they seemed one
> (*CP*, 316)

—an ultimacy which leads to: "It comes to this that we use the same faculties when we write poetry that we use when we create gods or when we fix the bearing of men in reality" (*OP*, 216).[21] Stevens' meditations on poetry, tending away from the narrowing effects of narcissistic absorption ("the quirk[s] of a self-conscious writer" [*OP*, 253]), find: "description is revelation" by which the words inscribe a world "intenser than any actual life could be" (*CP*, 344). For the mariners of the fable, the question of whether the land is actually one of elm trees or of lemon trees does not arise. When the trees are "redescribed," it is "an alteration / Of words that was a change of nature."[22]

These figurative usages of "poet" and "poetry" divide Stevens' work from Romanticism's investment in the poet's messianic role. Though he identifies the poet as one who supplies aesthetic fictions that "help people to live their lives" (*NA*, 29), he makes it plain with regard to the directly "sociological or political . . . obligation of the poet" that "he has none" (*NA*, 27). He would scarcely say, with Shelley, that "poets are the unacknowledged legislators of the world" (*Shelley's Critical Prose*, 36); and only in the most metaphorical context could he assent to Shelley's "poets . . . are the institutors of laws, and the founders of civil society, and the inventors of the arts of life, and the teachers, who draw into a certain propinquity with the beautiful and the true, that partial apprehension of the agencies of the invisible world which is called religion" (*Shelley's Critical Prose*, 7). Stevens, as has been seen, deconstructs the "invisible"—whether transcendentalism, theogony, Platonism—for the sake of a new clairvoyance of the "visible." At "one of the limits of reality" (*CP*, 374) within the integrations of "Credences":

> . . . The trumpet cries
> This is the successor of the invisible.
> (*CP*, 376)

In Shelley's view, "A poet participates in the eternal, the infinite, and the one; as far as relates to his conceptions, time and place and number are not" (*Shelley's Critical Prose*, 7); for Stevens, again, "It Must Change" (*CP*, 389): "Death is the mother of beauty."

A similar divergence between Stevens and Whitman allows Whitman's "Passage to India" to greet the poet as "the true son of God" in whose poems "Trinitas divine shall be gloriously accomplish'd and compacted" and "Nature and Man shall be disjoin'd and diffused no more" (*Leaves of Grass*, 415–16). Whitman's poet would undo the Fall from Paradise, restoring a prelapsarian state of grace; and by "the poet" Whitman intends an actual future poet (not "any man of imagination") whose poems would effect a lasting change in the human situation.

While a diluted account of Stevens' "major man" and "hero" might take them to be incarnations of the poet as the Whitmanian "true son of God," and while Stevens expresses (in an October 1948 letter) the wish that "the novelists, the actors, the poets could once more get the upper hand of the politicians and their conspiracies" (*Letters*, 621), Stevens' central interest remains "the poetic [not the political] side of life"—an interest different from the prospect that

> Finally shall come the poet worthy that name,
> The true son of God shall come singing his songs.
> (*Leaves of Grass*, 415)

Stevens' poet, rather than leading us forward (or backward) to an ideal state, discovers a way of living with "things as they are" (and as they "are changed") at present: "What a modern poet desires, above everything else, is to be nothing more than a poet of the present time" (*OP*, 244). And Stevens sees Whitman-as-poet accordingly: "It seems to me . . . that Whitman is disintegrating as the world, of which he made himself a part, disintegrates" (*Letters*, 871).

Forging a consonancy between Stevens and Whitman, Riddel tells us: "In his only explicit reference to Whitman, Stevens characterizes the American mythmaker as an incarnate cosmic voice, the oracle of vitalism" ("Functions of a 'Literatus,'" 31)—referring to an often-quoted passage at the beginning of "Like Decorations" (*CP*, 150):

> In the far South the sun of autumn is passing
> Like Walt Whitman walking along a ruddy shore.
> He is singing and chanting the things that are part of him,
> The worlds that were and will be, death and day.
> Nothing is final, he chants. No man shall see the end.
> His beard is of fire and his staff is a leaping flame.

Vendler describes these lines as "the mythologizing of Whitman-as-sun into a prophetic figure" (*On Extended Wings*, 66), and Pearce postulates that "Stevens [like Whitman] is another sun ('son?') of autumn. (Generally in the poems 'sun'='reality,' and 'autumn'—like 'spring'—=the poet's season, since it is one in which he is protected from the sun, yet is not, as in winter, denied it.) His chant is Whitman's, as is his subject" (*Continuity of American Poetry*, 379). But the passage primarily lionizes the sun (though "passing") and not Whitman himself. The sun's appearance is like Walt Whitman's, with its "beard . . . of fire" and its "staff" of "flame"—an incandescent visible similarity. The sun is autumnal, low on the horizon—as if "walking along a ruddy shore"; "the far South" dis-locates it from Whitman-of-Mannahatta but is in touch with Stevens' view "that Whitman is disintegrating": a sun which seemingly/ultimately burns itself up/out. Stevens' description overturns Whitman's desire for union with the eternal: the sun is represented as

> . . . singing and chanting the things that are part of him,
> The worlds that were and will be, death and day.
> Nothing is final, he chants. . . .

"The things that are part of him" is a version of the disintegrating "world of which he made himself a part"; but as transformed by Stevens' present poetry, the sun (and Stevens, through the sun) sings the non-Whitmanian chant of the finite, for which only change is sustained. The "chant" evokes "Sunday Morning"'s "ring of men" chanting "in orgy on a summer morn / Their boisterous devotion to the sun" (*CP*, 69–70). This is the world in which one can be a "pupil of the gorgeous wheel." And when the solar image from "Like Decorations" is reprised in "The News and the Weather," it is with reference to the sun only:

> The blue sun in his red cockade
> Walked the United States today,
>
> Taller than any eye could see,
> Older than any man could be.
> (*CP*, 264)

And Pearce's construction of spring and autumn into Stevens' "poet's seasons" forgets the ecstatically affirmative tone of "Credences of Summer," the celebrations of summer's sun in "Sunday Morning," the noonday sun in "Notes." Without doubt, spring and autumn are "the poet's seasons" for the Romantics, but Stevens turns the seasons to his own use. Spring is the locus of the Shelleyan "invisible," summer the center of the Stevensian "visible":[23]

> The weight of primary noon,
> The ABC of being,
>
> The ruddy temper, the hammer
> Of red and blue, the hard sound—
> Steel against intimation—the sharp flash,
> The vital, arrogant, fatal, dominant X.[24]
> (CP, 288)

Allegiance to the visible also separates Stevens from Emersonian transcendentalism—undercutting Pearce's association of Stevens with Emerson (rather than Eliot) via the "Adamic" tradition. About Emerson, Pearce says, "The opposition, self against what he in fact called the anti-poetic world, is evident everywhere in his work. It is especially sharp in the poems, where it becomes a means of transmutation of the world into something freshly seen, fully found, and so a manifestation of the Adamic principle itself" (*Continuity of American Poetry*, 153).[25] "Fully found" borrows from Stevens' "Credences," where summer's integration becomes "this hard prize, / Fully made, fully apparent, fully found" (CP, 376); but while Emerson's world may be "fully found," it is not, in Stevens' sense, "fully made." Emerson's poet excavates a pre-existing Truth: "There is a property in the horizon which no man has but he whose eye can integrate all the parts, that is, the poet" (*Nature*, 23). Stevens' integrations, as improvisations of the poet (or "any man of imagination") and not revelations of the otherwise-veiled Ideal, pursue a different idea of "order."[26] At the conclusion of "The Man on the Dump," Stevens satirizes the Emersonian "the world is emblematic" (35), and "nature is a sea of forms" (30):

> Is it to hear the blatter of grackles and say
> *Invisible priest;* is it to eject, to pull
> The day to pieces and cry *stanza my stone?*
> Where was it one first heard of the truth? The the.
>
> (*CP*, 203)

In Stevens' anti-Logistical "variations" and "seemings": "Words are not forms of a single word" (*CP*, 204). It is, therefore, only in a sharply delimited usage (poetry-as-transcendent-analogue) that one can assert, as Richard Eberhart does: "in spite of himself Wallace Stevens is a transcendentalist" ("Emerson and Wallace Stevens," 64); and at that point the terms are better altered.[27]

Cassirer contends, in a passage Stevens uses in "Imagination as Value" (*NA*, 136): "Imagination [for Romanticism] is no longer that special human activity which builds up the human world of art. It now has universal metaphysical value.... The true poem ... is the universe itself, the one work of art which is forever perfecting itself" (*Essay on Man*, 155–56). While the Romantic poets frequently disparage religious orthodoxy, they are inevitably drawn to the metaphysical "invisible." To Stevens, on the other hand, "it is important to believe that the visible is the equivalent of the invisible; and once we believe it, we have destroyed the imagination; that is to say, we have destroyed the false imagination, the false conception of the imagination as some incalculable *vates* within us, unhappy Rodomontade" (*NA*, 61). This decreation frees imagination from preternatural preoccupations, restoring it to the region where "revelations are not the revelations of belief."

For Stevens, a transcendentalist predisposition (and the meliorist tendency which accompanies it) shares in the sentimentality he broadly attributes to Romanticism. Stevens, replacing transcendental "truth" (and the "sentimental") with poetic "fiction" (as food for "contemplation"), explains: "Supreme poetry can be produced only on the highest possible level of the cognitive" (*Letters*, 500). Along these lines, it is interesting to recall Richards' "Most, if not all, sentimental fixations and distortions of feeling are the result of inhibitions, and often when we discuss sentimentality we are looking at the wrong side of the picture" (*Practical Criticism*, 252)—which buttresses Stevens' contention that "Romanticism is to poetry what the decorative is to painting" (*OP*, 169). "In the long run" (*OP*, 180), Stevens views Romanticism's over-emphasis on "feeling" (including metaphysical attachment, and devotion to Nature) as a sentimental phenomenon resulting from a poverty of genuine feeling: "The ideal is the actual become anaemic. The romantic is often pretty much the same thing" (*OP*, 164).[28]

CHAPTER III

The ABC of Being

Stevens' "The Figure of the Youth as Virile Poet" divides philosophic from poetic "truth"—the former as "the official view of being," the latter "an unofficial view" (*NA*, 40). The differentiation is interesting in two respects: it recognizes divergent kinds of truths, and it refers to poetry as a "view of being." Although attention to the relative merits of poetry and philosophy as vehicles for truth has a long history in English and American literature,[1] separating truth itself into two disparate realms indicates a distinctly modern (nineteenth- and twentieth-century) turn—one closely related to philosophical re-evaluations of metaphysics.[2] And Stevens' choice of the phrase "view of being" reinforces the disjunction by suggesting that poetry advances an alternative to philosophical ontology.

As we have begun to see, Stevens' "poetic truth"—unlike its ideal metaphysical or ontological counterpart—is not incomplicate, either in any single poem or over the course of his poetic evolution. The difficulty—especially of the sparser, more contemplative later poems marked by long, sometimes cryptic, discussions of abstract questions—which has stimulated decreationist hypotheses, has also produced, in the light of Stevens' phrase "view of being," a spectrum of criticism defining the later poetry as a "poetry of being" (or "nothingness"). This strategy, like the decreationist, assumes a decisive break between earlier and later poetry—in this case effected by a desire to experience being/nothingness-as-such (à la Heidegger), generally bypassing "pure reality" (the thing-in-itself).

The phrase "poetry of being," popularized by Miller in "Wallace Stevens' Poetry of Being," has become useful to those sharing the idea that Stevens' later poetry seeks a deeper experience of being-as-such[3]—though for this approach generally and for individual critics, there seems to be underlying confusion as to both the nature of "being" and the role of the "being question" in Stevens' thought. Miller himself on one occasion construes "being" as "nothing" (157), on another sees it as "the humanlike figure which the mind is always confronting at every extreme" (160), and elsewhere seems to equate it with "reality"; while Hines, reading Stevens as a Heideggerian, tells us that "Das Sein des Seinenden [sic] ist nicht selbst ein Seiendes" (*The Later Poetry of Wallace Stevens*, 119),[4] yet also speaks of "The figure of Being" (129). According to Miller, "being" as "nothing," is

the universal power, visible nowhere in itself, and yet visible everywhere in all things. It is what all things share through the fact that they are. Being is not a thing like other things, and therefore can appear to man only as nothing, yet it is what all things participate in if they are to exist at all. All Stevens' later poetry has as its goal the releasing of the evanescent glimpse of being which is as close as man can come to a possession of the ground of things. ("Stevens' Poetry of Being," 157)

And Hines, taking a similar position, describes "Being" (capital B) as "ground or source of both the mind and the world. It is that by virtue of which the things that exist are present" (20n).

Such terminology draws heavily on Heidegger's ontological speculation; at the same time, the contemporary language masks a conception of mystical force (or "power") more metaphysical than Heideggerian, and resembling the Romantic "Spirit of Beauty" in Shelley's "Hymn to Intellectual Beauty": "The awful shadow of some unseen Power / Floats though unseen among us" (*Poetical Works of Shelley*, 356).[5] And although it is evident that in the later poetry (as in the earlier[6]) Stevens wants to capture something—"this hard prize" (*CP*,

376), "one thing . . . / No greater than a cricket's horn" (*CP*, 247), "the palm at the end of the mind" (*OP*, 117)—it is less clear that this projection retraces the ontological or metaphysical ruminations intrinsic to an "official view" and inherent in the notion of a "poetry of being."

Miller describes a dialectic of decreation and re-creation which, for Stevens, can within a given poem move so rapidly from one extreme to the other that the "oscillation" at last "becomes a blur in which opposites are touched simultaneously, as alternating current produces a steady beam of light, and the cycle of decreation and imagining, hopelessly false if the poet goes through it at leisure, becomes true at last to things as they are if he moves through it fast enough" ("Stevens' Poetry of Being," 151).[7] That is, the rapid motion finally, in effect, becomes a static state, and this poetically devised stasis momentarily reveals a depth of "being." By this view, Stevens simultaneously grasps both poles of the imagination/reality dichotomy, and "as the tension between imagination and reality diminishes there is an unperceived emptying out of both, until, at the moment they touch, in the brevity of a poem which includes beginning and ending in a breath, the poet finds himself face to face with a universal nothing." And, reversing Hegelian dialectic, "the nothing is not nothing. It is. It is being" ("Stevens' Poetry of Being," 157).

The strength of this account (over the decreative) is its appreciation of the reciprocal referentiality of imagined and real—a principle with ample theoretical precedent. Cassirer, for example, tells us: "Language and art are constantly oscillating between two opposite poles, an objective and a subjective pole. No theory of language or art could forget or suppress either one of these poles, though the stress may be laid now on the one and now on the other" (*An Essay on Man*, 138).[8] And Joseph Warren Beach's explication of such views as the Coleridgean and Emersonian offers a Romantic variation: "The life of the imagination has two poles, the real and the ideal, and poetry is in perpetual oscillation between these poles" (*A Romantic*

View of Poetry, 111). But while the general point that imagination and reality are necessarily related suits Stevens, the notion that the poetry exposes, advocates, or engages idiosyncratic forms of oscillation between the two for the sake of ontological revelation is, as we have indicated, more problematic.

Reading the language of certain poems as critical vocabulary, Miller transports Stevens' phrases into theory. Section IX of "It Must Change" in "Notes" (*CP*, 396–97), for instance, becomes a Milleresque discussion of oscillation. The poem offers:

> The poem goes from the poet's gibberish to
> The gibberish of the vulgate and back again.
> Does it move to and fro or is it of both
>
> At once? Is it a luminous flittering
> Or the concentration of a cloudy day?

A polarity is established in this passage, "a luminous flittering" between poles suggested, yet the passage shows the possibility of embracing "both at once" as an alternative to, and not the result of, the "flittering" back and forth. Though the essential elements of Miller's scheme seem present, the appearance of disjunction subverts his cause/effect relationship, preventing Stevens' "luminous flitterings" from condensing into the "concentration of a cloudy day"—that is, from becoming a viable example of "oscillation . . . in which opposites are touched simultaneously." The lines' descriptions are interrogatives in a collect of interrogations into change. The indication of the questions may be that the poem's "peculiar speech" instrumentalizes both analogizing "flitter" and metaphorizing "concentration" in composing the "peculiar potency of the general"—a potentiality inherent in language-as-such. But the description of the "poem" reformulates the "intricate evasions of as" in the confounding compaction of metaphor. And, as with these interrogative musings, the sense of Stevens' metaphorizing/analogizing transformations is often patiently meditative, leisurely. The series of hypotheticals which discloses the "poem" in Part II of "The Rock," for example, allows a gradual growth of fictive "leaves" which, "if they broke into bud, / If they broke into bloom, if they bore fruit," would (and do) become/reveal, again in metaphor, "the poem, the icon and the man" (*CP*, 526–27)[9]—a metapoetic amplification of the tempo and imagery in the earlier poem "The Man with the Blue Guitar," with its intimation of the gradual, progressive action of thought on the real: "Slowly the ivy on the stones / Becomes the stones" (*CP*, 170), and

> Deeper within the belly's dark
> Of time, time grows upon the rock.
> (*CP*, 171)[10]

Delineating his own version of the "rapid shift," Macksey finds: "The poet can move with the speed of light from the bare 'winter branch' to 'the bough of summer'" ("The Climates of Wallace Stevens," 187) (a reference to the 1915 poem "Sunday Morning"); and, as with Miller, this takes place in the context of a coincidence of "being" and "nothingness." By way of explanation Macksey, consulting Hegel, submits that "Stevens begins, as did Hegel in the *Logik*, by confronting pure Being; it vanishes before his attention and is displaced by its antithesis, the nothingness which is to play an increasingly vital role in his thought" (191).[11] Macksey, referring to "The Snow Man" (*CP*, 9–10), contends that the poem "becomes a dialogue with the self where mood, understanding, and language (Heidegger's formula) allow man, standing in the 'no-thingness' of being, to reveal nothingness" (198)—congruent with Miller's: "Only the snow man, the man who is 'nothing himself,' is free of imagination's fictions and can behold 'nothing that is not there and the nothing that is'" ("Stevens' Poetry of Being," 155). Although "The Snow Man," like "Sunday Morning," appears in *Harmonium*, while "poetry of being" is primarily applied to the later poetry, it may be Stevens' poem in which a sense of "nothingness" most explicitly predominates; but this "nothing" does not become the indeterminacy that in Hegelian terms (and in Miller's reversal) would leave "being" and "nothing" indistinguishable.[12] The winter scene—as it includes pines, junipers, spruces, "the sound of the wind"—does not attempt to effect the wholly indeterminate; and if not indeterminacy, then the "nothing" is not "being" (or vice-versa).

The poem's wintry landscape, a decreated scene (in Stevens' usage), reveals "nothingness" as a condition existing at an ebb in integrations—the ground for the new beginnings (or fictions) of spring. The decreation is a dis-integration: a falling apart of complicate integrations, as when, in "Credences,"

> A complex of emotions falls apart,
> In an abandoned spot.
>
> (CP, 377)

"The Snow Man" calls on images of desolateness or sparsity continuous with other "poems of winter," both early and late: the snow-covered trees, the "bare place," the empty sound of the wind, and, of course, "the listener" who is "nothing himself"—prefiguring the imagination which "adds nothing, except itself." The poem rejects the concatenation by which we might imagine a "misery in the sound of the wind"—consonant with the "misery" of "nothing to have at heart" in "Poetry Is a Destructive Force" (CP, 192). Here again, however, the imagined is not wholly absent. As in "The Plain Sense of Things," for which "the absence of the imagination had / Itself to be imagined" (CP, 503), in "The Snow Man": "One must have a mind of winter,"

> ... not to think
> Of any misery in the sound of the wind,
> In the sound of a few leaves,
>
> Which is the sound of the land
> Full of the same wind
> That is blowing in the same bare place.

The poem is not passive absorption; a "mind of winter" is needed to appreciate the "weather"—"To discover an order as of / A season, . . . / To discover winter and know it well." "The January sun" symbolizes this wintry integration—not identical with summer's expansiveness, yet providing the imaginative compass of the scene. Stevens says in a 1944 letter to Hi Simons: "I shall explain The Snow Man as an example of the necessity of identifying oneself with reality in order to understand it and enjoy it" (*Letters*, 464).[13] The "nothing" of the poem simultaneously reveals a "plain reality" which harbors no mystical (or onto-mystical) element and (as with "The Plain Sense of Things") an ironic act of mind ("identifying oneself with reality").

De-centering this fictionality, Bové offers: "It is by virtue of the awareness that there is no center [meaning that there is only a central "nothingness"] that Stevens is able to rethink specific centered myths and metaphors and show them to be fiction in a radical sense in the early poetry" (*Destructive Poetics*, 186). Like Miller and Macksey (and with an affinitive point in mind), he turns to "The Snow Man" for confirmation, reading the poem as "the earliest certain demonstration of Stevens' knowledge of the nothingness at the heart of fiction" (189–90). Referring to the "abyss of metaphor, of absence which is the being of the poem," he describes "The Snow Man" as an "anti-poem" which, "as an *ars poetica*, shows how literally poetry, linguistic discourse of the highest order, is a metaphysical fiction based on nothing. . . . 'The Snow Man' shows that all poems have nothingness at their center and that other poems and poets, unconscious of this, while delusively trying to name the center and thus to obscure the nothing of what is, always disclose the omnipresence of mere metaphor in poetry" (192).[14]

Compatible with the destruction of "metaphysical fictions," "Connoisseur of Chaos" (*CP*, 215–16) declares that we "cannot go back" to the time "when bishops' books / Resolved the world"—books propounding the essential unity of human experience within a universal design. But Bové's extension— that Stevens undercuts all fictional or experiential "centers"—

neglects the connoisseur's insistence that although the "squirming facts exceed the squamous mind," it remains that

> ... relation appears,
> A small relation expanding like the shade
> Of a cloud on sand, a shape on the side of a hill.

And in the same way, "centralities" figure positively and repeatedly in Stevens' poems: "A Primitive Like an Orb" refers, as we have seen, to the "essential poem at the centre of things" (*CP*, 440); affirming the integrations of "Credences," the poet proclaims: "this, this is the centre that I seek" (*CP*, 373); in "Reply to Papini" he writes that the poet:

> Increases the aspects of experience,
> As in an enchantment, analyzed and fixed
> And final. This is the centre.
>
> (*CP*, 447–48)

And in "The Snow Man" itself such "relation appears" in the way the "mind of winter" identifies itself "with reality in order to understand it and enjoy it."

Bové's rhetorically Heideggerian account of "the nothing" would ensconce Stevens as a theoretician/practitioner of "destructive phenomenological" praxes:

The result of phenomenological destruction and interpretation is a return to actuality, to an acknowledgement of Being-in-the-World as a fundamental temporal constituent structure of Dasein. Since the poet is free to blast away the "aesthetic" interpretations in language by "re-thinking" the "centers" and revealing their Being as a fiction, he performs and discloses movements which are possible only in the medium of life and not in art. (*Destructive Poetics*, 189)[15]

This "destructive" program moves toward the decreationist as Bové sees the poet promoting "a return to actuality."[16] Yet, other difficulties aside, he has said, paradoxically, regarding "The Snow Man" both that "poetry . . . is a metaphysical fiction based on nothing" and that "what is" ("actuality"?) is "nothing." And this problematic construct carries forward to the late poem "The Rock," whose central figuration is reduced by Bové to the image of "an image of the nothingness of what-is": "The rock . . . represents a complete barrenness, an ultimate progression downward toward no goal" (*Destructive Poetics*, 209). But Stevens' description gives us the rock's eventuality as "the habitation of the whole" and as

> . . . the gate
> To the enclosure, day, the things illumined
>
> By day, night and that which night illumines
> (*CP*, 528)

—by which the poem contemplates the rock as both ground and surrounding for the possibility of an imaged wholeness, richness, and fullness, and, far from "metaphysical fiction based on nothing," presents the poetry itself as anti-metaphysical fiction based in integration of the "real" and "unreal."

Displaying this Stevensian conjunction of "being" and "nothingness"—and in relation to the question of fictionality and actuality—"Seventy Years Later," Part I of "The Rock" (*CP*, 525–26), doubts the reality of old memories: "It is an illusion that we were ever alive." A remembered encounter seems:

> An invention, an embrace between one desperate clod
> And another in a fantastic consciousness,
> In a queer assertion of humanity:
>
> A theorem proposed between the two—
> Two figures in a nature of the sun,
> In the sun's design of its own happiness,
>
> As if nothingness contained a métier
> A vital assumption, an impermanence
> In its permanent cold, an illusion so desired
>
> That the green leaves came and covered the high rock,
> That the lilacs came and bloomed, like a blindness cleaned,
> Exclaiming bright sight, as it was satisfied,
>
> In a birth of sight. The blooming and the musk
> Were being alive, an incessant being alive,
> A particular of being, that gross universe.

Though the language associates the "rock" with the "gray particular of man's life," Miller, much like Bové, finds that "the rock of reality seems not to be a substantial reality, material and present before the poet's eyes. It seems to have come from nothingness. If it has come from nothingness, its source still defines it" ("Stevens' Poetry of Being," 156). The present, initially, seems empty in this scene, and the past like "an illusion," but again, as in "The Snow Man," this emptiness is not an attribute of being-as-such (or being-as-nothing). The poem speaks of past integrations, now "rigid in rigid emptiness," and concludes: "The lives these lived in the mind are at an end." Again, a wintry "nothingness" occurs—a seemingly "permanent cold," which Stevens identifies with lapsed imaginative energies. The sun, emblem of differentiating/unifying originative energy, is present only in distant retrospect, existing in memory, illuminating the seemingly hypothetical ("A theorem proposed between the two")—a temporal version of

> The sun of Asia creeps above the horizon
> Into this haggard and tenuous air,
> A tiger lamed by nothingness and frost
> ("Like Decorations," *CP*, 153)

or, from the later poem "Two Illustrations That the World Is What You Make of It" (1952),

> It was not the shadow of cloud and cold,
> But a sense of the distance of the sun—
> The shadow of a sense of his own.
> (*CP*, 513)

Stevens' "Adagia" assert that "reality is a vacuum" (*OP*, 168); the poetry adds that this is so in that its "emptiness" (or "indifference") calls for a stroke of imagination (in this case, both past and present)—"As if nothingness contained a métier." "The blooming and the musk" of the integration were "a particular of being"—once-vivid manifestations that now arouse lifeless memories and give them life ("an incessant being alive," about which it can, again, be said: "As if nothingness contained a métier"). The métier seemingly contained as a "vital assumption" affiliates the "nothingness" with naked Alpha (the infant A), which as signification contains the assumption of Omega. Without such integrations there is no "being," that is, no sense of life.

Miller's essay "Stevens' Rock and Criticism as Cure" gives another and still more elaborate account of poetic fictionality, nevertheless preserving the central importance of "nothingness" (as the "abyss"):

> Since all referentiality in language is a fiction, the aboriginal trope or turning away from the abyss, the blind spot, the referentiality of language is its fall, its unconquerable penchant toward fiction. All words are initially catachreses. The distinction between literal and figurative is an alogical deduction or bifurcation from that primal misnaming. The fiction of the literal or proper is therefore the supreme fiction. (29)

On this view, the supreme fiction is a meta-fiction resulting from a meta-misconception, and, by extension, "notes toward" such a fiction lead us through the unsettling permutations of a *mise en abyme* within the terrain of a metalinguistic aporia.[17] This radically augments Miller's earlier supposition that Stevens, disturbed by the "evaporation" of the gods (which Miller connects with the original subject/object schism ["Stevens' Poetry of Being," 145]) and concerned with overcoming the exposed duality, inscribes a poetry which, despite language's distortional inclination, gets at the "being" of things. By the earlier, the gods, seen as imaginative superstructure, "reveal themselves to be [supreme?] fictions, aesthetic projections of man's gratuitous values" ("Stevens' Poetry of Being," 144); the poetry (or certain eccentric aesthetical qualities), with its eye toward "being," in some sense transcends fictionality. The later view, though seeming to accept the fictional "substrate" of language, sustains "nothing"/"the abyss" as if as a residue of the "truth of being": Stevens' poem now gets at the truth of the abyss.[18] Both tactics are distracted, by philosophical earnestness, from the pleasures of the texture/textuality of the merely going round—Stevens' supreme fictionality, which is the extravagantly positive moment of the "turquoise rock." Stevens' fiction of "The Rock" images "poetic truth" (the "unofficial view of being"), even "blessedness":

> The fiction of the leaves is the icon
>
> Of the poem, the figuration of blessedness,
> And the icon is the man.
>
> (*CP*, 526)[19]

As this positive a "fiction" becomes the "supreme fiction," a play on "supreme being" used humorously in "A High-Toned Old Christian Woman" and more seriously in "Notes" to name the poetical counterpart of the metaphysical. For Stevens, fictive offerings are in no way inferior to "official" truth; on the contrary, the usual sense of truth carries negative connotation in such poems as "On the Road Home" and "The Latest Freed Man." And for the significance (as opposed to falsity) of "supreme fiction," one can recall Stevens' autobiographical note from February 1954: "The author's work suggests the possibility of a supreme fiction, recognized as a fiction, in which men could propose to themselves a fulfilment. In the creation of any such fiction, poetry would have a vital significance. There are many poems relating to the interactions between reality and the imagination, which are to be regarded as marginal to this central theme" (*Letters*, 820).

At the end of his career, designating the fictional (and particularly "a supreme fiction") as his "central theme," Stevens also shows that the supreme fiction—while such that "men could propose to themselves a fulfilment"—is not deception, since it would be "recognized as a fiction." The supreme fiction would, as in "Of Modern Poetry," "be the finding of a satisfaction" (*CP*, 240), of "what will suffice" (*CP*, 239)—an instrumentation of

> Sounds passing through sudden rightnesses, wholly
> Containing the mind, below which it cannot descend,
> Beyond which it has no will to rise.
>
> (*CP*, 240)

Though language may be, from an ontological or epistemological point of view, originative distortion, that, we could say, is the problem of the philosopher; the poet, on the other hand, experiences and extends the "vital ambiance" of language (and its seemings), as by a

> ... grandiloquent
> Locution of a hand in a rhapsody.
> Its line moves quickly with the genius
>
> Of its improvisation until, at length,
> It enfolds the head in a vital ambiance.
> (CP, 379)

Part I of "The Rock" (in which "being" and "nothingness" appear) evidences such an adequacy: in the fiction of leaves and blooms, the desire for an integration is "satisfied, // In a birth of sight" (CP, 526). Other objections, for the moment, aside, failure to take full measure of the "supreme fiction" and, more generally, to preserve Stevens' positive sense of fiction seems an insoluble difficulty for the "poetry of being" (and "nothingness").

"Nothingness" and the "sense" of "being" (as a vitalness) again commingle in the late poem (1955) "A Clear Day and No Memories" (OP, 113):

> Today the air is clear of everything.
> It has no knowledge except of nothingness
> And it flows over us without meanings,
> As if none of us had ever been here before
> And are not now: in this shallow spectacle,
> This invisible activity, this sense.

Once more there is a winter integration—a "sense" in which the past (with its fictions) has vanished with the "sun" that once illuminated it. The clear air of the present moment has "no knowledge except of nothingness / And it flows over us without meanings." The indifference of the air, to the present as well as the past, is an indifference to the human, reminiscent of the indifferent night ("the color of the heavy hemlocks" [*CP*, 8]) in the early poem "Domination of Black" (1916). But as in "Domination," the indifferent (what seems objective) is so only in our apprehension of it. By the doubled meaning of the lines, the clear air, in the "invisible activity" of air, "flows over" this "invisible activity" which is ourselves. As he often does, Stevens exposes the full shape of the poem by the turn of the last line. Our "invisible activity" (which again is like the light that "adds nothing . . . ") is not simply a sense; it is "this sense": of what was, of what is, and of the indifferent "sense" of the air.[20]

The late poem (1954) "Conversation with Three Women of New England" (*OP*, 108–9) similarly affirms the existential variances in our "sense of things":

> The mode of the person becomes the mode of the world,
> For that person, and, sometimes, for the world itself.
> . . . .
> It follows that to change modes is to change the world.

The "three women" of the poem figure modes of comprehension/feeling which shape one's "sense of being" such that they become indistinguishable from the world(s) in which one lives. At the conclusion of the poem the speaker asks:

> In which one of these three worlds are the four of us
> The most at home? Or is it enough to have seen
> And felt and known the differences we have seen
> And felt and known in the colors in which we live,
> In the excellences of the air we breathe,
> The bouquet of being—enough to realize
> That the sense of being changes as we talk,
> That talk shifts the cycle of the scenes of kings?

The rhetorical question intimates that it is "enough" to have lived in the chromatic innovations of experience—"the excellences of the air we breathe." In these we find the "bouquet of being"—the "flower" of existence: a sense of life articulated (though not too exactly labeled) and including the realization that "the sense of being changes as we talk," since in conversing we change the mode, alter the color, and, consequently, "change the world." In the note of the final line, "talk shifts the cycle of the scenes of kings," Stevens reprises the theatrical imagery of "Of Modern Poetry," in which poetry, facing a "change of scene," must create a new mode—a fiction which "will suffice," and of which we are told:

> It has to be living, to learn the speech of the place.
> It has to face the men of the time and to meet
> The women of the time. . . .
> . . . It has
> To construct a new stage. It has to be on that stage
> And, like an insatiable actor, slowly and
> With meditation, speak words that in the ear,
> In the delicatest ear of the mind, repeat,
> Exactly, that which it wants to hear, at the sound
> Of which, an invisible audience listens,
> Not to the play, but to itself, expressed
> In an emotion as of two people, as of two
> Emotions becoming one. . . .
> (CP, 240)

And this meditatively textured life which makes such convergence possible also generates the variations—the divergences—of the final lines of "Esthétique du Mal":

> And out of what one sees and hears and out
> Of what one feels, who could have thought to make
> So many selves, so many sensuous worlds,
> As if the air, the mid-day air, was swarming
> With the metaphysical changes that occur,
> Merely in living as and where we live.
> (CP, 326)

"What we see in the mind is as real to us as what we see by the eye," according to the "Adagia" (OP, 162); and so the "self" creates its "sensuous world"—"With the metaphysical changes that occur, / Merely in living as and where we live."

Though the poetry frequently reaffirms that these modes of

apprehension, in "the generations of thought," devise world-constituting "ideas of order," Regueiro, advancing a decreative version of the "poetry of being," holds that "the poems that seek this creation of order are ultimately anecdotes, preludes, asides, extracts, notes, prologues, nuances, metaphors that turn against the symbol that creates it" (*The Limits of Imagination*, 165)—brushing aside such poems as "Anecdote of the Jar," "Asides on the Oboe," "Extracts from Addresses to the Academy of Fine Ideas," and, of course, "Notes toward a Supreme Fiction." And as has been seen, in the later poetry she finds imagination "reveal[ing] its incapacity to validly create and inhabit the world" (210). This "revelation" is, in her view, not a note of resignation; it is foundational in Stevens' development toward the exemplary "Of Mere Being": "If consciousness and imagination are the alienating entities that separate the poet from the natural world, the imaginative act that undercuts its own validity brings the poem into contact with natural time" (211).[21] By this de-metaphorizing strategy, the imagination, preparing the way for its withdrawal in favor of an experience of "mere being," sets the stage for the event itself: "Consciousness has been transformed by paradoxically moving to annihilate itself. And the poem has touched the unimaginable reality by undercutting the creative act that generated it. As creation and decreation become simultaneous, and in fact a single act, Stevens' poetry becomes the rite of passage into a world that lies beyond its reach" (213).

Regueiro's explication, consistently portraying the furtive "being" as the objective real, nonetheless retreats toward mystification as it describes the means to an experience of "being." And in the conjunction of creation and decreation her theory intersects Miller's:[22] self-annihilation of the imagination serves essentially the same purpose as Miller's "rapid oscillation." Like Bové, both find at the center of the poem an emptiness: a "nothingness" or a "core of silence"—a central void in which the essential perception occurs.

On this last, their theories approach Benamou's regarding

the later poetry: "A completely new Stevens appears at the very end of his life, when he has broken the ego's will, erased the Self's projections into marriageable opposites, and . . . cure[d] his mind of 'the indulgences' of the moon, the encroachments of anima, by a heroic *askesis*; he had to sever and reunite the giant of abstraction with the 'fat girl terrestrial'" (*Stevens and the Symbolist Imagination*, 138). Both Benamou and Regueiro look to "Of Mere Being" (*OP*, 117–18) as the realization of this "cure":

> The palm at the end of the mind,
> Beyond the last thought, rises
> In the bronze distance [decor],
>
> A gold-feathered bird
> Sings in the palm, without human meaning,
> Without human feeling, a foreign song.
>
> You know then that it is not the reason
> That makes us happy or unhappy.
> The bird sings. Its feathers shine.
>
> The palm stands on the edge of space.
> The wind moves slowly in the branches.
> The bird's fire-fangled feathers dangle down.[23]

Benamou encourages a Heideggerian slant, reading the poem's central image as "unsymbolized" (*Stevens and the Symbolist Imagination*, 139) and calling the poem a "revelation of existential dasein" (138). And for Regueiro:

It is perhaps "Of Mere Being" . . . that comes closest to the unmediated experience. Here the poem seems to stretch itself ineffably to the point of breakage in an attempt to "poematize" the mere being it cannot reach. . . . In positing a world beyond the enclosed space and terming it "foreign," the imagination undercuts its own space, its own enclosure, and moves out into the space it cannot reach. . . . The poetic imagination is silencing itself before it can speak, placing reality in a realm into which it cannot transgress.

There is thus a core of silence in the poem, a refusal to image, order, or transform the natural world. The poetic imagination cannot inhabit reality. But it can experience reality by thrusting the poem into the silence of mere being. (*The Limits of Imagination*, 213–16)

This view particularly depends on: "at the end of the mind, / Beyond the last thought" and "You know then that it is not the reason / That makes us happy or unhappy." Here Regueiro assumes that rejection of one conscious process is rejection of all. But "thought" and "reason" in the poem indicate rational modes (source of the "official view") not encompassing poetic imaginings and their "unofficial view." In company with Regueiro, Frye supposes that, for "Of Mere Being," "the only unchanging thing about being is that it remains external, 'at the end of the mind,' 'beyond the last thought'" ("Stevens and the Variation Form," 401). This, too, overlooks the precision of Stevens' language; "at the end of the mind, / Beyond the last thought" does not interchange with "beyond the mind," or "external." What, then, lies "beyond the last thought"? Stevens proposes in his 1951 essay "A Collect of Philosophy" that it is imagination itself:

Does not philosophy carry us to a point at which there is nothing left except the imagination? If we rely on the imagination (or, say, intuition), to carry us beyond that point, and if the imagination succeeds in carrying us beyond that point (as in respect to the idea of God, if we conceive of the idea of God as this world's capital idea), then the imagination is supreme, because its powers have shown themselves to be greater than the powers of the reason. (*OP*, 200)

The language here so closely parallels "Of Mere Being" that the poem reads as a conscious illustration of the prose passage.[24] The palm rises at that juncture where, within the terrain of conscious experience, "thought" lapses and, in Stevens' words, "we rely on the imagination . . . to carry us beyond that point." Stevens elsewhere asserts: "As the reason destroys, the poet must create" (*OP*, 164); "Of Mere Being" answers this imperative.

Abandoning the discursiveness which marks much of the later poetry, the poem, reminiscent of the brilliant, finely crafted imagery of *Harmonium* described by Miller as "The finished unity ... which makes [the poems] seem like elaborately wrought pieces of jewelry" ("Stevens' Poetry of Being," 146), returns Stevens to the gaudier style of his early work.[25] As if underscoring the viability of metaphor, "Of Mere Being" invests in a concentrated, flamboyant symbol (a gold-feathered bird singing in a palm), which affords a satisfaction. The vitality of "beingness" appears—accomplished through the effects of an affirmation of supremely conscious symbolization. The palm, appropriating religious associations and tropical exoticism, is, after all, an odd vehicle for unmediated experience—unadorned Being/Reality. Ronald Sukenick, coming nearer the point, speaks of "an acute awareness of existence itself, the palm, in 'Of Mere Being'" (*Wallace Stevens*, 31); but as elsewhere with Stevens, the existence figured by the palm is an infused, embellished one. In "A High-Toned Old Christian Woman" (*CP*, 59), for instance, the palm symbolizes both the Celestial and its replacement, "the supreme fiction"; in "Description without Place" the palm stands at the perceptual horizon (as in "Of Mere Being") and seems to image the symbolizing process itself:

> ... Description is
> Composed of a sight indifferent to the eye.
>
> It is an expectation, a desire,
> A palm that rises up beyond the sea,
>
> A little different from reality:
> The difference that we make in what we see
>
> And our memorials of that difference,
> Sprinklings of bright particulars from the sky.
> (*CP*, 343–44)

This description of description (in which the "palm that rises up beyond the sea" prefigures the "palm at the end of the mind") is a matter of getting "beyond the last thought" to a signification (a "substitute in stratagems / Of the spirit" [*CP*,

376])) commensurate with "the idea of God," within the province of the supreme fiction. Likewise, the heightened sense of our "beingness" which "Of Mere Being" depicts, while, in a sense, grounding our conceptions of being-as-such and the real itself, is not either of these. The palm that "rises / In the bronze decor" (not a natural setting) is, like the palm of "Description without Place," "A little different from reality: / The difference that we make in what we see."

The palm—habitat of the gold-feathered bird—arises within the region where, as Cassirer says, the symbolic form "produces and posits a world of its own. In these realms the spirit exhibits itself in that inwardly determined dialectic by virtue of which alone there is any reality, any organized and definite Being at all" (*Language and Myth*, 8).[26] Riddel speculates that "what one knows of mere being is an image on the edge of space, at that point where being becomes nothingness. Is this not to prove the ultimate creativity of self, of the mind which must always conceive a reality beyond form or metaphor?" (*The Clairvoyant Eye*, 266). Still, the poem relishes the metaphorical quality of palm and bird (a "reality" existing as metaphor)—not incompatible with Cassirer's contention that we originally (and ultimately) apprehend being, existence, reality in their inseparability from symbolizing configurations: "The special symbolic forms are not imitations, but *organs* of reality, since it is solely by their agency that anything real . . . is made visible to us. The question as to what reality is apart from these forms, and what are its independent attributes, becomes irrelevant here" (*Language and Myth*, 8).

Doggett, drawing attention to the form of the bird which sings in the palm, offers: "Stevens' final image of individual being is given in one of his last poems, 'Of Mere Being,' a symbolic portrait of the glory of the animate, of the living creature in its simple existence and as a creature only, the essence of animation conceived even beyond the point at which it is human" (*Stevens' Poetry of Thought*, 3). But the bird, gold feathers and foreign song, displaying more than simple animate existence, is a hypothetical evocation that flaunts its own artifice—reminiscent of Yeats'

> ... such a form as Grecian goldsmiths make
> Of hammered gold and gold enamelling
> To keep a drowsy Emperor awake;
> Or set upon a golden bough to sing
> To lords and ladies of Byzantium
> Of what is past, or passing, or to come.
> (*Collected Poems*, 192)

Within Stevensian variations, the singing bird recalls the description of aesthetic "elevation" from "The Figure of the Youth as Virile Poet": "In this state of elevation we feel perfectly adapted to the idea that moves and *l'oiseau qui chante*" (*NA*, 51).

And what of the "inhuman" quality of the bird's song, as it "sings ... without human meaning, / Without human feeling, a foreign song"? The denial of humanness may seem to exclude imaginings, yet as we have seen, the specificity of the next lines—"You know then that it is not the reason / That makes us happy or unhappy"—dispels this seeming, harmonizing the passage with "A Collect"'s reliance on "imagination" as surpassing reason ("human meaning") or emotion ("human feeling"). And if we think of the poem as an originative moving beyond the point where philosophy ends, to produce/entertain a fiction as supreme, then the trope extends—imaging the rejection of

> ... an over-human god,
> Who by sympathy has made himself a man
> And is not to be distinguished, ...
> ....
> A too, too human god, self-pity's kin
> And uncourageous genesis ...
> ("Esthétique du Mal"; *CP*, 315)[27]

As for the finite counterpart, "humanism" (as utopian political philosophy), Stevens says in a letter of January 1943, "The trouble with humanism is that man as God remains man, but there is an extension of man, the leaner being, in fiction, a possibly more than human human, a composite human" (*Letters*, 434); and in May of the same year he writes, "The chief defect of humanism is that it concerns human beings. Between humanism and something else, it might be possible to create an acceptable fiction" (*Letters*, 449). He objects in each case to what "Notes" calls the "apotheosis" of man (*CP*, 387), favoring fictions which would sublate the human into the realm of the "more than human." In the paradoxical language of "Less and Less Human, O Savage Spirit," "It is the human that is the alien" (*CP*, 328).

Stevens uses the expression "mere being" once other than in the title of the poem; he writes in May 1943: "Miami Beach . . . was once an isolated spot by the sea, where it was as easy to enjoy mere 'being' as it was to breathe the air" (*Letters*, 449). And as for "pure being," he writes in a letter of January 1953: "I suppose . . . the time will arrive [for me] when just to *be* will take in everything without the least *doing* since even the least doing is irrelevant to pure being" (*Letters*, 767). From these two playfully prosaic uses of the term we see, again, that "being" is the profoundly "unique experience, the item of ecstasy" (*OP*, 213), of life-worth-living—the subject, according to *The Necessary Angel*'s concluding passage, of all artists and "of all study":

> It would be tragic not to realize the extent of man's dependence on the arts. . . . It is enough to have brought poetry and painting into relation as sources of our present conception of reality, without asserting that they are the sole sources, and as supports of a kind of life, which it seems to be worth living, with their support, even if doing so is only a stage in the endless study of an existence, which is the heroic subject of all study. (*NA*, 175–76)

Recognizing art as a source of one's conception of life particularizes Stevens' view that the experience of "being" is initiated in imagination's genius—by which, improvisational energies compass/compose Stevensian reality. He speaks in the early poem "Another Weeping Woman" (*CP*, 25) of

> The magnificent cause of being,
> The imagination, the one reality
> In this imagined world.

And if imagination is the source of "being," that from which "being" arises, it is so in the sense conspicuous in the later poetry: fictive integrations, producing a "vital ambiance," create "an incessant being alive." Neither "universal power" nor "ground and source of both the mind and the world," "being" for Stevens is this sense of things, of life, original to "imagination."

Within this alternative context the Miller/Hines naming of the "river of rivers" (*CP*, 533) as the river of "being" (Miller, "Stevens' Poetry of Being," 158; Hines, *Later Poetry*, 258–59) takes on new meaning:

> The mere flowing of the water is a gayety,
> Flashing and flashing in the sun . . .

evidences a joy to be derived from life's fluid/fluent appearances, intimately related (in sense, sound, and image) to "the going round":

> And round and round, the merely going round,
> Until merely going round is a final good
>   (*CP*, 405)

—a celebration of "mere being" (the merely/merrily going round). And Doggett's more traditional reading of the river as "the river of time that flows nowhere" (*Stevens' Poetry of Thought*, 71) is expanded to take in the symbolizing temporality of human existence. In Cassirer's parallel images: "The symbolic process is like a single stream of life and thought which flows through consciousness, and which by this flowing movement produces the diversity and cohesion, the richness, the continuity, and constancy, of consciousness" (*Phenomenology of Knowledge*, 202). Stevens' river gives concrete presence to this flow of consciousness and, in the richness of the imagaic confluence, becomes the "river of rivers" (of nature/time/consciousness/life/thought/language: metaphor). This is the opposite extreme from Benamou's "unsymbolized" symbol; here, as with the palm in "Description without Place," the specific symbol signifies the symbolizing process in general. Thus, the river of being "is not to be seen beneath the appearances / That tell of it"; or, as the opening of "Description without Place" suggests,

> It is possible that to seem—it is to be,
> As the sun is something seeming and it is.
> (CP, 339)

And when the poem says the river "is the third commonness with light and air," it reenacts the "world of words" (CP, 345)[28] in which "Description is an element, like air or water" (OP, 170). If for Stevens, "the stream of consciousness is individual, the stream of life, total" (OP, 157), this relation modulates toward identity (as it is in the intricacies of as) in "the theory / Of poetry is the theory of life"—the "unofficial view of being."

CHAPTER IV

The Phenomena of Perception

The "poetry of being" and "decreationist" readings often depend, as we have seen, on the relation between Husserlian/Heideggerian language and the vocabulary of Stevens' poetry and poetics. This has influenced and been influenced by a narrower trend in Stevens criticism which understands the poetry strictly in Husserlian or Heideggerian terms. Such an approach is not wholly unfounded. Both thinkers provide viable support for general features of Stevens' phenomenological inclination. Stevens is interested in the experienced ("subjective/objective") as perceived within, or by way of, the matrices of meaning that perception entails—matrices which figure indispensably in Husserl's phenomenology.[1] Likewise, though Heidegger studiously avoids subject/object terminology, his emphasis on Dasein in *Being and Time* sees the "authentic" human perspective as central. But what of the particulars of fitting the idiosyncrasies of Stevens' poetry to the nuances of Husserlian or Heideggerian analysis? As Stevens says at the beginning of "An Ordinary Evening in New Haven," "Of this, / A few words, an and yet, and yet, and yet—" (*CP*, 465).

Disenfranchising the usual notions of real or unreal, Stevens, with Husserl, delineates objects of perception as phenomena. Along this line, Riddel notices that Stevens' "reality," consisting of "ordinary appearance, commonplace events, or the texture of social reality[,] . . . is a perceiver's reality, not an ontologist's or metaphysician's" (*The Clairvoyant Eye*, 26).[2] Riddel's point is readily confirmed by Stevens' prose. In a letter of June 1948 Stevens speculates that "thinking about the nature of our relation to what one sees out of the window . . . without any effort to see to the bottom of things, may some day disclose a force capable of destroying nihilism" (*Letters*, 602). Still more directly, "A Note on Samuel French Morse" speaks of "a book of first poems" by a new author as "a fresh opportunity to become aware that the people in the world, and the objects in it, and the world as a whole, are not absolute things, but, on the contrary, are the phenomena of perception" (*OP*, 266–67). And "Effects of Analogy" asks: "What is the poet's subject? It is his sense of the world" (*NA*, 121).

The Husserlian perspective, exploring the subject/object distinction, views consciousness and world relationally—and presents this relationality from both sides: "Objects exist for me, and are for me what they are, only as objects of actual and possible consciousness" (*Cartesian Meditations*, 65), and at the same time, "Conscious processes are also called *intentional*; but then the word intentionality signifies nothing else than this universal fundamental property of consciousness: to be conscious *of* something; as a *cogito*, to bear within itself its *cogitatum*" (*Cartesian Meditations*, 33). Macksey interprets this interrelatedness as showing "consciousness and reality in a way cancel[ing] each other out in the very unity of perception, a simultaneous creation and decreation which . . . suggests the essential oscillations of Stevens' poetry, from winter to summer, day to night, and from world to imagination" ("The Climates of Wallace Stevens," 193). But for the Husserlian articulation (and somewhat differently for Stevens) the opposite holds true on both counts. Husserl underscores the importance of seeing subject distinguished from object, intention from intentional object (no mutual cancellation), yet within an invariable interdependence which leaves no question of "oscillation" between them. For Husserl, as for Stevens, the "rock" (though elementally double-natured) "cannot be broken. It is the truth" (*CP*, 375): every *cogito* must "bear within itself its *cogitatum*." Or, from the *Ideas*, "An object that has being in itself (*an sich seiender*) is never such as to be out of relation to consciousness and its Ego" (148).

Husserl's phenomenological method, which Cambon, Macksey, and Hines identify as analogous to Stevens' "poetry as a process of dialectical discovery" (Cambon, *The Inclusive Flame*, 237), defines essentially three "reductive" phases—phenomenological, transcendental, and eidetic—directing Husserlian meditations and effectively overcoming the "natural standpoint," the naïve perspective in which "This 'fact-world,' as the word already tells us, I find to *be out there*, and also *take it just as it gives itself to me as something that exists out there*" (*Ideas*, 106). With the phenomenological reduction: "*We put out of action the general thesis which belongs to the essence of the natural standpoint*, we place in brackets whatever it includes respecting the nature of Being" (*Ideas*, 110), though it "still remains there like the bracketed in the bracket, like the disconnected outside the connexional system" (*Ideas*, 108). The phenomenological *epoché* alters our view (though not our perceptual vision) of what from the natural standpoint is the Real world: the Reality claim is suspended; "the things that are" are seen as phenomena, the world as phenomenal field. Within this alteration, "Consciousness in itself has a being of its own which in its absolute uniqueness of nature remains unaffected by the phenomenological disconnexion" (*Ideas*, 113). In other words, the first reduction makes possible the next, the "transcendental"—rendering accessible a "pure," or "transcendental," consciousness: consciousness as the "*phenomenological residuum*" (*Ideas*, 113) remaining after divesture ("bracketing") of psychological/empirical elements. In this condition all phenomena refer us back to the constituting ego; phenomenology becomes an investigation of "a sense-giving consciousness" for which "all real unities are 'unities of meaning'" (*Ideas*, 168). The subject is no longer "subjected" to

"Reality"; the perceiving "transcendental ego" sees subject and object relationally within the sphere of transcendental subjectivity.[3] Husserl writes: "I, the meditating phenomenologist, set myself the all-embracing task of *uncovering myself*, in my full concreteness—that is, with all the intentional correlates that are included therein" (*Cartesian Meditations*, 38). The "transcendental-phenomenological" is complemented by "eidetic reduction," which in its final distillation reduces things to their essential form, giving us a field of essences which includes all imaginative variations on the de facto phenomenal field. It encompasses every manifestation of what is in essence apprehensible.[4] The eidetic reduction likewise reveals an eidetic ego, effecting the transition from "my ego" to a "*transcendental ego as such*, which comprises all pure possibility-variants of my de facto ego and this ego itself qua possibility" (*Cartesian Meditations*, 71). The "ego" is now viewed as the essentially possible ego, and its objects and world in their essentialities.

Hines sketches a correspondingly tripartite "Husserlian method" in Stevens' poetizing:

As Stevens accomplishes these steps of rejection (a process that is analogous to Husserl's original intuition), reduction (a process that is similar to Husserl's demand for perception without preconceptions), and decreation (which is similar to Husserl's demand for minimal level of interaction between perceiver and the object of perception), he proceeds toward an apprehension of reality that is similar to Husserl's goal of the "essence of the thing itself" (*Later Poetry*, 36).

Leaving "reduction" momentarily to the side, Stevensian decreation, as a necessary participant in the creative cycle, only tangentially conjoins with Husserl's investigations of intention and intentional object. Stevens unifies "decreation" and "rejection" since decreation describes an effective rejection of obsolete mythologies ("making pass from the created to the uncreated"); section VIII of "Esthétique du Mal" (*CP*, 319) displays such rejection/decreation:

> The death of Satan was a tragedy
> For the imagination. A capital
> Negation destroyed him in his tenement
> And, with him, many blue phenomena.

The "capital negation" of this passage, rejecting the myth of Satan, results in the "destruction" of "blue phenomena"—imaginative constructs that constellated around the myth. And a similar destruction of "phenomena" accompanies the demythologizing of Deity, as with "the idea of God is the ultimate poetic idea." Such "capital negations," as we have seen, guide Stevens' "Modern reality is a reality of decreation, in which our revelations are not the revelations of belief, but the precious portents of our own powers."

With respect to "reduction," Stevens, as noted, welcomes the phenomena of the world as phenomena: "Things seen are things as seen" (*OP*, 162); and the question of this category as a point of intersection between Husserl and Stevens arises naturally out of the poetry. Section XIX of "The Man with the Blue Guitar" (*CP*, 175) makes use of *reduce*: "That I may reduce the monster to / Myself, and then may be myself / / In the face of the monster." This dramatizes Stevens' interest in the world as phenomenal and, consequently, in relation to the perceiving consciousness. He explains that "Monster = nature, which I desire to reduce: master, subjugate, acquire complete control over and use freely for my own purpose, as poet" (*Letters*, 790). But to advocate an important similarity between Stevens' poetic reduction and Husserl's "scientific" term promotes equivocation more than meaningful equivalence. Stevens' usage of "reduction" circumscribes the poet's struggle with reality (in its ordinary sense)—an impossible face-to-face confrontation between language and nature, suggested by the image of "the lion in the lute / Before the lion locked in stone." Stevens elaborates: "I want to face nature the way two lions face one another—the lion in the lute facing the lion locked in stone. I want, as a man of the imagination, to write poetry with all the power of a monster equal in strength to that of the monster about whom I write. I want man's imagination to be completely adequate in the face of reality" (*Letters*, 790).

Beyond philosophical clarification of the relation between self and nature, the poet intends to capture this relation, to make it a part of himself and an instrument of poetic sight. Stevens' "Effects of Analogy" refers to "the imagination as a power within [the poet] to have such insights into reality as will make it possible for him to be sufficient as a poet in the very center of consciousness. This results, or should result, in a central poetry" (*NA*, 115). While Husserl's phenomenology engages in a systematic pursuit of the "things themselves," the poet speaks of his desire to:

> . . . reduce the monster and be,
>
> Two things, the two together as one,
> And play of the monster and of myself,
>
> Or better not of myself at all,
> But of that as its intelligence.

Returning to the opening dictum of "The Comedian as the Letter C," "man is the intelligence of his soil" (*CP*, 27), Stevens again (as in "The Snow Man") confirms the necessity of empathizing with nature "in order to understand it and enjoy it"; yet we see also that it is poetic scrutiny which shapes and reshapes our surroundings. And as "Imagination as Value" tells us, "poetic value . . . is not the value of knowledge. It is not the value of faith. It is the value of the imagination" (*NA*, 149).

This sense of innovative struggle with what is other recurs in section VII of "Credences" (*CP*, 376):

> Three times the concentred self takes hold, three times
> The thrice concentred self, having possessed
>
> The object, grips it in savage scrutiny,
> Once to make captive, once to subjugate
> Or yield to subjugation, once to proclaim
> The meaning of the capture, this hard prize,
> Fully made, fully apparent, fully found.

The thrice-occurring "taking hold" of "the object" may tempt an association with Husserl's methodology, but here, too, the equation is no more than superficial. The emphasis once more falls on "capture," on appropriation of the "object" as *materia poetica*, or, more generally, as material for the imagination—congruent with "The poet's native sphere . . . is what he can make of the world" ("A Collect of Philosophy"; *OP*, 198). The captured thing, both "fully found" and "fully made," is known in and through integrative transformations. For Stevens, "The habit of probing for an integration seems to be part of the general will to order" (*OP*, 196), and it is this "probing" which, as we recall, forms the principal motif of "Credences." The "hard prize" (the captived, subjugated, proclaimed) is a multiplied reality like the "rock of summer" of the poem's previous section (*CP*, 375).

Cambon finds that "both Husserl and Stevens aim at a focused apprehension of the *essences* of things (*Wesenheiten*) by a process of 'stripping' or 'unhusking' . . ., which Stevens calls 'abstraction' and which appears in so many of his poems as a kind of preliminary negation of the given object, or of our construed interpretations" (*The Inclusive Flame*, 237). On this view, by means of Husserlian "bracketing," or "reduction," "consciousness 'discovers' the object as if for the first time and corrects the incrustations of history. All of *Notes toward a Supreme Fiction* is conformable to this principle" (237). But while "Notes" assiduously cancels "construed interpretations"—"the incrustations of history"—this clears the way for new interpretations, not for a Husserlian apprehension of essence; and Stevens' use of the "object" displaces Husserl's reductive program, as he remedies the monotony of phenomenal change ("inconstant objects of inconstant cause / In a universe of inconstancy" [*CP*, 389]) with the "freshness of transformation" (*CP*, 397). It is, again, the metaphysical assumption Stevens overturns, telling us early in "It Must Be Abstract," "The death of one god is the death of all" (*CP*, 381), and advancing the decreative strategy with the later turn: "It feels good as it is without the giant, / A thinker of the first idea" (*CP*, 386). The underlying opposition in these lines obtains between fictions: the unself-consciously generated and the self-conscious. As has been seen, Stevens is drawn less to the "essences of things" than to a fictionality ("The fiction that results from feeling" [*CP*, 406]) foreign to Husserl's "phenomenological science": "to find the real" is "to be stripped of every fiction except one." "Abstraction" in the poem, not fitted to Husserlian *epoché*, is that fictional intention of the "supreme fiction" separating it from "literal" notions of deity; the "supreme fiction," to be more than thoughtless repetition, "must be abstract" and understood as abstraction. Stevens makes the point this way: "Underlying ["Notes"] is the idea that, in the various predicaments of belief, it might be possible to yield, or to try to yield, ourselves to a declared fiction" (*Letters*, 443).

Husserlian observations are, as Hines indicates, not altogether inimical to imagination and its "fictions" (*Later Poetry*, 75). With the casual effect of an aside, Husserl remarks in the *Ideas*: "If anyone loves a paradox, he can really say, and say with strict truth if he will allow for the ambiguity, that the *element* which *makes up the life of phenomenology as of all eidetical science* is 'fiction,' that fiction is the source whence the knowledge of 'eternal truths' draws its sustenance" (201). Necessarily, the eidetic ego, in apprehending the *eidos*, the essence of the object, apprehends its "ideal extension" as "all ideally possible perceptions" of the object (*Cartesian Meditations*, 70); and in order to escape the closed horizon (and solipsism) to which the de facto ego is prey, it thinks itself as "every imaginable ego" (75). Exploration of similarly possible perceptions appears as a motif in Stevens' early poems—including "Thirteen Ways of Looking at a Blackbird," "Metaphors of a Magnifico," and "Sea Surface Full of Clouds"—though these particularly stress the variances without pointing to an eidetic form of the experience.

In the later poem "Bouquet of Roses in Sunlight" (*CP*, 430–31), as "our sense of these things changes and they change," Stevens' "black reds, / Pink yellows, orange whites," while more than variations, again confound the residually Platonic quality of the *eidos*.⁵ They are "like a flow of meanings with no speech" for which the fluid unreality of the sensation becomes the source of its "truth"—a pause, a concentration, a certain quietude:

> And yet this effect is a consequence of the way
> We feel and, therefore, is not real, except
> In our sense of it, our sense of the fertilest red,
>
> Of yellow as first color and of white,
> In which the sense lies still, as a man lies,
> Enormous, in a completing of his truth.

The last two lines especially are in the spirit of Aphorism 107 of Nietzsche's *Gay Science*: "We do not always keep our eyes from rounding off something and, as it were, finishing the poem; and then it is no longer eternal imperfection that we carry across the river of becoming—then we have the sense of carrying a *goddess*, and feel proud and childlike as we perform this service" (163).⁶ As "The Figure of the Youth as Virile Poet" finds: "If the end of the philosopher is despair, the end of the poet is fulfillment, since the poet finds a sanction for life in poetry that satisfies the imagination" (*NA*, 43). The thematized art-as-perfection departs decisively from the Husserlian play of perceptual/eidetic variation: through the vehicle of variation the poet seeks a provisional "satisfaction"—"description that makes it divinity" (*CP*, 475). This is the "meaning of the capture, this hard prize, / Fully made, fully apparent, fully found" of "Credences": a perception of the object in which, punningly, "the sense lies still, as a man lies, / Enormous, in a completing of his truth"—the "man" of these lines serving as both perceiver and image of the concept which "satisfies."

The roses of the poem are proposed as ("Say that it is") "things that in being real / Make any imaginings of them lesser things"; they are "too much as they are to be changed by metaphor." Without discarding metaphor or the imagination's vitalness, the roses affirm aesthetic depths in experience by which "sense"—the poet's sense ("this invisible activity, this sense")—"exceeds all metaphor." But as the poem continues, we see that the metaphorizing "sense," as a "flow of meanings," is, finally, viable only in its metaphors. In "yellow as first color," Stevens returns, not with a cognitive but with a sensuous vision, to the "first idea" of "Notes"—the idea of "this invented world, / The inconceivable idea of the sun" (*CP*, 380); and in "the fertilest red" he suggests the generative energy of imagination, as when in "Notes," the lion "reddens the sand with his red-colored noise" (*CP*, 384). Revisiting these colors/ideas, the "meanings" of the roses become, in a "sense," a locus of the "supreme fiction." The play on the word *lies* underscores the "truth" of the self-confessed illusion the roses present—a perfection actualized as "white, / In which the sense lies still . . . "[7]

This view of art, or imaginative acts generally, as a satisfaction carries us beyond the Husserlian sphere. Husserlian variation methodologically anchors the eidetic ego's realm of possibility; Stevensian variation "enhances the sense of reality, heightens it, intensifies it" (*NA*, 77). Husserl's philosophic concerns demand a definitive discrimination, even within phenomenological matrices, between "perceived" and "fancied" (corresponding to "Real" and "imagined" in the natural standpoint), privileging that which is "perceived" over that which only seems: "Every such experience in the form of fancy is characterized not as being really present, but as being 'as though' (*gleichsam*) it were present. . . . Every perceived item is characterized as 'really present Being'; every parallel item in the form of fancy is characterized as the same in content, but as 'mere fancy,' 'as though it were' present Being" (*Ideas*, 315).[8] But for Stevens' poetic interest, the "as though it were" of the fictive is "like / A new knowledge of reality" (*CP*, 534) surpassing that of "really present Being." As Cassirer sees: "The artistic eye is not a passive eye that receives and registers the impression of things. It is a constructive eye, and it is only by constructive acts that we can discover the beauty of natural things" (*Essay on Man*, 151). And, returning us to the question of reality's structure: "Art gives us a richer, more vivid and colorful image of reality, and a more profound insight into its formal structure" (*Essay on Man*, 170). Here Cassirer's view (conjoining amplification and "insight") begins to suggest those complications within "reality" which, for Stevens, "prove" the "theory of poetry" as the "theory of life." Stevens' convolution, "if we desire to formulate an accurate theory of poetry, we find it necessary to examine the structure of reality, because reality is the central reference for poetry" ("Three Academic Pieces"; *NA*, 71), may intentionally reproduce Cassirer's language; at the least, Cassirer's articulation illumines Stevens' curious emphasis, in that piece and elsewhere, on examining the "structure" of reality (rather than reality itself) in relation to poetry.[9] The results of these "examinations" are improvisations on the ordinary for which, regardless of season, "The World Is Larger in Summer" (*CP*, 514)—that is, in the integration imaged by summer.

"As You Leave the Room" (*OP*, 116–17), a late poem and one of Stevens' most autobiographical, elaborates on the range of his exploration/reflection; the poet, looking back over his work, wonders:

> . . . have I lived a skeleton's life,
> As a disbeliever in reality,
>
> A countryman of all the bones in the world?

This mood of skeptical, analytical rumination occasions the amplifying integration, which, setting aside momentary doubt, reaffirms imaginative instrumentation:

> Now, here, the snow I had forgotten becomes
>
> Part of a major reality, part of
> An appreciation of a reality
>
> And thus an elevation, as if I left
> With something I could touch, touch every way.

> And yet nothing has been changed except what is
> Unreal, as if nothing had been changed at all.

Simply by changing "what is unreal," the language of the poem creates, out of the memory of snow (emblem for the decreative), an aspect of a "major reality"—an "elevation" such that, in Nietzsche's words, "then it is no longer eternal imperfection that we carry across the river of becoming."

This same view—of poetry as enhancement—opens a gulf between Stevens and Heidegger; the sufficing "fiction" is as antithetical to Heidegger's study of "Being" as it is essential to Stevens' poetry. Heidegger defines poetry as "the saying of the unconcealedness of what is" (*Poetry, Language, Thought*, 74);[10] Stevens preserves an imaginative play, juxtaposing "Poetry is often a revelation of the elements of appearance" and "Poetry is a renovation of experience" (*OP*, 177). Walter Biemel tells us, in his essay "Poetry and Language in Heidegger," that for Heidegger, "the essence of poetry . . . is establishing the truth, the articulated clearing in which Being comes to pass" (78). For Stevens, on the other hand, enigmatically "In the long run the truth does not matter" (*OP*, 180).

Calling the poet "a 'shepherd of Being' who is 'housed in language,'" Cambon submits, "Heidegger's metaphors are highly suggestive of the posture of symbiotic acceptance of reality that underlies so much of Stevens' writing" (*The Inclusive Flame*, 238).[11] But "symbiotic acceptance of reality" undercuts Stevens' emphasis on innovation ("the lion in the lute"). Heidegger's account of language as "the precinct (*templum*), that is, the house of Being" (*Poetry, Language, Thought*, 132) does not at all correspond to Stevens' identification of "the imagination" as "the magnificent cause of being" (*CP*, 25), nor to the invention of values, in the Nietzschean sense, which pervades the poetry. When Heidegger says, "*Der Mensch ist der Hirt des Seins*" (*Wegmarken*, 162), he means, as William J. Richardson explains, "man helps conserve and guard the truth of Being" (*Heidegger*, 525).

Heidegger's "truth," to be sure, is not the religious/metaphysical truth that Stevens specifically rejects, yet it is a non-posited truth, as he makes clear in "The Word of Nietzsche: 'God Is Dead.'" He contends, "Nietzsche articulated the first value-principle of the metaphysics of the will to power in still another form: 'We possess *art* lest we *perish of the truth*'" ("The Word of Nietzsche," 93)—a view that Heidegger opposes: "The value-thinking of the metaphysics of the will to power is murderous in a most extreme sense, because it absolutely does not let Being itself take its rise, i.e., come into the vitality of its essence" ("The Word of Nietzsche," 108). By extension, the idea that art and its "fictions" can "take the place / Of empty heaven and its hymns" (*CP*, 167) associates with vestiges of metaphysics and, so, with a failure to "let Being itself take its rise." Stevens' concept of "supreme fictions" as homocentric substitutes for deity resides with Nietzsche's will to artistry—conflicting with Heidegger's essentially passive/receptive understanding of Being's "coming to presence in its truth."

Art for Heidegger is, or should be, "the letting happen of the advent of the truth of what is" (*Poetry, Language, Thought*, 72). Stevens contends that "the poet . . . creates the world to which we turn incessantly and without knowing it and . . . gives to life the supreme fictions without which we are unable to conceive of it" (*NA*, 31)—in keeping with: "The author's work suggests the possibility of a supreme fiction, recognized as a fiction, in which men could *propose to themselves* a fulfilment." Neither does Heidegger's ontological seriousness meet with the characteristically Stevensian sentiment expressed in "On the Road Home":

> It was when I said,
> "There is no such thing as the truth,"
> That the grapes seemed fatter.
> The fox ran out of his hole.
>
> (*CP*, 203)

Heidegger would mark as evasive Stevens' successors to "the truth"—"poetic truths" like those represented in "Mrs. Alfred

Uruguay" by the "figure of capable imagination" who "passed her there on a horse all will" (*CP*, 249). Stevens' "imaginative man" finds that his "pleasure is the pleasure of powers that create a truth" (*NA*, 58).

Considering Heidegger's antipathy to the notion of "creative imagination," there seems less to recommend a Heideggerian than a Husserlian interpretation of Stevens; yet the Heideggerian has generated greater enthusiasm. Bové's extended discussion on Stevens' relation to Heidegger ignores Husserl entirely; Hines treats Stevens' relationship to Husserl as preliminary to what he sees as an ultimate comparability between Stevens and Heidegger.

Though Hines maintains that Husserlian method defines steps which effect Stevens' poetry of "perception," he sees the poetry, after *The Man with the Blue Guitar*, diverted from "conceptual essence" toward the possibility of "non-conceptual essence" aligned with Heidegger's investigations: "As Stevens rejects the division between mind and world, he also finds that the clear perceptions that were available through the processes of reduction that he had developed in *Ideas of Order* and *The Man with the Blue Guitar* were inadequate for his aesthetic purposes" (*Later Poetry*, 26–27). *Parts of a World* enacts a return, for Hines, to a prephilosophical "natural standpoint"—which, he believes, eliminates the subject/object dichotomy: "As long as the poet assumed, like Husserl, the notion that consciousness is inescapably different from the object of consciousness, the attempts to resolve this dualism ended in an unresoluble conflict" (114). Accordingly, Stevens' rejection of Husserlian "dualism" inclines him to "the world of Martin Heidegger's *Dasein*, where existence is described as always given in a world where the self and world are unified" (114).[12]

Hines, following Miller and others, maps Stevens' approach to "being" by way of cyclic "creation and decreation"; but in Hines' hands the lower-case "being" (already, for Miller, something more than "existence," or "life") becomes the specifically Heideggerian "Being":

I want to make it clear that Being, being, and existence are going to have different senses in my study. Being with a capital B will stand for the ground or source of both the mind and the world. It is that by virtue of which the things that exist are present.... [I]t is used in a sense that is distinct from "being," which (as in the term *human being*) simply means existent or something that exists, and from "beings," which are things that exist (objects, animals, humans, etc.). (*Later Poetry*, 20n)[13]

He puts this special usage to work with respect to "The Countryman" (*CP*, 428–29), who, walking beside the Swatara River,

> ... is there because he wants to be
> And because being there in the heavy hills
> And along the moving of the water—
>
> Being there is being in a place,
> As of a character everywhere,
> The place of a swarthy presence moving,
> Slowly, to the look of a swarthy name.

By Hines' reading, the Swatara "suggests 'a swarthy presence' in which 'being there is being in a place,' a line that would sound like pure Heidegger if translated into German (for example, *Da-Sein ist in-der-Welt-sein*)" (254). Yet in the poem the "swarthy presence" is not "suggested"; it appears directly—as the mere appearance of the river, which in its dark muddiness is the incarnation of its "swarthy name." And more broadly, it is easy to recognize, without special knowledge of Heidegger, the risks of such literal transpositions of technical philosophical terminology. Here the result confuses by both introducing a convolution extraneous to the poem and, in the process, misconstruing the meaning of Heidegger's Dasein. Stevens' "being there" ("in the heavy hills") *is* "being in a place"; but as Michael Gelven notes in *A Commentary on Heidegger's "Being and Time"*: "*Da* [in Dasein] ... must be distinguished from *dort*, which means 'there' in the sense of 'at that place'" (22).

Interpretation via idiosyncratic philosophical jargon invites faux pas of this sort, often compounding the obscurity of the poem with an obscuration of theory. In apparent reference to Stevens' use of the word *ecstasy*, Macksey says that "after the poet's ascesis the effect is transport (*ekstasis*)" ("The Climates of Wallace Stevens," 217), thus confusing, for instance, the "ecstatic identities" of "Extracts from Addresses to the Academy of Fine Ideas" (*CP*, 258) with Heidegger's notion of "*ekstasis*," which—rather than *ecstasy* in the sense of joy, as in Stevens' poetry—designates a "standing outside" or "standing forth" that finds itself existing in a world and with respect to "Being" (*Being and Time*, 377n).[14] Similarly, Macksey's discussion of the "alien voice" in Heidegger's *Being and Time* derives:

This homeless voice exposes for Stevens the nothingness at the center of human existence, the nothingness behind entities and the nothingness that annihilates the external world as an object of direct connatural knowledge in the very act of apprehending it. Yet this realization makes possible the endless creation of pseudo-objects, ambiguous marriages of nothingness and being, neither wholly real nor wholly unreal. ("The Climates of Wallace Stevens," 198–99)

Earlier objections to this application of the "nothingness" aside, the passage in question (*Being and Time*, 320–22) does not postulate a nothingness "behind entities"; and "the nothingness that annihilates" belongs more to Sartre than to Heidegger.[15] To the extent to which Heidegger indicates a "nothingness at the center of human existence," he points toward an authentic awareness of mortality which sustains a certain "anxiety in the face of death" (*Being and Time*, 298).[16] The "alien voice" is that of "Dasein in its uncanniness" (*Being and Time*, 321), for whom, as Heidegger tells us:

Being-towards-death is the anticipation of a potentiality-for-Being of that entity whose kind of Being is anticipation itself. In the anticipatory revealing of this potentiality-for-Being, Dasein discloses itself to itself as regards its uttermost possibility. But to project itself on its ownmost potentiality-for-Being means to be able to understand itself in the Being of the entity so revealed—namely, to exist. (*Being and Time*, 307)

"Nothingness" is "at the center" not as an immediate condition but as a present recognition of a potentiality for nonexistence—for the termination, at any time, of one's existence. By this view, the realization that one is "going to [one's] death"—that one's being bears in its being the negation of its being—separates one off from the "they-self" of inauthentic existence, brings one's own life into relief in its singularity and totality (circumscribed by birth and death), and grounds ontological understanding.

Leaving behind the issue of "nothingness" for that of "nothingness" in Heideggerian ontology, Hines finds no better result: "In 'A Primitive Like An Orb,' the principle evoked 'is and / It is [sic] not and therefore is' (CP, 440). In this case, it is and yet is not a thing. Heidegger's 'ontological difference' is alluded to in these lines" (*Later Poetry*, 251).[17] At best, Hines' "it is and yet is not a thing" is unhelpfully ambiguous; at worst, it badly misconstrues the "ontological difference"—the difference between "Being" and "beings." In *What Is Called Thinking?* Heidegger traces the etymology of "Being," reinterpreting the term in a verbal sense which distinguishes it from "beings" (214) such that it can be said that Being "is" and that it is not a thing; but this does not render "Being" a paradoxical entity which both "is and is not a thing." *Being and Time* puts it straightforwardly: "The Being of entities 'is' not itself an entity" (26).

Equally important, Hines' Heideggerian analysis is inattentive to Stevens' lines in context:

> We do not prove the existence of the poem.
> It is something seen and known in lesser poems.
> It is the huge, high harmony that sounds
> A little and a little, suddenly,
> By means of a separate sense. It is and it
> Is not and, therefore, is. In the instant of speech,
> The breadth of an accelerando moves,
> Captives the being, widens—and was there.
> (CP, 440)

The subject here is "the essential poem at the centre of things" (*CP*, 440)—the central innovation implied in "The Man with the Blue Guitar" in the phrase "Poetry is the subject of the poem" (*CP*, 176) and explicit in "The Noble Rider and the Sound of Words": "There is, in fact, a world of poetry indistinguishable from the world in which we live" (*NA*, 31). This "poem" is revealed by "a difficult apperception"—perception as a poetically deliberative act by which the perceived is continually, but discontinuously, rediscovered. Again Stevens stresses the integrative as means, and necessary component, of appreciation and understanding; fixed "in an eternal foliage," the "poem" is fully made and fully found, "by means of a separate sense." The elusive lines in which Hines finds Heidegger's "difference" (reading the "it" as "Being") further describe the "existence" of the "poem at the centre of things," which is "the huge, high harmony." Constituted by "harmony," the "poem" becomes like "Sounds passing through sudden rightnesses, wholly / Containing the mind." It doubly "is and it / Is not and, therefore, is." Stevens tells us, "The chord destroys its elements by uniting them in the chord. They then cease to exist separately" (*Letters*, 363)—the "harmony," like the "chord," opposing the discord of ordinary experience. And the "poem" is captured in (and captures) the mind momentarily, "in the instant of speech"—in an illusion of permanence produced by language—then slips away as the moment's integration is lost.

For Heidegger, "Being" is that which is uniquely "there" for man by virtue of his ontological disposition. Conversely, man is Dasein, the "there-Being"—the one who, by his "nature" ("essential tendency-of-Being" [*Being and Time*, 35]), apprehends Being as such. Neither objective (or material) reality nor subjective (or spiritual) reality, "Being" does not so much absorb the categories of subject and object as subvert them, in effect replacing the traditional dichotomy with the "ontological difference."[18] Bypassing the problematic of imagination/reality, Heidegger's investigations focus on a singular constitutive aspect of human existence: the human situation as disclosed by the fact of the Being question.[19] But this "question" has little interest in Stevensian "fictions" as they "discover" the world in the changing nuances of imaginative language. For Heidegger, as Richardson explains: "λόγος (Being) is a coming-into-the-Open that can and must be attended to; it is only by attending to, therefore docility toward, λόγος that the There-being can be authentically itself as the There of Being (λόγος); it is only this docility to λόγος that grounds the authentic use of words; the true poets and the true thinkers achieve this docility" (*Heidegger*, 294). By this, all poetry and thought lead back to the fundamental "understanding-of-Being which belongs to existent Dasein" (*Being and Time*, 488). Whatever the "fictions" of the age—regardless of the turn of hermeneutical interpretation—always Dasein is the one for whom there is a world, for whom there is "Being." Heidegger's interest quests for authentic understanding of Dasein's being and the meaning of "Being" as such. In *Being and Time* "authenticity," exposing Dasein's primordial relation to Being, provides a "disclosure of Being" which includes a specific denial of "subjective discretion"[20] incommensurate with Stevens' view that "reality is an activity of the most august imagination" (*OP*, 110)—and elsewhere: "the world is what you make of it" (*CP*, 513), "to change modes is to change the world" (*OP*, 108), "our sense of these things changes and they change" (*CP*, 431),[21] "thou art not August unless I make thee so" (*CP*, 251) (passages which range in time from 1940 to 1954).

Heidegger's later work dwells increasingly on language as a middle term that gives rise to man as man, Being as Being; and in poetry's foundational use of language, he finds Being's disclosure. At the same time, however, he reinforces the characterization of Dasein as docile perceiver: "*Language speaks*" (*Poetry, Language, Thought*, 190); "Mortals speak insofar as they listen" (*Poetry, Language, Thought*, 209). Heidegger's poet primarily experiences, not as Hines supposes, "a sense of freedom" (*Later Poetry*, 120)[22] or beauty, but rather the ontological leverage of language as responsibility. For Heidegger, "only speech enables man to be the living being he is as man. It is as one who speaks that man is—man" (*Poetry, Language, Thought*, 189). Stevens counters with: "Man is the imagination or rather the imagination is man" (*OP*, 177).

Despite Heidegger's later emphasis on language as "the house of Being" and on poetry as a mode for disclosure of the "truth of Being," these remain participants in what Stevens would see as an "official view." Hines himself notices something of this disjuncture: "The difference, then, between the philosophy of Being and the poetry of Being is best defined by Stevens' fiction of fulfilled Being, which is neither available nor important to philosophy" (*Later Poetry*, 212).[23] But Stevensian fictionality is not merely lacking from Heidegger's philosophy; it opposes that philosophy. Once the idea of the "supreme fiction" (or the imagination's possible "genius") is introduced, "the saying of the unconcealedness of what is" is no longer in question.

CHAPTER V

Sun and Symbol

"The Figure of the Youth as Virile Poet" distinguishes: "The philosopher proves that the philosopher exists. The poet merely enjoys existence" (*NA*, 56). In this atmosphere, philosophical exegesis runs a risk of obliterating the difference—subverting the pleasures of the poetry.[1] Yet despite difficulties, already explored, of systematizing Stevens by way of certain "official views," the poetry is indelibly thoughtful, and more congenial philosophical approaches encourage less reductive critical strategies.[2] Nietzschean tropes and Cassirerian aesthetics succeed in this, suggesting artful and theoretical beginnings for Stevens' "central fictions."

Bloom's recognition of Stevens/Nietzsche (in *The Poems of Our Climate*) sees Nietzsche as a conduit through which Emerson's Romantic spirit passes to Stevens. Others acknowledging the Nietzschean in the poetry have tended to subordinate those aspects to the possible influences of Santayana, Vaihinger, or William James.[3] Milton Bates' recent account begins to right the balance: "Nowhere else in Stevens does one have an intellectual influence whose sources and extent can be specified with as much certainty" (*Wallace Stevens*, 248). But Bates, emphasizing the shared motifs of the hero (overman/major man) and "will to power" (as will-to-domination),[4] gives little attention to a range of other Nietzschean themes apparent in Stevens' figurations—including the "three metamorphoses," "death of God," solar images, and "eternal return."⁵ No poet has dealt with these Nietzschean figures as explicitly, persistently, and insightfully as Stevens (in prose, and from his earliest major poems—"Sunday Morning" and "Peter Quince"—to the last).

In *The Gay Science* Nietzsche writes:

> Have you not heard of that madman who lit a lantern in the bright morning hours, ran to the market place, and cried incessantly: "I seek God! I seek God!" . . . "Whither is God?" he cried; "I will tell you. *We have killed him*—you and I. All of us are his murderers. But how did we do this? How could we drink up the sea? Who gave us the sponge to wipe away the entire horizon? What were we doing when we unchained this earth from its sun? Whither is it moving now? . . . Has it not become colder? Is not night continually closing in on us? Do we not need to light lanterns in the morning? (181)

The madman's anguish is met through *Thus Spoke Zarathustra*'s "three metamorphoses of the spirit": "the spirit becomes a camel; and the camel, a lion; and the lion, finally, a child" (137). In the first stage, that of the scholarly or religious ascetic submissive to the burden of history and culture: "What is difficult? asks the spirit that would bear much, and kneels down like a camel waiting to be well loaded" (138). This first is overcome by the second: "The creation of freedom for oneself and a sacred 'No' even to duty—for that, my brothers, the lion is needed. To assume the right to new values—that is the most terrifying assumption for a reverent spirit that would bear much" (139). As in Stevensian decreation, the negation clears the ground for the newly positive. By the third metamorphosis, the creative act of the child engages humanity's affirmative destiny: "The child is innocence and forgetting, a new beginning, a game, a self-propelled wheel, a first movement, a sacred 'Yes.' For the game of creation, my brothers, a sacred 'Yes' is needed: the spirit now wills his own will, and he who had been lost to the world now conquers his own world" (139).⁶ The overthrow of ritual duty, old values (Zarathustra's "Dead are all the gods: now we want the overman to live" [191])⁷ makes possible the self-conscious assertion of finite creativity: "the spirit now wills his own will."

The "three metamorphoses," structurally/thematically central to *Zarathustra*, are archetypal transformations intrinsic to individual enlightenment and the historical development of self-consciousness. In the first stage one must go into the "desert": endure scarcity and isolation, learn patience, duty, reverence for what may lie beyond, abstain from (pro)creation, cultivate recollection essential for the discipline of the will. Only on the basis of such restraint is the next metamorphosis possible. The lion comes forward when man has become "a grave burden for himself . . . [carrying] on his shoulders too much that is alien to him . . . [such that] life [itself] seems a desert" (305). The lion's "No" conquers the "thou shalt" with "I will," conquers "values, thousands of years old," creates "freedom for oneself for new creation" (138–39).

Stevens' "Two or Three Ideas," touching on both tragic and affirmative aspects of the "metamorphoses," mixes Zarathustra's images within a distinctly Nietzschean spectrum of implication:

To see the gods dispelled in mid-air and dissolve like clouds is one of the great human experiences. . . . It was their annihilation, not ours, and yet it left us feeling that in a measure, we, too, had been annihilated. It left us feeling dispossessed and alone in a solitude, like children without parents, in a home that seemed deserted, in which the amical rooms and halls had taken on a look of hardness and emptiness. . . . At the same time, no man ever muttered a petition in his heart for the restoration of those unreal shapes. There was always in every man the increasingly human self, which instead of remaining the observer, the nonparticipant, the delinquent, became constantly more and more all there was or so it seemed; and whether it was so or merely seemed so still left it for him to resolve life and the world in his own terms. (*OP*, 206–7)

Here is the lion's "sacred 'No'": the refusal to speak "a petition in his heart for the restoration of those unreal shapes"; and the child's "Yes": the wish "to resolve life and the world in his own terms."

Stevens, with Nietzsche, dismisses the abstruse structures of metaphysics in favor of the intricacies of poetic form. He answers the rhetorical question of "Sunday Morning"—"And shall the earth / Seem all of paradise that we shall know?"— with:

> The sky will be much friendlier then than now,
> A part of labor and a part of pain,
> And next in glory to enduring love,
> Not this dividing and indifferent blue.
>
> (*CP*, 68)

In its broad affirmativeness (rejecting only the divisively indifferent) the Nietzschean sentiment of the passage embraces the expansively human: labor, pain, glory, love.

This positive turn undercuts criticism that traces only the abysmal aspect of the madman's loss—confuting Regueiro's derogative extrapolation that after "the heavens" have been "emptied by the death of the gods," Stevens sees the world as merely bare (*The Limits of Imagination*, 168) and Miller's "In this impoverishing of the world when the gods disappear man discovers himself, orphaned and dispossessed, a solitary consciousness" ("Stevens' Poetry of Being," 145). The bleakness of alienation in a world without transcendent dimension becomes, as we recall, the critics' backdrop for Stevens' contemplative poetry and his interest in subject/object dualism: "Stevens is left in a world made of two elements: subject and object, mind and matter, imagination and reality. Imagination is the inner nothingness, while reality is the barren external world with which imagination carries on its endless intercourse. Stevens' problem is to reconcile the two" (Miller, "Stevens' Poetry of Being," 145).

But "Sunday Morning" compasses the sky-as-heaven (the divine habitat) as "dividing and indifferent." If (as for Stevens) the Creator is an absolute incarnation of our own sublimity, the resulting self-alienation leaves us (as with Nietzsche's madman, who, like Professor Eucalyptus, "seeks god") finding, that, in Hegelian terms, the "'other' cannot be found where it is sought" (*Phenomenology of Mind*, 258). Demythologized, "the sky will be much friendlier then than now"—as in Zarathustra's "I love even churches and tombs of gods, once the sky gazes through their broken roofs with its pure eyes, and like grass and red poppies, I love to sit on broken churches" (340–41). The new nearness (and for Nietzsche, "purity") depends on a sense that "the mind that in heaven created the earth and the mind that on earth created heaven were, as it happened, one" (*OP*, 176). Divisiveness, not the absence of deity, draws Stevens' complaint. In "Dezembrum":

> This great world, it divides itself in two,
> One part is man, the other god:
> Imagined man, the monkish mask, the face
> (*CP*, 218)

and again in "An Ordinary Evening":

> . . . Why, then, inquire
> Who has divided the world, what entrepeneur?
> No man. The self, the chrysalis of all men
>
> Became divided in the leisure of blue day
> And more, in branchings after day. One part
> Held fast tenaciously in common earth
>
> And one from central earth to central sky
> And in moonlit extensions of them in the mind
> Searched out such majesty as it could find.
> (*CP*, 468–69)

This self-division between earth and sky—humanity and divinity—for Stevens (and Nietzsche) effectively devalues the earth and leaves "heaven" an "icy Élyseé" (*CP*, 56). For both poet and thinker the division is healed, its effects overcome, in the conviction that "the imperfect [the earthly] is our paradise" (*CP*, 194).[8] Nietzsche speculates: "perhaps man will rise ever higher as soon as he ceases to *flow out* into a god" (*Gay Science*, 230); and "man has [as yet] felt too little joy: that alone . . . is our original sin" (*Thus Spoke Zarathustra*, 200). Agreeing, Stevens' early poem "The Surprises of the Superhuman" directly advocates a Nietzschean "Übermenschlichkeit":

> The palais de justice of chambermaids
> Tops the horizon with its colonnades.
>
> If it were lost in Übermenschlichkeit,
> Perhaps our wretched state would soon come right.
>
> For somehow the brave dicta of its kings
> Make more awry our faulty human things.
>
> (*CP*, 98)

"Evening without Angels" tells us that

> Sad men made angels of the sun, and of
> The moon they made their own attendant ghosts,
> Which led them back to angels, after death.
>
> (*CP*, 137)

The poetry conceives this unhappy manipulation—the deprivation of our fully human (partly divine) potentiality—in a negative light, while the clear air of a "bare night" (and houses, in this positive, "our own") is greeted affirmatively:

> Bare night is best. Bare earth is best. Bare, bare,
> Except for our own houses, huddled low
> Beneath the arches and their spangled air.
>
> (*CP*, 137–38)

To the conventional notion of paradise section XXVI of "Like Decorations" responds,

> This fat pistache of Belgian grapes exceeds
> The total gala of auburn aureoles.
> *Cochon!* Master, the grapes are here and now.
>
> (*CP*, 154)

And in "Sunday Morning" the "beyond" does not satisfy the mind:

Sun and Symbol

> ... Or do the boughs
> Hang always heavy in that perfect sky,
> Unchanging, yet so like our perishing earth,
> With rivers like our own that seek for seas
> They never find, the same receding shores
> That never touch with inarticulate pang?
>
> (*CP*, 69)

This meta-physically surreal image of earth foregoes temporality for eternity, pregnancy for stasis. Stevens' decreation, displacing the surreal (or Real) with the "real," discovers in the "here and now" of our beginnings and endings, "the unique experience, the item of ecstasy which we have been isolating and reserving for another time and place, loftier and more secluded" (*OP*, 213). "Death is the mother of beauty" not as presage of eternal contentment but because it makes the present more precious:

> In a world without heaven to follow, the stops
> Would be endings, more poignant than partings, profounder,
> And that would be saying farewell, repeating farewell,
> Just to be there and just to behold.
>
> To be one's singular self, to despise
> The being that yielded so little, acquired
> So little, too little to care, to turn
> To the ever-jubilant weather, to sip
>
> One's cup and never to say a word,
> Or to sleep or just to lie there still,
> Just to be there, just to be beheld,
> That would be bidding farewell, be bidding farewell.
>
> (*CP*, 127–28)

The weather is "ever-jubilant" because its nonteleological changes are the "freshness of transformation" in a human paradise of imperfection. The unchanging perfection of the eternal disclaims creation/fruition; in reaction, Zarathustra proclaims, "It is of time and becoming that the best parables should speak: let them be a praise and a justification of all impermanence. Creation—that is the great redemption from suffering, and life's growing light" (*Thus Spoke Zarathustra*, 198–99).

Stevens' figures of metamorphosis (including seasonal phases) progress in parallel with the Nietzschean metamorphoses—camel to lion to child. His first stage, that of the "doctor," shares in the "sublime metaphysical illusion" Nietzsche ascribes to Western philosophy: an "unshakable faith that thought, using the thread of causality, can penetrate the deepest abysses of being, and that thought is capable not only of knowing being but even of *correcting* it" (*Birth of Tragedy*, 95).[9] Stevens' pejorative references to "doctors" and their "doctrines" (metaphysical pursuits of truth) attack an exclusive reliance on reason. "The Doctor of Geneva" is "A man so used to plumb / The multifarious heavens" (*CP*, 24); and the "doctors" of "Notes," viewing the statue of General Du Puy and

> ... having bathed
>
> Themselves with care, sought out the nerveless frame
> Of a suspension, a permanence, so rigid
> That it made the General a bit absurd,
>
> Changed his true flesh to an inhuman bronze.
>
> (*CP*, 391)

Stevens' "autumn" often images this sort of confident rigidity, when the flesh of belief has ironically changed to "an inhuman bronze." Thought, fixed on a particular sublime, loses its generative energy. This prelude to an inevitable winter of unbelief is the time of the Stevensian/Nietzschean "ascetic":

With a swelled chest and like one who holds in his breath, he stood there, the sublime one, silent, decked out with ugly truths, the spoil of his hunting, and rich in torn garments; many thorns too adorned him—yet I saw no rose.

As yet he has not learned laughter or beauty. Gloomy this hunter returned from the woods of knowledge. (*Thus Spoke Zarathustra*, 228–29)

Sun and Symbol

The description displays the inherent inadequacy of the "camel" (self-determined by withdrawal and self-denial) as paradigm for thought (and spirituality). Intellectual asceticism, bent on purging the spirit (or intelligence) of the earth-bound and anti-rational, abandons the simple starting point of reflection: wonder at the extraordinary phenomenon of existence. The logical/metaphysical search for absolute grounding uproots us; Nietzschean aphorisms insistently vitalize thinking, re-turn thought to its poetic ground. For this, Nietzsche argues, philosophy must also be artistry, coupling Dionysian intoxication (uncritical abandonment to life) and Apollonian imagination (formal, aesthetic perspective).

Stevens' "anti-master-man, floribund ascetic" in "Landscape with Boat" (*CP*, 241–43), a variant on Nietzsche's ascetic,

> ... never supposed divine
> Things might not look divine, nor that if nothing
> Was divine then all things were, the world itself,
> And that if nothing was the truth, then all
> Things were the truth, the world itself was the truth.

The anti-master-man's floribundness, perverting the rose-potentiality of the class floribunda, renders it a rosaceous equivalent of the moribund. His deadening asceticism extracts beauty/truth from the human context, places them out of reach. His detached "suppositions" leave him unable to discover the Zarathustran "grass and red poppies":

> Had he been better able to suppose:
> He might sit on a sofa on a balcony
> Above the Mediterranean, emerald
> Becoming emeralds. He might watch the palms
> Flap green ears in the heat. He might observe
> A yellow wine and follow a steamer's track
> And say, "The thing I hum appears to be
> The rhythm of this celestial *pantomime*."
>
> (*CP*, 243)

Stevens' projection/rejection of asceticism probes the rational/metaphysical bias (that intellect "can penetrate the deepest abysses of being") underlying the scientific orientation of Western thinking—a presumption satirized in "Crude Foyer" (*CP*, 305):

> Thought is false happiness: the idea
> That merely by thinking one can,
> Or may, penetrate, not may,
> But can, that one is sure to be able—
>
> That there lies at the end of thought
> A foyer of the spirit in a landscape
> Of the mind, in which we sit
> And wear humanity's bleak crown.

Anticipating the formulation that "it is not the reason / That makes us happy or unhappy" ("Of Mere Being"), the first stanza's ineffectual syntax parodies a vacantly precise rationality directed toward an otherworldly "foyer of the spirit"—the antithesis of "Mere Being"'s sensuous "palm" (with its "gold-feathered bird") which stands "at the end of the mind." Stevens' warning joins with Zarathustra's "Beware of the scholars! . . . for they are sterile. . . . before them every bird lies unplumed" (*Thus Spoke Zarathustra*, 402). The palm, like the grapes of "Like Decorations," is prolifically "here and now," while in the foyer, ambiguously, "we sit / And wear humanity's bleak crown; / / In which we read the critique of paradise."[10] The consolation of the foyer as imitative illusion, resting on the rhetoric of hyper-rationality, is a

> False happiness, since we know that we use
> Only the eye as faculty, that the mind
> Is the eye, and that this landscape of the mind
>
> Is a landscape only of the eye; and that
> We are ignorant men incapable
> Of the least, minor, vital metaphor, content,
> At last, there, when it turns out to be here.[11]

False happiness, since the intellectual ascetic's self-denial is ultimately self-deception. The terrain, the context for his "crude foyer" (and humanity's thorny/metaphysical "bleak crown"), originates in the "eye" for which, again ambiguously, "the mind is the eye": the mind/eye gathers the phenomena of "perception" for its landscapes. In the mixed meanings of the last lines, this essential relationality, if captived by the essentially relational "vital metaphor" (subverting the "meta-foyer") would produce a "vital ambiance," bringing the "beyond" near: the "there" is decreated by Stevens' sense of "here"—underscoring "The brilliance of the earth is the brilliance of every paradise" ("Three Academic Pieces"; *NA*, 77).

Stevens' turn away from the meta-physical kingdom's "bleak crown" emulates Nietzsche's "In the loneliest desert... the second metamorphosis occurs: here the spirit becomes a lion who would conquer his freedom and be master in his own desert" (*Thus Spoke Zarathustra*, 138). And the language of Stevens' opening lines in section V of "It Must Be Abstract" ("Notes") directly appropriates this Zarathustran "challenger":

> The lion roars at the enraging desert,
> Reddens the sand with his red-colored noise,
> Defies red emptiness to evolve his match,
>
> Master by foot and jaws and by the mane,
> Most supple challenger....
>
> (*CP*, 384)

Nietzsche's expanded desert realm also appears (as it prepares for, or transforms into, the region of the child's affirmation) in Stevens' scheme of things as "being without description": at times a winterscape, at times the formless night or the ubiquitous hue of morning mist. The leonine freedom, preserved in the child's innocence, is that of Stevens' "Latest Freed Man" (*CP*, 204–5), who, "having just / Escaped from the truth," rises early and finds that "the morning is color and mist, / Which is enough." Emancipation from the pseudo-permanence of "doctrine" brings him into vivid contact with the transient. The way "the sun came shining into his room" produces an experience of "the ant of the self changed to an ox / . . . changed / From a doctor into an ox"—fulfilling Nietzsche's wish for the "ascetic of the spirit": "He should act like a bull, and his happiness should smell of the earth, and not of contempt for the earth. I would like to see him as a white bull, walking before the plowshare, snorting and bellowing; and his bellowing should be in praise of everything earthly" (*Thus Spoke Zarathustra,* 229). These metamorphoses, for Stevens and Nietzsche, transmute metaphysical to physical, invisible to visible; the camel's burden is shed by the lion's "no." The "latest freed man" knows

> . . . that the change and that the ox-like struggle
> Come from the strength that is the strength of the sun,
> . . . .
> It was being without description, being an ox.

The sun's power ("the strong man vaguely seen"), which is his own, overcomes the debilitating effects of "old descriptions":

> It was everything being more real, himself
> At the centre of reality, seeing it.

In this centrality, his light is like the "rabbit-light" in "A Rabbit as King of the Ghosts":

> . . . The trees around are for you,
> The whole of the wideness of night is for you,
> A self that touches all edges,
>
> You become a self that fills the four corners of night.
>
> (*CP,* 209)

The luminous sensibility of the "freed man," likewise, broadens to fill/encompass the reality it apprehends.

"Ploughing on Sunday" (*CP,* 20) presents an earlier form of the "freed man." Sunday, reclaimed as the day of the sun, becomes a day for the ploughman's natural exaltation:

Sun and Symbol

> Remus, blow your horn!
> I'm ploughing on Sunday,
> Ploughing North America.
> Blow your horn!

These deceptively simple lines open onto a complex of allusion. The ploughman, like Nietzsche's white bull, ploughs the earth and bellows his exuberance. Celebrating work on the Sabbath, the ploughman is in company with Christ's radically freeing "It is lawful to do well on the sabbath days" (Matthew 12:12). Fittingly, the poem's "Remus" (literally "an oar," ploughlike and propelling) may be both the freed slave invented by Joel Chandler Harris to plough the soil of the rural South with homely fables and another Remus (like Christ, of virgin birth), co-founder of the "eternal" city of Rome. The horn-blowing proclaims a coalescence like that of the Second Coming, to be announced by "a great sound of a trumpet" while angels "gather together his elect from the four winds" (Matthew 24:31).[12] Stevens' poem concludes with the cross-fertilization: "Water in the fields. / The wind pours down."

A similar exuberance breaks into the quiet meditation of "Sunday Morning," as the "ring of men" chant in a pagan "orgy" of

> ... boisterous devotion to the sun,
> Not as a god, but as a god might be,
> Naked among them, like a savage source.
> (CP, 70)

Again Stevens' use of "the strength of the sun" joins with Nietzsche's pervasive solar imagery. Nietzsche's geotropism is an anti-Platonist heliotropism—a turn toward life-sustaining solar heat and light.[13] Nietzsche concludes *Zarathustra* with a passage that seems more than coincidentally close to Stevens' description of the "latest freed man": "'Zarathustra has ripened, my hour has come: this is *my* morning, *my* day is breaking: *rise now, rise, thou great noon!*' Thus spoke

Zarathustra, and he left his cave, glowing and strong as a morning sun that comes out of dark mountains" (439).

For Stevens,

> The greatest poverty is not to live
> In a physical world, to feel that one's desire
> Is too difficult to tell from despair.
>
> (*CP*, 325)

Replacement of the intangible with the visible, present sun reinstates "physicality"—as if we were "completely physical in a physical world" (*CP*, 325). "On the Road Home" accents this piquancy:

> It was when you said,
> "The idols have seen lots of poverty,
> Snakes and gold and lice,
> But not the truth";
>
> It was at that time, that the silence was largest
> And longest, the night was roundest,
> The fragrance of the autumn warmest,
> Closest and strongest.
>
> (*CP*, 204)

The experience (as in Nietzsche's *Twilight of the Idols*) of freedom from the old order (from the mythoi of the serpent in Eden and the serpent lifted up in the wilderness) amplifies the Nietzschean desire "no longer to bury one's head in the sand of heavenly things, but to bear it freely, an earthly head, which creates a meaning for the earth" (*Thus Spoke Zarathustra*, 144). Here the seemingly direct passing from "ascetic" to "child" suggests the way in which (as with Stevens' conjunction of "but not the truth" and the "rounding" of night) the child's "yes" is anticipated in the lion's "no": "To create new values—that even the lion cannot do; but the creation of freedom for oneself for new creation—that is within the power of the lion" (*Thus Spoke Zarathustra*, 139).

The metamorphoses from acceptance to negation to affirmation are captured by Stevens' "Esthétique du Mal" in a passage recalling Nietzsche's title *The Birth of Tragedy*:[14]

> ... The mortal no
> Has its emptiness and tragic expirations.
> The tragedy, however, may have begun,
> Again, in the imagination's new beginning,
> In the yes of the realist spoken because he must
> Say yes, spoken because under every no
> Lay a passion for yes that had never been broken.
>
> (*CP*, 320)[15]

The poetry assumes that, again, such "tragic expirations" (here referring to the "capital negation" of "Satan") are the fate of all "gods" and "demons"—all objects of belief. Since, for Stevens, humanity "invented the Gods[,] ... put into their mouths the only words they have ever spoken!" (*OP*, 167), a certain restlessness with the delimitations of these articulations is inevitable. But the dissatisfaction is not a nihilism; it contains "a passion for yes"—and for the "tragic" cycle. In the changing currents of belief, the "yes of the realist," though containing (in each particular utterance) the seed of its destruction, sustains both "passion" and cycle.

The "yes" which begins the tragedy entails a Nietzschean "great health" (*Gay Science*, 346): "the ideal of a human, superhuman well-being and benevolence that will often appear *inhuman*"—with which the "*great seriousness* really begins, ... the real question mark is posed for the first time, ... the destiny of the soul changes, the hand moves forward, the tragedy *begins*" (*Gay Science*, 347). This is the Zarathustran "health" which insists, "We have no wish whatever to enter into the kingdom of heaven: we have become men—*so we want the earth*" (*Thus Spoke Zarathustra*, 428). Stevens' "freed man" flourishes in the transparence of "all gods are poets' parables, poets' prevarications" (*Thus Spoke Zarathustra*, 240).[16] The "yes," even of the "realist," cultivates the satisfaction of the metaphorizing impulse: "After one has abandoned a belief in god, poetry is that essence which takes its place as life's redemption" (OP, 158)[17]—but as an inherent "form of life or . . . sound or color of life" continuous with ("often indistinguishable from") "life itself" (OP, 158). Belief, redirected by the demise of "the metaphysicals" (CP, 325), exists in the cleared air of section XX of "The Man with the Blue Guitar":

> What is there in life except one's ideas,
> Good air, good friend, what is there in life?
>
> Is it ideas that I believe?
> Good air, my only friend, believe,
>
> Believe would be a brother full
> Of love, believe would be a friend,
>
> Friendlier than my only friend,
> Good air. . . .[18]
>
> (CP, 175–76)

The poet breathes the Zarathustran "good air" of the earth.[19] "Poetry is a health" (OP, 176), Stevens remarks in his "Adagia," following the Nietzschean formulation; and in this healthful atmosphere, the freed man builds "a chapel of breath, an appearance made / For a sign of meaning in the meaningless" ("St. Armorer's Church from the Outside"; CP, 529):

> The chapel underneath St. Armorer's walls,
> Stands in a light, its natural light and day,
> The origin and keep of its health and his own.
> And there he walks and does as he lives and likes.
>
> (CP, 530)

And in "Parochial Theme":

> . . . This health is holy,
> This halloo, halloo, halloo heard over the cries
>
> Of those for whom a square room is a fire,
> Of those whom the statues torture and keep down.
>
> This health is holy, this descant of a self,
> This barbarous chanting of what is strong, this blare.
>
> (CP, 191)[20]

Sun and Symbol

The Stevensian/Nietzschean "health" reconstitutes the problematic of the "human" and "inhuman" in an extended, ironical play of terms by which the static (inhuman/dehumanized) and the egocentric (over-human/all-too-human) oppose the generative positive (inhuman/more-than-human). Like the statue of General Du Puy in "Notes," "Parochial Theme"'s statues—dehumanized doctrinal molds into which humanity tries to fit itself—"torture" and "keep [us] down." In the course of becoming fully human in a human world, the freed man, with his "barbarous chanting of what is strong," says "no" to the statues and is "changed / From a doctor into an ox." The statues, relics of the past, are "stale perfections" (*CP*, 293). Stevens tells us in "Dutch Graves in Bucks County" that

> Freedom is like a man who kills himself
> Each night, an incessant butcher, whose knife
> Grows sharp in blood.
>
> (*CP*, 292)

Nietzsche asserts that life is "continually shedding something that wants to die.... Constantly being a murderer" (*Gay Science*, 100). By such metaphorical violence humanity overcomes the past, becomes itself by its continual self-overcoming:[21] "the *great health*—that one does not merely have but also acquires continually, and must acquire because one gives it up again and again, and must give it up" (*Gay Science*, 346).

Again, in the ironies of "Esthétique"'s dialectics of human and inhuman (inverting the motif of "indifference"):

> The fault lies with an over-human god,
> Who by sympathy has made himself a man
> And is not to be distinguished.
>
> (*CP*, 315)

These lines reprise the anecdote in "Sunday Morning" that "Jove," being of "inhuman birth" (*CP*, 67), envied humanness, and so, "commingled" his blood with humanity's, engendering a "chimera" (*CP*, 68)—half-man, half-god.[22] "Nuances of a Theme by Williams" admonishes the morning star:

> Be not chimera of morning,
> Half-man, half-star.
>
> (CP, 18)

The "over-human god" of "Esthétique," inflicting the devastation of his human-like pity, is such a "chimera":

> If only he would not pity us so much,
> Weaken our fate, relieve us of woe both great
> And small, a constant fellow of destiny,
>
> A too, too human god, self-pity's kin
> And uncourageous genesis ... It seems
> As if the health of the world might be enough.
>
> (CP, 315; ellipsis is Stevens')

The vilification of the "too, too human god"—suggesting, as it does, Nietzsche's *Human, All-Too-Human*[23]—mirrors *Zarathustra*'s "God died of his pity for man" (202) and "when you say, 'From pity, a great cloud approaches; ... all great love is over and above its pity'—O Zarathustra, how well you seem to me to understand storm signs" (378).

Set against the tyrannous sympathy, humanity's newly sufficing fiction would, ironically, transcend the over-human/all-too-human. As in "Of Mere Being," it would be "without human meaning, / Without human feeling, a foreign song." "Less and Less Human, O Savage Spirit" (CP, 327–28) remonstrates:

> If there must be a god in the house, must be,
> Saying things in the rooms and on the stair,
>
> Let him move as the sunlight moves on the floor,
> Or moonlight, silently, as Plato's ghost
>
> Or Aristotle's skeleton. Let him hang out
> His stars on the wall. He must dwell quietly.

Instead of the "overpitying" witness:

> If there must be a god in the house, let him be one
> That will not hear us when we speak: a coolness,
>
> A vermilioned nothingness ...

Sun and Symbol

The poem calls for Nietzsche's "gods of Epicurus who [without the divisiveness of pity, envy, deliberate indifference] have no care and are unknown," effectively encouraging appreciation of our own dexterities and the natural tones of life's surprising rightnesses—"the wonderful harmony created by the playing of our instrument" (*Gay Science*, 224). The title of the poem indirectly marks the sun—the "savage source" in "Sunday Morning"—and the movement back toward that sun/ source at the beginning of "Notes":

> How clean the sun when seen in its idea,
> Washed in the remotest cleanliness of a heaven
> That has expelled us and our images . . .
> ....
> Phoebus is dead, ephebe. But Phoebus was
> A name for something that never could be named.
> There was a project for the sun and is.
>
> (*CP*, 381)

In Stevens' matrix of figuration the Nietzschean sun supplants the Romantic moon (and "moonlit extensions . . . in the mind"). The moon's pale imitation—lacking the original's ruddy vitality—distances us from the "source": "The moon follows the sun like a French / Translation of a Russian poet" (*CP*, 234).

The sun as original ("gold flourisher"), being "in the difficulty of what it is to be," becomes emblem of willful invention (re-cognized with the "expulsion" of the obsolete); and it is the Nietzschean expression "will to power" that Stevens chooses for "Mountains Covered with Cats":

> Regard the invalid personality
> Instead, outcast, without the will to power
> And impotent, like the imagination seeking
> To propagate the imagination or like
> War's miracle begetting that of peace.
>
> (*CP*, 368)

The "impotence" resulting from the absence of "will" is countered by the figure of Nietzsche himself in "Description without Place" "in a kind of total affluence":

> Nietzsche in Basel studied the deep pool
> Of these discolorations, mastering
>
> The moving and the moving of their forms
> In the much-mottled motion of blank time.
>
> His revery was the deepness of the pool,
> The very pool, his thoughts the colored forms,
>
> The eccentric souvenirs of human shapes,
> Wrapped in their seemings, crowd on curious crowd,
>
> In a kind of total affluence, all first,
> All final, colors subjected in revery
>
> To an innate grandiose, an innate light,
> The sun of Nietzsche gildering the pool,
>
> Yes: gildering the swarm-like manias
> In perpetual revolution, round and round . . .
>   (*CP*, 342; ellipsis is Stevens')

The colorations, the movement of "forms" in the mind, the "gildering" force of the Nietzschean sun as it produces "an innate grandiose, an innate light": all these details speak of a subtle, affinitive understanding of Nietzschean philosophy.[24] The "perpetual revolution" of the final line conspicuously refers to Nietzsche's "*Ewige Wiederkehr*," mentioned in "A Collect of Philosophy" (*OP*, 194)[25] as an example of a poetic concept in philosophy—and impelling section IX of "It Must Give Pleasure" in "Notes":

> . . . These things at least comprise
> An occupation, an exercise, a work,
>
> A thing final in itself and, therefore, good:
> One of the vast repetitions final in
> Themselves and, therefore, good, the going round
>
> And round and round, the merely going round,
> Until merely going round is a final good,
> The way wine comes at a table in a wood.

> And we enjoy like men, the way a leaf
> Above the table spins its constant spin,
> So that we look at it with pleasure, look
>
> At it spinning its eccentric measure. Perhaps,
> The man-hero is not the exceptional monster,
> But he that of repetition is most master.
>
> (*CP*, 405–6)[26]

Repetition as "a final good" furthers the earlier "It Must Change," so that—in contrast to the fixed ("final") sobriety of the statue of General Du Puy—we "enjoy like men." The "master" of the repetition, characterized by a Nietzschean "*amor fati*" (*Gay Science*, 223), embraces/wills his fate. Nietzsche, in "Description without Place," is such a master, converted by the poem into an image of his own philosophy.

The repetitions perpetuate a gaiety, "in which we pronounce joy like a word of our own," as Stevens says in "Of Bright & Blue Birds & the Gala Sun":

> . . . a bright *scienza* outside of ourselves,
>
> A gaiety that is being, not merely knowing,
> The will to be and to be total in belief.
>
> (*CP*, 248)

Hines associates this "gaiety" with Heidegger (and *ekstasis*[27]) (*Later Poetry*, 137); but the "gaiety that is being" for Stevens is, as has been seen, an extravagant joyfulness—the Zarathustran "I would believe only in a god who could dance" (*Thus Spoke Zarathustra*, 153). And the "*scienza*" of Stevens' poem is very likely a direct allusion to "*la gaya scienza*," the Italian title under which *The Gay Science* was originally published (*Gay Science*, 29). The significant consequence of the "gaiety" of existence in a demythologized world in which "the grapes seemed fatter[,] / . . . the night was roundest, / The fragrance of the autumn warmest, / Closest and strongest" (*CP*, 203–4)—in which "the ant of the self [is] changed to an ox / . . . everything being more real" (*CP*, 205)—is compressed in the Nietzschean maxim: "To esteem is to create" (*Thus Spoke Zarathustra*,

171). Love of the transitory restores creative "innocence"—which takes tentative shape in the "ephebe" of "Notes" and "An Ordinary Evening" and more vigorous ("savage") form in section X of "Esthétique," where

> ... home
> Was a return to birth, a being born
> Again in the savagest severity,
> Desiring fiercely, the child of a mother fierce
> In his body, fiercer in his mind, merciless
> To accomplish the truth in his intelligence.
> (CP, 321)

The reborn persona experiences "life itself" as "innocence":

> ... That he might suffer or that
> He might die was the innocence of living, if life
> Itself was innocent ...
> (CP, 322)

—a reformation of the traditional return to innocence (childlikeness) as a rite of passage into the "kingdom."

The child's innocence connotes an emerging spring, portending summer, as in "A Discovery of Thought":

> One is a child again. The gold beards of waterfalls
> Are dissolved as in an infancy of blue snow.
> It is an arbor against the wind, a pit in the mist,
>
> A trinkling in the parentage of the north,
> The cricket of summer forming itself out of ice.
> (OP, 95)

Vendler, indicating that "certain late poems, taken together, make up what we may call Stevens' poem of infancy, as his west touches his east" (*On Extended Wings*, 310), finds: "This extraordinary creature, Stevens' last mythical invention, is the child one becomes in second childhood, in that sickness where the eyes dim, where the body is a chill weight, and the old winning fairy tales of bearded deities become irrelevant" (312). But in "Discovery," as elsewhere, the advent of the "child" does not signal decrepitude; it is a Stevensian/Nietzschean "new beginning," a re-formation out of the open potentiality of the winter landscape:

> Pronouncing its new life and ours, not autumn's prodigal returned,
> But an antipodal, far-fetched creature, worthy of birth,
> The true tone of the metal of winter in what it says:
>
> The accent of deviation in the living thing
> That is its life preserved, the effort to be born
> Surviving being born, the event of life.
>
> (OP, 96)

It renews possibility, effects a return from "hierophant Omega" to "naked Alpha" (CP, 469)—prefigured in the "form gulping after formlessness, / Skin flashing to wished-for disappearances / And the serpent body flashing without the skin" (CP, 411)[28] of "The Auroras of Autumn":

> So, then, these lights are not a spell of light,
> A saying out of a cloud, but innocence.
> An innocence of the earth and no false sign
>
> Or symbol of malice. That we partake thereof,
> Lie down like children in this holiness,
> As if, awake, we lay in the quiet of sleep,
>
> As if the innocent mother sang in the dark
> Of the room and on an accordion, half-heard,
> Created the time and place in which we breathed ...
>
> (CP, 418-19; ellipsis is Stevens')

The sky, now innocent (neither pitying nor "dividing and indifferent blue"), harbors no ominous mutterings among the clouds. For the human perceiver, such innocence is "blindness" to dogmatisms, a blindness

> ... in which nothing has been lost,
> Sight least, but metaphysical blindness gained,
>
> The blindness in which seeing would be false,
> A fantastic irruption ...
>
> (OP, 94-95)

—in which vision would retain the afterimages of "truths" incongruent with present "reality"; and "metaphysical blindness" is

> A freedom at last from the mystical,
> The beginning of a final order,
> The order of man's right to be
> As he is, the discipline of his scope
> Observed as an absolute, himself.
> (*OP*, 101)

This blindness-as-freedom shares in the possibility of the "ignorant man," named in an October 1945 letter as "perhaps the only really happy man, or the only man with any wide range of possible happiness" (*Letters*, 512). Like the "child," the "blind" or "ignorant" man is "innocence and forgetting"— the prelude of "the cricket of summer forming itself out of ice." The previous summer's "inamorata" (*CP*, 484) has been banished, but the whisperings of her successor begin to be audible:

> The dress is lying, cast-off, on the floor.
> Now, the first tutoyers of tragedy
> Speak softly, to begin with, in the eaves.
> (*CP*, 428)

The spell of estrangement from "things as they are" having been broken by the lion's "no":

> It may be that the ignorant man, alone,
> Has any chance to mate his life with life
> That is the sensual, pearly spouse.
> (*CP*, 222)

"Ignorance" as a sense of, and reliance on, one's own capacity, "without external reference" (*CP*, 251),[29] becomes "one of the sources of poetry" (*OP*, 173).

Nietzsche insists that "what is good and evil *no one knows yet*, unless it be he who creates. He, however, creates man's goal and gives the earth its meaning and its future. That any-

Sun and Symbol

thing at all is good and evil—that is his creation" (*Thus Spoke Zarathustra*, 308). Stevens' reformulation in "Imagination as Value" refers specifically to Nietzsche:

> Nietzsche walked in the Alps in the caresses of reality. We ourselves crawl out of our offices and classrooms and become alert at the opera. Or we sit listening to music as in an imagination in which we believe. If the imagination is the faculty by which we import the unreal into what is real, its value is the value of the way of thinking by which we project the idea of God into the idea of man. (*NA*, 150)

This prose description isolates the essential quality of Stevens' accord with Nietzsche, condensing into a single phrase the demise of metaphysics, the potency of the "sun," and the "sacred yes": the projection of "the idea of God into the idea of man"—the axis for the metamorphoses of Stevensian "belief."[30]

Cassirer's investigations augment the Nietzschean emphasis on the symbolizing and artistic, articulating philosophical bases for the Stevensian aesthetic. Nietzschean figurations (directly and through Stevens' friend Henry Church) exerted a pervasively overt influence on Stevens' thought and poetic sensibility.[31] Cassirer, though more kindred spirit than direct influence,[32] was a source of ideas circulating at the time Stevens was writing his middle and late poetry—ideas that repeatedly surface in Stevens' work. Cassirer clearly delineates key assumptions that activate Stevens' poetry—most importantly, the notion of a sufficing fiction: the "idea of order" which becomes the poet's "new knowledge of reality." Stevens' poetry and prose share the Cassirerian view that aesthetic fiction, self-consciously understood, rivals other means of knowing: showing us "life and reality in a form in which we feel we have never known it before . . . a *knowledge* which cannot be grasped in abstract concepts" (*Logic of the Humanities*, 85).[33]

For Cassirer, as Donald Verene says, "to know is to elicit order and to elicit order is to symbolize" ("Cassirer's Concept of Form," 18). Cassirer maintains: "the forms of art . . . are not empty forms. They perform a definite task in the construction and organization of human experience" (*Essay on Man*, 167); and: "By a pure activity of the imagination we can . . . inject a definite content into parts of a sensuous totality that have been left empty by direct experience" (*Phenomenology of Knowledge*, 426).³⁴ Though "phenomenological," Cassirer's thought provides for that "enhanced reality" excluded by Husserlian and Heideggerian phenomenologies.³⁵

Making this point with ethical forms in mind, he sharply separates his thinking from the Heideggerian as the difference plays itself out in terms of the "*Geworfenheit*": Heidegger "speaks of the *Geworfenheit* of man (the being-thrown of man). To be thrown into the stream of time is one of the fundamental and unalterable conditions of human life. Man cannot emerge from this stream, and he cannot change its course. He has to accept the historical conditions of his existence; he has to submit to his fate" (*Symbol, Myth, and Culture*, 229). Accordingly, Heidegger's emphasis on "thrownness" leaves humanity as if "curbed under the yoke of a dire and inexorable fatality" (229);³⁶ and by extension: "a philosophy whose whole attention is focused on the *Geworfenheit*, the Being-thrown of man, can no longer do its duty," since it loses sight of the essential role of the "active faculties" in forming "individual and social life" (230).

Cassirer's assumption that, as John Michael Krois notes, "the formation of humanity occurs in the sphere of meaning" within which the "creations of individuals" make themselves felt (*Cassirer*, 166), gives rise to the kind of multifaceted possibility central to Stevens' poetry. Displacing Heidegger's concern that "prevailing thing-concepts obstruct the way toward the thingly character of the thing" (*Poetry, Language, Thought*, 31), Cassirer underscores the symbolical character of reality: "The function of the concept now [since Kant] no longer appears as merely formal and analytical; it is a productive constructive function—no longer a more or less remote and pale copy of some absolute, self-subsisting reality, but a presupposition of experience and hence a condition of the possibility of its objects" (*Phenomenology of Knowledge*, 315). Umberto Eco observes about Cassirer: "He deals with the Kantian theory of knowledge as if it were a semiotic theory (even though Cassirer's a priori is more similar to a cultural product than to a transcendental structure of human mind): the symbolic activity does not 'name' an already known world, but establishes the very conditions for knowing it" (*Semiotics and the Philosophy of Language*, 135).[37] The liberation of concepts from the "merely formal and analytical" affords a rudimentary semiological basis for the creation of Stevens' fictions, even the supreme fiction.

In *Ideas of Order* and afterward, Stevens concentrates more and more explicitly on the ability of the concept, as in "Mud Master" (*CP*, 147–48), to order and clarify a "muddy" disorder:

> There is a master of mud.
> The shaft of light
> Falling, far off, from sky to land,
> That is he—
>
> The peach-bud maker,
> The mud master,
> The master of the mind.

Here the concept, the "shaft of light," masters the muddy mind/reality so that the "muddy rivers of spring" achieve midsummer's brilliance. Diverging from Heidegger's insistence that to appreciate "the thingly character of the thing," one must "leave the thing to rest in its own self" (*Poetry, Language, Thought*, 31), such "ideas" establish reflective/refractive categories which shape and vary the reality of experience ("emerald becoming emeralds"). This experience of the "concept" promotes the Stevensian/Cassirerian ascendancy of the fictional/aesthetic—and Stevens' "supreme fiction."

If in phenomenological terms conceptions of deity weaken, it is because, Cassirer shows, religious consciousness (dependent for its understanding on the meaning of the image) is inevitably at war with itself, torn between the "sensuous existence" of its images and continuous striving "toward a progressively purer spiritualization" (*Mythical Thought*, 260–61) in which no image (but therefore no guiding concept) would remain. But aesthetic consciousness and image provide a necessary and "sufficing" alternative:

> It is only the aesthetic consciousness that leaves this problem truly behind it. Since from the outset it gives itself to pure "contemplation," developing the form of vision in contrast to all forms of action, the images fashioned in this frame of consciousness gain for the first time a truly immanent significance. They confess themselves to be illusion as opposed to the empirical reality of things; but this illusion has its own truth because it possesses its own law. In the return to this law there arises a new freedom of consciousness: the image no longer reacts upon the spirit as an independent material thing but becomes for the spirit a pure expression of its own creative power. (*Mythical Thought*, 261)

Disrupting the tension between symbol and symbolized, aesthetic consciousness exceeds the mythico-religious; thus Stevens' "It is possible to establish aesthetics in the individual mind as immeasurably a greater thing than religion" (*OP*, 166). The new, self-consciously produced transcendence is not divisive; as the self-confessed "expression of [the spirit's] own creative power," it has "a truly immanent significance." This aesthetic mode of consciousness, which renews/reveals the potency of word and image, "elicit[ing] a sense of the imagination as something vital" (*NA*, 139), proves equal to its predecessors—and more than equal:

> Word and mythic image, which once confronted the human mind as hard realistic powers, have now cast off all reality and effectuality; they have become a light, bright ether in which the spirit can move without let or hindrance. This liberation is achieved not because the mind throws aside the sensuous forms of word and image, but in that it uses them both as *organs* of its own, and thereby recognizes them for what they really are: forms of its own self-revelation. (*Language and Myth*, 99)[38]

Sun and Symbol

As a manifest instance of the complex awareness which generates the symbol, the image attains a newly possible sufficiency. Cassirer holds that "it is only in the reciprocal movement between the 'representing' and the 'represented' that a knowledge of the ego and of objects, ideal as well as real, can arise. Here we feel the true pulse of consciousness, whose secret is precisely that every beat strikes a thousand connections" (*Phenomenology of Knowledge*, 203). Whether as "Thirteen Ways of Looking at a Blackbird" or five ways of looking at a November morning near Tehuantepec, the intricacy of the poetic image (its perspectives, figures, rhymes, and rhythms) becomes a reflection of the "thousand connections," satisfying one's sense of things. It is on this ground that poetic fiction becomes object of "belief"; and with this, as "Asides on the Oboe" asserts,

> The prologues are over. It is a question, now,
> Of final belief. So, say that final belief
> Must be in a fiction. It is time to choose.
> (*CP*, 250).

And, as we have seen, for Stevens (in company with Cassirer) political "fictions," as successors to the mythico-religious, likewise evade the depth (and breadth) of the aesthetic.[39] Spurred by criticism (particularly Stanley Burnshaw's) that *Ideas of Order* exhibited inadequate social responsibility during the troubled Depression era (Morse, *Wallace Stevens*, 148), Stevens in *Owl's Clover* takes pains to demonstrate the deficiency of the political (and specifically communism) as "a phenomenon of the imagination" (*NA*, 143):

> Men gathering for a mighty flight of men,
> An abysmal migration into a possible blue.
> (*OP*, 51)

And later, in "Imagination as Value":

Surely the diffusion of communism exhibits imagination on its most momentous scale. This is because whether or not communism is the measure of humanity, the words themselves echo back to us that it has for the present taken the measure of an important part of humanity. With the collapse of other beliefs, this grubby faith promises a practicable earthly paradise. The only earthly paradise that even the best of other faiths has been able to promise has been one in man's noblest image and this has always required an imagination that has not yet been included in the fortunes of mankind. (NA, 143)

"This grubby faith" indicates a lesser order of transcendence—a substitution of values based in the collective will for the "grand flights" (CP, 222) of what-has-been-lost. Its poverty is marked in "Description without Place" by the contrast between "Nietzsche in Basel," in a "total affluence," and the "grubby" figure of Lenin:

> The slouch of his body and his look were not
> In suavest keeping. The shoes, the clothes, the hat
>
> Suited the decadence of those silences,
> In which he sat. All chariots were drowned. The swans
>
> Moved on the buried water where they lay.
>
> (CP, 343)

The "decadence" and insufficiency here attributed to communism are signs of the peripheral nature of the political imagination: "The imagination that is satisfied by politics, whatever the nature of the politics, has not the same value as the imagination that seeks to satisfy, say, the universal mind, which, in the case of a poet, would be the imagination that tries to penetrate to basic images, basic emotions, and so to compose a fundamental poetry even older than the ancient world" (NA, 144–45). Communism is "a phenomenon of the imagination" since it proposes as a "final fiction" an idealized, utopian version of society. But this utopian projection is not a Zarathustran self-transcendent "leaner being" (CP, 387); it is only the average man collectively made larger.

The Man with the Blue Guitar and *Parts of a World* extend the examination of the poet's value/responsibility. His role is not to play an unambiguous version of

> A tune upon the blue guitar
> Of things exactly as they are.
>
> (CP, 165)

Rather, he must struggle against "the pressure of reality": "the pressure of an external event or events on the consciousness to the exclusion of any power of contemplation" (NA, 20). He must resort to "nobility": that faculty of mind Stevens defines as "a violence from within that protects us from a violence without[,] . . . the imagination pressing back against the pressure of reality" (NA, 36).

The "Adagia" tell us: "The bare image [as with Williams' "no ideas but in things"] and the image as a symbol are the contrast: the image without meaning and the image as meaning" (OP, 161). And in a letter of August 1940 Stevens writes: "The idea of pure poetry, essential imagination, as the highest objective of the poet, appears to be, at least potentially, as great as the idea of God, and, for that matter, greater, if the idea of God is only one of the things of the imagination" (Letters, 369). Again, what satisfies the poet and likewise his receptive audience is the complicate/fluent image which—speaking words that "In the delicatest ear of the mind, repeat, / Exactly, that which it wants to hear"—is a matter of "sounds passing through sudden rightnesses." Cassirer states the principle in terms strikingly relevant to Stevens: "Even though the image may be recognized and, as it were, epistemologically exposed as a fiction, it has reality as a fiction—that is, it arises according to definite and necessary laws of the imagination—and that suffices" (Phenomenology of Knowledge, 192).

Stevens' poetry rests on such a view of the adequacy of fiction. The conception of supreme fictionality requires both that fictions can, in some sense, "suffice" and that at its origin all belief is intrinsically metaphorical. This position, devastating to traditional metaphysical assumptions, is essential to the aesthetical. "The Pure Good of Theory" maintains:

> To say the solar chariot is junk
>
> Is not a variation but an end.
> Yet to speak of the whole world as metaphor
> Is still to stick to the contents of the mind
>
> And the desire to believe in a metaphor.
> It is to stick to the nicer knowledge of
> Belief, that what it believes in is not true.
>
> (*CP*, 332)

These lines join with Stevens' notion from the "Adagia": "Aesthetics is independent of faith" (*OP*, 166). It is precisely the knowledge "that what it believes in is not true," in any ordinary sense, which frees the mind for discoveries dependent on its own metaphorizing—recognized, as Cassirer says, as a form "of its own self-revelation": "The exquisite truth is to know that it is a fiction and that you believe in it willingly" (*OP*, 163). This willful "willingness" comprehends Cassirer's "Art gives us a new kind of truth—a truth not of empirical things but of pure forms" (*Essay on Man*, 164).[40]

Stevens describes "Notes toward a Supreme Fiction" as "three notes by way of defining the characteristics of supreme fiction" (*Letters*, 407) and explains the poem as "not the statement of a [systematic] philosophic theory. . . . [T]hese are Notes; the nucleus of the matter is contained in the title. It is implicit in the title that there can be such a thing as a supreme fiction" (*Letters*, 430). Also implicit is an orientation seeing the poet's task as analogous to the musician's, the "notes" as musical notes leading toward "the complicate, the amassing harmony" (*CP*, 403) of section VI of "It Must Give Pleasure." Sections VII and VIII conjure this harmony as an angel plucking a heavenly instrument. In the angel's flight from "the gold centre, the golden destiny" (*CP*, 404) of heaven, the imaginer feels himself a part of the decreative/creative movement—sharing the angel's experience by virtue of his momentary belief in its fictional reality. As if to illustrate the contention that "it is the explanations of things that we make to ourselves that disclose our character: The subjects of one's poems are the symbols of one's self or of one of one's selves" (*OP*, 164),[41] the persona asks:

> Is it he or is it I that experience this?
> Is it I then that keep saying there is an hour
> Filled with expressible bliss, in which I have
>
> No need, am happy, forget need's golden hand,
> Am satisfied without solacing majesty,
> And if there is an hour there is a day,
>
> There is a month, a year, there is a time
> In which majesty is a mirror of the self:
> I have not but I am and as I am, I am.
>
> (*CP*, 404–5)

The poem recasts "eternal bliss" as the single hour of aesthetic satisfaction, "without solacing majesty": an illusionally suspended moment like "Credences"'s "last day of a certain year / Beyond which there is nothing left of time." The implied self-sufficiency of the extended figurations is attuned to Cassirer's "A great painter or musician [and to this we can add the poet] is not characterized by his sensitiveness to color or sounds [or language] but by his power to elicit from his static material a dynamic life of forms" (*Essay on Man*, 160). In these forms "inexpressible bliss" is replaced by the "expressible bliss" of the poetic image, a finite "I am" succeeds the infinite "I am" of Yahweh, and "majesty"—no longer "beyond"—becomes "a mirror of the self." "Effects of Analogy," discussing the creation of such transcendent images (and their relation to reality), concludes:

These are the pictorializations of men, for whom the world exists as a world and for whom life exists as life. . . . Their words have made a world that transcends the world and a life livable in that transcendence. It is a transcendence achieved by means of the minor effects of figurations and the major effects of the poet's sense of the world and of the motive music of his poems and it is the imaginative dynamism of all these analogies together. Thus poetry becomes and is a transcendent analogue composed of the particulars of reality, created by the poet's sense of the world, that is to say, his attitude, as he intervenes and interposes the appearances of that sense (NA, 129–30).[42]

Without "solacing majesty" we are like the "ephebe" of "An Ordinary Evening," who, "defining" a "fresh spiritual," enjoys, as Stevens humorously says,

> A strong mind in a weak neighborhood and is
> A serious man without the serious.
>
> (CP, 474)

If poetry-as-transcendent-analogue redirects the transcendent impulse toward the image-as-meaning, then, as Stevens contends, "it is not too extravagant to think of resemblances and of the repetitions of resemblances as a source of the ideal. In short, metaphor has its aspect of the ideal" (NA, 81–82). This follows, according to "Of Ideal Time and Choice,"

> Since thirty mornings are required to make
> A day of which we say, this is the day
> That we desired, a day of blank, blue wheels,
>
> Involving the four corners of the sky,
> Lapised and lacqued [sic] and freely emeraldine[43]
> In the space it fills, the silent motioner
>
> There, of clear, revolving crystalline;
> Since thirty summers are needed for a year
> And thirty years, in the galaxies of birth,
>
> Are time for counting and remembering,
> And fill the earth with young men centuries old.
>
> (NA, 88)

And in this fictive transcendence, we find that

> ... we ourselves
> Stand at the center of ideal time,
> The inhuman making choice of a human self.
>
> (NA, 89)[44]

Sun and Symbol

This overarching sufficiency, established by the subtleties of metaphor, produces a "vivid transparence" ("Notes"; *CP*, 380) in "the excellences of the air we breathe." "The Pediment of Appearance" chronicles the search for such transparence:

> Young men go walking in the woods,
> Hunting for the great ornament,
> The pediment of appearance.
>
> They hunt for a form which by its form alone,
> Without diamond—blazons or flashing or
> Chains of circumstance,
>
> By its form alone, by being right,
> By being high, is the stone
> For which they are looking:
>
> The savage transparence. . . .
>
> (*CP*, 361)

The poem's emphasis on form-as-appearance again composes a transcendent analogue for phenomenological discovery, accentuating that "the reality of the phenomenon cannot be separated from its representative function. . . . It is mere abstraction to attempt to detach the phenomenon from this involvement, to apprehend it as an independent something outside of and preceding any function of indication" (*Phenomenology of Knowledge*, 141).

"Esthétique" transposes the "vivid transparence" of the image into its own variation on musical metaphor:

> When B. sat down at the piano and made
> A transparence in which we heard music, made music,
> In which we heard transparent sounds, did he play
> All sorts of notes? Or did he play only one
> In an ecstasy of its associates,
> Variations in the tones of a single sound,
> The last, or sounds so single they seemed one?
>
> (*CP*, 316)

Here "transparence" is experienced as the essential product of the artist's endeavor—variegating Stevens' much earlier contention (in "Peter Quince at the Clavier") that "music is feeling, then, not sound" (*CP*, 90). And the intimation that the pianist plays "only one [note] / In an ecstasy of its associates, / . . . or sounds so single they seemed one," suggests the transcendence/transparence of a transitory ultimacy—"The fiction of an absolute" (*CP*, 404)—around whose point of reference the phenomena of sound (or color, etc.) congregate. In the same spirit Cassirer writes: "If art is enjoyment it is not the enjoyment of things but the enjoyment of forms" (*Essay on Man*, 159–60).

Stevens' 1949 poem "Study of Images I" (*CP*, 463–64) proposes that "the study of his images / Is the study of man" and that

> . . . in images we awake,
> Within the very object that we seek,
>
> Participants of its being. It is, we are.[45]

Stevens' improvisational structurings, in the later poetry as in the earlier, attempt to "penetrate to basic images" which form the texture/truth of contemporary experience. As with Cassirer, this is a complex truth of which fiction is a vital part: we are participants in the symbolic value of the image seen, accepted, and understood as image. Stevens writes that "poetic truth is an agreement with reality, brought about by the imagination of a man disposed to be strongly influenced by his imagination, which he believes, for a time, to be true, expressed in terms of his emotions or, since it is less of a restriction to say so, in terms of his own personality" (*NA*, 54).[46] Such "agreement" is

> . . . not false except
> When the image itself is false, a mere desire,
>
> Not faded, if images are all we have.

Sun and Symbol

> They can be no more faded than ourselves.
> The blood refreshes with its stale demands.
> (CP, 463–64)

This Stevensian/Nietzschean/Cassirerian emphasis on humanity's imaging and symbolizing nature, redefines *animal rationale*, in Cassirerian terms, as *"animal symbolicum"* (*Essay on Man*, 26).

CHAPTER VI

The Marriage of the Rest

Stevens' poem "Connoisseur of Chaos" concludes with a two-line stanza:

> The pensive man . . . He sees that eagle float
> For which the intricate Alps are a single nest.
> (*CP*, 216; ellipsis is Stevens')

The "connoisseur" is one who knows, one who can appreciate. But what does he know? What is that eagle which floats for the pensive man—the one who, as Stevens says in "Asides on the Oboe," "has had the time to think enough" (*CP*, 250)—for whom the intricate Alps of our experience, the chaos of which the connoisseur partakes, assume the ordered comprehensibility and hospitable familiarity of the single nest?[1]

The "no" of Stevens' poetry is clearly defined—a Nietzschean/Stevensian decreative assertion carrying the intensity of the Melvillean "NO! in thunder" (*Moby-Dick*, 555); the specific projections of the subsequent "yes" are more problematic. As we have seen, Stevens' early poem "A High-Toned Old Christian Woman" identifies poetry itself as the "supreme fiction."[2] Stevens repeats this assertion years later in a letter to Henry Church (December 8, 1942), saying that "in the long run, poetry would be the supreme fiction; the essence of poetry is change and the essence of change is that it gives pleasure" (*Letters*, 430). But scarcely a month afterward, he tells Hi

The Marriage of the Rest

Simons (in letters of January 28 and 12, 1943) that "the Supreme Fiction is not poetry" (*Letters*, 438). In fact, he says, "I don't know what I mean. The next thing for me to do will be to try to be a little more precise about this enigma. I hold off from even attempting that because, as soon as I start to rationalize, I lose the poetry of the idea" (*Letters*, 435). As it turns out, Stevens (to the surprise of no one familiar with his explanations) was never very exact about the enigma; yet this seeming uncertainty contains a consistent, if not precisely delineated, sense of the supreme fiction's double nature: it is poetry as such and, also, something more difficult to sort out—so difficult, indeed, that Stevens scholarship has been hard-pressed to bring into focus this aspect which the poet himself, in deference to the poetry of the idea, would not specify.

Poetry as supreme fiction is the axis for any and all imaginative integrations. Along this line, Stevens tells us that "the knowledge of poetry is a part of philosophy, and a part of science; the import of poetry is the import of the spirit. The figures of the essential poets should be spiritual figures" (*Letters*, 378).[3] But this sense of poetry itself as the highest—most fundamental—mode of fiction leads toward that other, more delimited but less easily "labelled" sense which serves as subject of "Notes" and chief premise of Stevens' poetry generally: the supreme fiction as a contemporary poetic perception—captured in a central complex of imagery—to which one could turn in an aesthetic version of "belief."

The conclusion of "A Collect of Philosophy" underscores poetry's resolution (both general and particularized) of the divergent pressures of modern reality and of belief: "It is as if in a study of modern man we predicated the greatness of poetry as the final measure of his stature, as if his willingness to believe beyond belief was what had made him modern and was always certain to keep him so" (*OP*, 202). If poetry is a matter of believing beyond belief, its central fictions are those intentionally postulated fabrications by which "men could propose to themselves a fulfilment." "Belief" of this sort shares an elemental irrationality as well as a "usefulness" with the "emotional belief" (contrasted with "intellectual") defined by Richards in *Practical Criticism*: "Given a need (whether conscious *as a desire* or not), any idea which can be taken as a step on the way to its fulfillment is accepted.... So far as the idea is useful ... it is believed, and the sense of attachment, of adhesion, of conviction, which we feel, and to which we give the name of belief, is the result of this implication of the idea in our activities" (259). But while Richards designates "emotional belief" as a "primitive," pre-intellectual attitude (258), Stevens indicates that aesthetic belief entertains its "ideas," as we recall, "at the highest possible level of the cognitive."[4] Describing a conversation with a student at Trinity College, he tells Church:

> I said that I thought that we had reached a point at which we could no longer really believe in anything unless we recognized that it was a fiction.... There are things with respect to which we willingly suspend disbelief; if there is instinctive in us a will to believe, or if there is a will to believe, whether or not it is instinctive, it seems to me that we can suspend disbelief with reference to a fiction as easily as we can suspend it with reference to anything else. (*Letters*, 430)

Hybridizing Coleridge's "willing suspension of disbelief" and William James' "will to believe," Stevens derives the more Nietzschean notion of willful belief in a particular "supreme fiction."[5]

The supreme fiction, in its narrower sense, speaks to the exigency of the present demythologized reality of decreation: "The need for a thesis, a music constant to move" (*OP*, 82). Stevens' "fictional belief", as the other side of his conviction that philosophical thinking takes us only to a certain point beyond which "we rely on the imagination (or, say, intuition),"[6] deconstructs Plato's notion that, while systematic thought (*dianoia*) achieves mathematical abstractness, intellectual intuition (*noēsis*) alone gives access to the *eidē*, or ideal forms.[7] Subordinating "intellectual" to aesthetic, eternal to temporal, the poetry insists that the human spirit "resides / In a permanence composed of impermanence" (*CP*, 472).⁸ Stevens' "The image must be of the nature of its creator" (*OP*, 118) shifts the focus of contemplation from the *summum bonum* (whether Divinity or the Platonic "Good") to the hypothetical *bon homme*—the "good man" (*CP*, 364).

About the fictional "Good Man" he says: "Through centuries he lived in poverty. / God only was his only elegance" (*CP*, 364). But, as "Asides on the Oboe" recounts:

> One year, death and war prevented the jasmine scent
> And the jasmine islands were bloody martyrdoms.
> How was it then with the central man? Did we
> Find peace? We found the sum of men. We found,
> If we found the central evil, the central good.
> We buried the fallen without jasmine crowns.
> There was nothing he did not suffer, no; nor we.
>
> (*CP*, 251)

Constituted in the language of central evil, central good, central man, the lines reiterate Stevens' improvisationally recentering decreationist hypothesis. Without the perfume of metaphysical assumption, we discover, again: "man's truth is the final resolution of everything." Stevens elaborates:

If one no longer believes in God (as truth), it is not possible merely to disbelieve; it becomes necessary to believe in something else. Logically, I ought to believe in essential imagination, but that has its difficulties. It is easier to believe in a thing created by the imagination.... In one ["Asides on the Oboe"] of the short poems that I have just sent to the HARVARD ADVOCATE, I say that one's final belief must be in a fiction. I think that the history of belief will show that it has always been in a fiction. (*Letters*, 370)⁹

As to the specific shape of this fictional object, the poet asks in "As at a Theater": "What difference would it make, / So long as the mind, for once, fulfilled itself?" (*OP*, 91)—suggesting that what "matters most" (*CP*, 345) is an enjoyment of the art of belief itself. Nonetheless, Stevens' poetry consistently revolves, and re-evolves, certain imagaic configurations as primary objects for contemplation. Section V of "Extracts from Addresses to the Academy of Fine Ideas" (*CP*, 255–56) details the emergence of such configurative abstractions in the changing "seasons of belief":

> The law of chaos is the law of ideas,
> Of improvisations and seasons of belief.
>
> Ideas are men. The mass of meaning and
> The mass of men are one. Chaos is not
>
> The mass of meaning. It is three or four
> Ideas or, say, five men or, possibly, six.
>
> In the end, these philosophic assassins pull
> Revolvers and shoot each other. One remains.

This singular outcome approaches the Nietzschean "to be a human being with one elevated feeling—to be a single great mood incarnate" (*Gay Science*, 231). Imagination uses this remaining one: "The mass of meaning becomes composed again. / He that remains plays on an instrument"; and "It is the music of the mass of meaning":

> ... that song
>
> Of the assassin that remains and sings
> In the high imagination, triumphantly.

If, in Stevens' view, "life is a composite of the propositions about it" (*OP*, 171)—the "sunny day's complete Poussiniana" of "Poem Written at Morning"—then, as he says elsewhere, "The world is the world through its theorists. Their function is to conceive of the whole and, from the center of their immense perspectives, to tell us about it" (*OP*, 232). As transposed by the concluding lines of "Description without Place":

> ... what we say of the future must portend,
>
> Be alive with its own seemings, seeming to be
> Like rubies reddened by rubies reddening.
>
> (*CP*, 346)

This projection images the process by which a "central" apprehension, conforming "world" to word, lends the texture of imaginative appropriation and deeply held sense of the redness of rubies, producing the stone which is the object of the rubescent experience. The fictional apperception, forming the poet's "mundo"—an articulate world—finds its figurative ground most often, for Stevens, in archetypal variations on "male" and "female": idea of experience and sense of experience, aesthetic apprehension and aesthetic appreciation, vital concept and vivid presence.[10]

Stevens' poetry repeatedly locates conceptualization within the scope of the male figure. In "The Well Dressed Man with a Beard" (CP, 247), the "well dressed man" personifies

> ... one thing that was firm, even
> No greater than a cricket's horn, no more
> Than a thought to be rehearsed all day,

which, if it could be retained and believed in, "would be / Enough"[11]—giving local habitation to the suggestion that "ideas are men," and illuminating the entire cast of male characters (the giant, the hero, major man) who people Stevens' poetry. The efficacy of these larger-than-life personages transforms the power of abstraction[12] into the poetized "peculiar potency of the general" (CP, 397).[13] As early as 1904, Stevens hints at this conclusion: "Moral qualities are masculine; whimsicalities are feminine. That seems hardly just but I think it is exact" (Souvenirs, 114). The male is the vigorous image of the idea; as "Study of Images I" puts it: "He is, we are" (CP, 463)—reformulating Descartes' *cogito ergo sum*. And Stevens uses this rationalist Cartesian context still more explicitly in "Life on a Battleship" in the transmutation of the "moral"-as-masculine. The "captain" of the ship *The Masculine* "drafted rules of the world, / *Regulae mundi*, as apprentice of / Descartes" (playing on Descartes' *Regulae ad Directionem Ingenii*)[14] according to which *The Masculine* itself could be:

>   . . . both law and evidence in one,
>   As the final simplification is meant to be.
>   It is clear that it is not a moral law.
>   It appears to be what there is of life compressed
>   Into its own illustration.
>
>   (*OP*, 78–79)

As the "giant," the male figure is a way of looking at the world: ranging from the "sprawling portent," embodying the spirit (or spiritlessness) of an age in *Owl's Clover* ("the form / Of a generation that does not know itself" [*OP*, 68]); to a view of the earth in "The Man with the Blue Guitar" (the "giant that fought / Against the murderous alphabet: // The swarm of thoughts, the swarm of dreams / Of inaccessible Utopia" [*CP*, 179]);[15] to the "giant of the weather" (*CP*, 385) in "Notes," of whom Stevens says, "The abstract does not exist, but it is certainly as immanent: that is to say, the fictive abstract is as immanent in the mind of the poet, as the idea of God is immanent in the mind of the theologian" (*Letters*, 434). Again we see the intimate relation between the poetic as "supreme" fictional alternative to metaphysics and the way fictive form (the supreme fiction's narrower sense) reveals its paradoxical condition as both concrete figure and that which does not violate conceptive abstractness—a quality expressed in "The Auroras"'s visible abstraction of the serpent-form "gulping after formlessness."[16] This figurative complication, inherent in the central musical metaphor of "Notes" and the "central poem" of "A Primitive Like an Orb," is circumscribed in the latter as "the poem of the composition of the whole" (*CP*, 442), whose masculine aspect becomes:

>   . . . the skeleton of the ether, the total
>   Of letters, prophecies, perceptions, clods
>   Of color, the giant of nothingness, each one
>   And the giant ever changing, living in change.
>   (*CP*, 443)

The giant appears here as a conceptual composite shaping one's vision of things (as they are). He "imposes power by the power of his form" (CP, 443). Reifying the "fictive abstract," the person of the giant (much like "*The Masculine*" in "Life on a Battleship")

> ... is an abstraction given head,
> A giant on the horizon, given arms,
> A massive body and long legs, stretched out,
> A definition with an illustration, not
> Too exactly labelled.
>
> (CP, 443)

He provides, as in "Things of August," "a new text of the world," which "evok[es] one thing in many men" (CP, 494). Constituting a sort of *Zeitgeist*, he summarizes Stevens' contention that "the centuries have a way of being male" (NA, 52).

As the "hero" the male figure is less the spirit of his age and more a locus of belief—in part a classical "hero," by whom "a last barrier between god and man falls away; the hero takes his place between them as an intermediary. Now the hero, the human personality, is raised to the divine sphere" (Cassirer, *Mythical Thought*, 197).[17] Mythologically, the hero's capacious sense of humanity spans the distance between transcendent and "all-too-human"; the "hero-hymns" of "A Thought Revolved" are:

> Hymns of the struggle of the idea of god
> And the idea of man, the mystic garden and
> The middling beast, the garden of paradise
> And he that created the garden and peopled it.[18]
>
> (CP, 185)

Doggett tells us: "Idealized as a fullness of being, as the man of summer, the hero stands, a concept rising above lesser versions of the idea of man. Finally, above and including the hero is the ultimate idealization: the idea of God as person, an embodiment of majesty" (120–21). But this conflation, rightly recognized by Doggett, of the hero figure (as idealization of man) with God (as a higher form of that idealization) proves an unsatisfactory object of aesthetic (as compared to mythic) belief. In so far as the portrayal of the hero too closely resembles the visage of an anthropomorphic deity, Stevens can say: "I throw knives at the hero, etc." (*Letters*, 409). "It Must Give Pleasure" of "Notes" rejects the stale irrelevance of:

> A lasting visage in a lasting bush,
> A face of stone in an unending red,
> Red-emerald, red-slitted-blue, a face of slate,
>
> An ancient forehead hung with heavy hair,
> The channel slots of rain, the red-rose-red
> And weathered and the ruby-water-worn,
>
> The vines around the throat, the shapeless lips,
> The frown like serpents basking on the brow,
> The spent feeling leaving nothing of itself.[19]
>
> (*CP*, 400)

Yet about the hero not as "large eye / And bearded bronze" (*CP*, 165)—"not the exceptional monster, / But he that of repetition is most master" (*CP*, 406)—Stevens seems thoroughly positive. This variation on the hero converts the impossible god-man, a figure stretched out between earth and heaven, to the possible "man-sun" (*CP*, 280)—an illumination like the "Phosphor Reading by His Own Light" (*CP*, 267).[20]

Such a "credible hero" (*OP*, 117) "crystallizes" most satisfactorily for Stevens as "major man"—combining the heroic with the transparency of musical metaphor. Stevens' January 19, 1909, letter to his wife supplies an early precursor (and a prefiguration of the "major weather" of "Notes"): "Music in minor tones is—but in major tones it delights. . . . Your letter was in major, the weather is in major. Your Spring is buoyant minor, and Autumn minor all in all" (*Letters*, 124). The view of spring and autumn as minor seasons resurfaces much later in "The Motive for Metaphor" (a title again suggesting the musical), where autumn is "half dead" and spring is characterized by "half colors of quarter-things" (*CP*, 288): half- and quarter-notes drawn in counterpoint to the full notes of summer, the "major" season. By extension, the concluding section of "Esthétique du Mal" finds that the idea of "paradise" is only

"The minor of what we feel," while in the ametaphysical experience of existence:

> The green corn gleams and the metaphysicals
> Lie sprawling in majors of the August heat.
> (*CP*, 325)

"Paisant Chronicle" says of the "major men":

> ... They are characters beyond
> Reality, composed thereof. They are
> The fictive man created out of men.
> They are men but artificial men. They are
> Nothing in which it is not possible
> To believe, more than the casual hero, more
> Than Tartuffe as myth, the most Molière,
> The easy projection long prohibited.
> (*CP*, 335)

With this passage in mind, Stevens writes to José Rodríguez-Feo in February 1945: "I have defined major men for you. I realize that the definition is evasive, but in dealing with fictive figures evasiveness at least supports the fiction. The long and short of it is that we have to fix abstract objectives and then to conceal the abstract figures in actual appearance" (*Letters*, 489). Stevens' formulation, reconsidering Marianne Moore's well-known "imaginary gardens with real toads in them" (quoted in "A Poet That Matters"; *OP*, 253),[21] instead proposes actual appearances that conceal abstractions—a version of his "poem as icon" (*CP*, 526). Major man's palpability preserves (as music does) the abstractness of the concept. His visage, antithetical to the "bearded bronze," is that more realizable form visualized at the conclusion of "Paisant Chronicle":

> ... see him for yourself,
> The fictive man. He may be seated in
> A café. There may be a dish of country cheese
> And a pineapple on the table. It must be so.
> (*CP*, 335)

The act of imagining the "fictive man" creates its own necessity; he is as we imagine him to be. This is, in its effect, a playful, humanized (fictive) conversion of Anselm's "ontological argument" that God's essence includes existence.[22] For Anselm (and for theology/philosophy generally) the argument necessarily applies only to Deity. But if the idea of God is taken to be a fiction (in Stevens' terms), the power of the proof can be seen as an assertion of the curious strength of the imagination itself[23]—a strength invested by the poetry in the imagination's highest ("major") forms.

Major man is "beyond / Reality, composed thereof"; while he is an "artificial" man, our sense of him grows out of actual men that we encounter. The last section of "It Must Be Abstract" in "Notes" explains:

> The major abstraction is the idea of man
> And major man is its exponent, abler
> In the abstract than in his singular,
>
> More fecund as principle than particle,
> Happy fecundity, flor-abundant force,
> In being more than an exception, part,
>
> Though an heroic part, of the commonal.
> The major abstraction is the commonal,
> The inanimate, difficult visage....
> (CP, 388)

As "exponent," major man represents the "commonal" (metaphorically, as advocate, actually as symbol) and raises the concept "man" to its highest power. He is

> Logos and logic, crystal hypothesis,
> Incipit and a form to speak the word
> And every latent double in the word
> (CP, 387)

—a transformation of the incipit and the Logos, the poet's answer to theology/philosophy.[24] His "flor-abundant force" counters the "anti-master-man, floribund ascetic" of "Landscape with Boat," in a transfiguration of the moribund into the abundant. Through his "heroic" aspect the idealized "visage" of the commonal appears, not as attempted reproduction but as "abstract" symbolic signification.

Humanity's present age is, according to "Notes," a tattered form, a figure of poverty in an "old coat" with "sagging pantaloons"; yet:

> It is of him, ephebe, to make, to confect
> The final elegance, not to console
> Nor sanctify, but plainly to propound.
> (CP, 389)

The poet's role, as has been seen, is not to design "sleek ensolacings" (CP, 322) to comfort us in our poverty (lack of a sufficing fiction); neither is it to deify "common man," since "apotheosis is not / The origin of the major man" (CP, 387). Instead, poetry must "abstract" from the "commonal" features which could inhere in a "final elegance"—an elaborated envisioning intrinsically appropriate to era and locale. Through major man (as "abstraction"), the poet, like the "figure of capable imagination" in "Mrs. Alfred Uruguay," conceives "the ultimate elegance: the imagined land" (CP, 250). Stevens writes to Rodríguez-Feo:

The major men, about whom you ask, are neither exponents of humanism nor Nietzschean shadows. I confess that I don't want to limit myself as to my objective, so that in NOTES TOWARD A SUPREME FICTION and elsewhere I have at least trifled with the idea of some arbitrary object of belief: some artificial subject for poetry, a source of poetry. The major men are part of the entourage of that artificial object. (*Letters*, 485)[25]

Though not the supreme fiction, major man is an element of the fiction, a part of the entourage, part of the commonal-as-idea. He is the homocentric sun of the poet's "fluent mundo" (CP, 407)—an alternative to the untenable absolute.

Matthew Arnold's essay "The Study of Poetry" formalizes, more simply than Stevens would be willing to do, a view of relations among poetry, idea, and the Absolute much like that contained in Stevens' "fictional belief": "Our religion has materialized itself in the fact, in the supposed fact; it has attached its emotion to the fact, and now the fact is failing it. But for poetry the idea is everything. . . . Poetry attaches its emotion to the idea; the idea *is* the fact" (1–2). Arnold's idea-as-fact is a forerunner of the "masculine" aspect of Stevens' "Idea of Order at Key West,"[26] which

> Mastered the night and portioned out the sea,
> Fixing emblazoned zones and fiery poles,
> Arranging, deepening, enchanting night.
> (CP, 130)

For Stevens, musingly, "imagination is the power that enables us to perceive the normal in the abnormal, the opposite of chaos in chaos" (NA, 153). Through the song the singer at Key West becomes an innovator of the real—"artificer of the world / In which she sang"—reflecting Stevens' "We live in the mind. . . . If we live in the mind, we live with the imagination" (NA, 140).[27] In the intricacies of Stevens' male/female figurations, though the singer is female, the song's musical images render Key West in a "major key," fashioning the singer's world, and for the listeners mastering the moment and place. Stevens' male figure, product of the "blessed rage for order" (CP, 130), satisfies the "need for a thesis." He is the major idea of oneself in relation to the world—visibly present but abstract—"what there is of life compressed into its own illustration."

Major man, associated with an ordering intellection, arrives

> Compact in invincible foils, from reason,
> Lighted at midnight by the studious eye.
> (CP, 388)[28]

—a re-turn of the "phosphor reading"; but Stevens tells us, in "The Figure of the Youth as Virile Poet," that "it is the *mundo* of the imagination in which the imaginative man delights and

The Marriage of the Rest

not the gaunt world of the reason" (NA, 57–58). The final section of "It Must Give Pleasure" ("Notes") reveals the poet's terrain as something beyond the rational:

> That's it: the more than rational distortion,
> The fiction that results from feeling. Yes, that.
>
> They will get it straight one day at the Sorbonne.
> We shall return at twilight from the lecture
> Pleased that the irrational is rational,
>
> Until flicked by feeling, in a gildered street,
> I call you by name, my green, my fluent mundo.
> You will have stopped revolving except in crystal.
>   (CP, 406–7)

The expansive illusion of the moment mixes with a perception of its finitude: the world "will have stopped revolving except in crystal."[29] The perspective of our distant, more abstract understanding—the "crystal hypothesis"—captures the revolutions of "the merely going round." But the crystalline quality is not identical with the integration—the poet's "mundo."[30] At the moment in which this "more than rational" experience of his world is "intensest," the poet speaks, naming a world that speaks. The depth of the experience affords a nonrational sense of the earth's arrested motion: a geocentric version of the mythical noonday at which the sun stands still—as when, in "What We See Is What We Think," "the trees stood green, / At twelve, as green as ever they would be. / . . . Twelve meant as much as: the end of normal time, / . . . The imprescriptible zenith" (CP, 459).[31] This other aspect, the "irrational"—the other integrant of the invented world—appears in Stevens' poetry as the female figure. In this same concluding section which chides the Sorbonne and its rationalism, she takes form as the "Fat girl, terrestrial, my summer, my night, / . . . familiar yet an aberration" (CP, 406).

Stevens observes in a letter to Church: "The fat girl is the earth: what the politicians now-a-days are calling the globe, which somehow, as it revolves in their minds, does, I suppose, resemble some great object in a particularly blue area" (*Letters*, 426). Taken alone, this encourages a hasty identification of the female with reality, the male only with imagination—that "particularly blue area" in which she revolves. But such delimitation oversimplifies a motif of figuration only seemingly simple. Mastering repetition, Stevens' fresh involutions foil even his own elaborate imagination/reality complex. One must, for example, consider the "male reality / And . . . that other and her desire" (*OP*, 99) of "Farewell without a Guitar." And in section IV of "It Must Give Pleasure" we find that the usual explanation of union between imagined and real does not engage the "mystic marriage in Catawba":

> The great captain loved the ever-hill Catawba
> And therefore married Bawda, whom he found there,
> And Bawda loved the captain as she loved the sun.
>
> They married well because the marriage-place
> Was what they loved. It was neither heaven nor hell.
> They were love's characters come face to face.
>
> (*CP*, 401)

A conventional reading of these lines (with the captain as imagination, Bawda as reality) leaves a significant third element out of play: Catawba, the place of their conjunction (reflected in the spelling of its name). If one of the marriageable opposites denotes the real, what of the discrete (as third) and indispensable existence of the beloved (by both) "marriage-place"? Here is what Stevens elsewhere calls a "venerable complication" (*CP*, 311).

Within Stevens' inclusive figurations, there are versions of a "male reality": that abstract "reality" of the "first idea" ("an imagined thing" [*CP*, 387])—"a myth before the myth began" (*CP*, 383); and a male imagination, possessed by the deific "thinker of the first idea" (*CP*, 386), inhabitant of that "particularly blue area" encompassing one's sense of the world. Likewise, the female principle includes a reality (interestingly, both earthly, as with the "fat girl, terrestrial," and heavenly, as with the "celestial paramours" of *Owl's Clover* [*OP*, 47]) and, at the same time, the way one feels about that reality—the innovative "sense of things" which, in changing, changes the experience of perception, as in "Bouquet of Roses in Sunlight" (*CP*, 430–31). This female "sense" depends on the male concept to determine her character, as the sunlight defines the way we feel about the roses. As with the green globe in blue space, the male principle provides the context within which the female sense appears. But conversely, the male principle depends on the female for its particular and sensuous immediacy. "Holiday in Reality" finds that each individual's sense of the world differs:

> . . . each had a particular woman and her touch[.]
>
> After all, they knew that to be real each had
> To find for himself his earth, his sky, his sea.
> (*CP*, 312)

And in the "whimsicalities" of "sense," life's eccentric divagations and sudden elevations happen spontaneously, without warning, as with "The Sense of the Sleight-of-Hand Man":

> One's grand flights, one's Sunday baths,
> One's tootings at the weddings of the soul
> Occur as they occur. . . .
> (*CP*, 222)

Ironically, the possessor of imagination, like the protagonist in "Things of August," is "the possessed of sense not the possessor" (*CP*, 492).

> The woman is chosen but not by him,
> Among the endlessly emerging accords
> (*CP*, 493)

—agreements within the relational multiplicities of male and female: "imagination"/"reality"/"sense," as they include conception, intuition, motion, stasis, universality, particularity, etc. Section IV of "It Must Change" postulates:

> Two things of opposite natures seem to depend
> On one another, as a man depends
> On a woman, day on night, the imagined
>
> On the real. This is the origin of change.
> Winter and spring, cold copulars, embrace
> And forth the particulars of rapture come.
>
> (CP, 392)

This motif of union/metamorphosis illustrates the thematic of change in various ways: man and woman marry and produce offspring; day arises out of night, night from day; the imagined grows out of the "real." And "winter and spring, cold copulars"—coupling Keats' "cold pastoral" ("Ode on a Grecian Urn") with Shakespeare's "country copulatives" (*As You Like It*, V.iv.53-54)—reconstitute the processes in the broad metaphors of Stevens' seasonal metamorphoses; winter's clarity, "embracing" spring's possibility, engenders the fullness of summer, the seasonal equivalent of Catawba's marriage-time: "At noon it was on the mid-day of the year" (*CP*, 401). Despite divergences among these assorted pairings, a specifically "unifying" principle binds them: the metaphorical marriage of "sense" and concept—male intellection with female intimation, diurnal force with nocturnal sensibility, imaginative potence with the potency of intuition, the distant abstractness of the winter sun with the palpable immediacy of spring, Keats' frozen artwork with Shakespeare's animated country scene. Significantly, the union of imagination/reality (both terms de-centered from the conventional by Stevens' usages) presents only one of a number of examples of a more generalized principle of "opposition," by which "the partaker partakes of that which changes him" (extending the overall theme of "It Must Change") and, in a celebratory elevation of dialectical interreferentiality, "forth the particulars of rapture come"— a poetic formulation of Stevens' "the essence of poetry is change and the essence of change is that it gives pleasure" (*Letters*, 430).

The Marriage of the Rest

If we locate the marriage in Catawba within this context of change as the vivifying source of the pleasure of existence, the suitability of earth as marriage-place becomes apparent. Displacing the dualism of unchanging perfection and endless suffering, "what they loved" is the changeable human world, where the "truth," inhabiting a poet's metaphors, "comes and goes and comes and goes all day." From this view, one marries not so much the earth as one's sense of the earth (a sense which, like the earth, changes), represented here by Bawda. The captain, descendent of the sun as "first idea," completes the sense, makes it comprehensive and comprehensible. The marriage of the two, participating in abstraction, relies on the significative nature of each:

>   Each must the other take as sign, short sign
>   To stop the whirlwind, balk the elements
>   (CP, 401)

—producing a specific unity which, though momentary, is believed as if it were eternal. Male and female figures, as halves of the human world, join to form the "fluent mundo"—an "elegant" vision of existence in which the world "will have stopped revolving except in crystal." This brilliant, fluent image speaks to us, becomes the shape of our world and an object of our love:

>   ... the mind
>   Turns to its own figurations and declares,
>   "This image, this love, I compose myself
>   Of these. In these, I come forth outwardly.
>   In these, I wear a vital cleanliness,
>   Not as in air, bright-blue-resembling air,
>   But as in the powerful mirror of my wish and will."
>   (CP, 246)

The "vital cleanliness" figures a more-than-abstract immaculateness—a return to the metaphoric innocence of the "first idea." The image, once again "of the nature of its creator" (OP,

118), reflects the union of male "will"—the horse which carries forward the "figure of capable imagination"—with female "wish"—"that other and her desire."³²

Cassirer shows that "the mythical symbol as such embraces the fundamental mythical opposition between the sacred and the profane. It is set up in order to make a separation between the two provinces, and to warn and frighten, to bar the uninitiated from approaching or touching the sacred" (*Phenomenology of Knowledge*, 201). The mythic symbol ordains that aspect of existence through which, as Stevens says,

> This great world, it divides its self in two,
> One part is man, the other god:
> Imagined man, the monkish mask, the face.
> (*CP*, 218)

But the aesthetic assimilation effects the opposite, commixing sacred and profane, heavenly and earthly, universal and particular. It is the artist's "search / For reality," an "exterior made / Interior" (*CP*, 481), as the green world revolves in a "crystal hypothesis"—which, unlike philosophical intellection, has the spectral possibility of the poem. In the late poem "The Bouquet," the flower arrangement becomes

> The infinite of the actual perceived,
> A freedom revealed, a realization touched,
> The real made more acute by an unreal.
> (*CP*, 451)

The "unreal"—the way of looking at the flowers—combines "wish" and "will," one's sense of the flowers and one's idea about them. Thus encountered, the bouquet appears as more than the seemingly simple reality of the flowers:

> It is a symbol, a sovereign of symbols
> In its interpretations voluble,
>
> Embellished by the quicknesses of sight,
> When in a way of seeing seen, an extreme,
> A sovereign, a souvenir, a sign,

The Marriage of the Rest

> Of today, of this morning, of this afternoon,
> Not yesterday, nor tomorrow, an appanage
> Of indolent summer not quite physical.
>
> (CP, 451)

Again, the integration intensifies the moment, extends it, separates it from our ordinary sense of time. The "way of seeing" produces an experience "like rubies reddened by rubies reddening." The "abstracted" floral colors image an inherent relation between inner and outer experience: "The rose, the delphinium, the red, the blue, / Are questions of the looks they get" (CP, 451)—just as the "black reds, / Pink yellows, orange whites" of "Bouquet of Roses in Sunlight" are "a consequence of the way / We feel." The arrangement of flowers in "The Bouquet"

> Is a drop of lightning in an inner world,
> Suspended in temporary jauntiness.
>
> The bouquet stands in a jar, as metaphor,
> As lightning itself is, likewise, metaphor
> Crowded with apparitions suddenly gone
>
> And no less suddenly here again, a growth
> Of the reality of the eye . . .
>
> (CP, 448)

As with Stevens' "sudden rightnesses," "The moment we pass from one form of vision to another, it is not only a single factor in the intuition, but the intuition itself in its totality, its unbroken unity, that undergoes a characteristic metamorphosis" (Cassirer, *The Phenomenology of Knowledge*, 134).

The icon of the "mundo" revolved in crystal comes back again in "Credences," translated as the "rock of summer":

> . . . a mountain half way green and then,
> The other immeasurable half, such rock
> As placid air becomes . . .
>
> (CP, 375)

—the mundo's green and its crystalline context preserved in the green of the "rock" and "placid air." Again the visible compounding is "the more than visible" (*CP*, 376)—as "The Rock" contends, "The starting point of the human and the end" (*CP*, 528). In "The Poem as Icon" (section II of "The Rock"; *CP*, 526–27), the "rock" appears first as a lesser manifestation—a version of the "gray particular," not yet "cured" by imagination.[33] As with ineffectual metaphors which obscure, an "insensible" vision of the rock, represented by leaves which would only cover it, cannot effect the cure;[34]

> And yet the leaves, if they broke into bud,
> If they broke into bloom, if they bore fruit,
>
> And if we ate the incipient colorings
> Of their fresh culls might be a cure of the ground.

These lines supplant Nietzsche's "ascetic of the spirit," for whom there is "no rose" and, returning to the "incipit" of major man, substitute the "incipient colorings" of the poem's flowers and "fruit" for sacramental bread and wine. Recalling the Eucharistic breaking of bread, the leaves break "into bud" "in the predicate [the hypothesis] that there is nothing else," as crystal breaks light into the colors of the spectrum:

> These leaves are the poem, the icon and the man.
> These are a cure of the ground and of ourselves,
>
> In the predicate that there is nothing else[35]

—nothing, that is, but the vital composure of integrations (poem, icon, man), which "is enough" (*CP*, 524).

The supreme fiction is "the poem of the whole" (*CP*, 442), which takes specific shape in the intricacy of the "icon," an imaged wholeness, as if both religious image and poetic verbal sign:

> The fiction of the leaves is the icon
>
> Of the poem, the figuration of blessedness,
> And the icon is the man . . .

—not as male figure but as humanity. Uniting the abstracted male and female, the hypothetical extension (blooms/fruit) of the leaves-as-icon transforms/becomes the rock—figurational descendant of the "rock of ages" and successor to lesser perceptions (barren particular or obscured/uncured "ground"). As with Cassirer's "true pulse of consciousness, whose secret is precisely that every beat strikes a thousand connections,"

> ... the poem makes meanings of the rock,
> Of such mixed motion and such imagery
> That its barrenness becomes a thousand things
>
> And so exists no more.

We have seen that it is not the imponderable "thing-in-itself" which becomes the "thousand things" in the imagination. The female, as figuration for "gray" particularity and "green" sense, is already integral to a "central poem"—a fiction of the whole. In section VIII of "It Must Change" (*CP*, 395–96), "Nanzia Nunzio" presents herself to "Ozymandias" as

> ... the woman stripped more nakedly
> Than nakedness, standing before an inflexible
> Order, saying I am the contemplated spouse.

The male figure is again a conceptualizing principle ("an inflexible order"); and Nanzia is the female sense, in its own way not reducible to the real-as-such: she is not naked but "more naked than nakedness."[36] She seeks through Ozymandias that hypothetical investiture which will complete her—as the "mundo" is "completed" by our conception of it:

> Speak to me that, which spoken, will array me
> In its own only precious ornament.
> Set on me the spirit's diamond coronal.
>
> Clothe me entire in the final filament,
> So that I tremble with such love so known
> And myself am precious for your perfecting.

But already in Ozymandias' sight:

> ... the spouse, the bride
> Is never naked. A fictive covering
> Weaves always glistening from the heart and mind.

In the terms of "The Sense of the Sleight-of-Hand Man," she is "the sensual, pearly spouse"—the essential interrelatedness-in-difference of the two figures evidenced in the literal play (man-nun/nan; dias-zia; ozy-zio—these last two, in effect, reversing each other).

The opening stanza of "Men Made out of Words" asks what we would be "without the sexual myth"; the second stanza responds: "Castratos of moon-mash" (*CP*, 355). The male/female union of "thought" (*OP*, 243) and sense, belief and love, produces a transcendence "achieved by means of the minor effects of figurations and the major effects of the poet's sense of the world."[37] By this semiologic "transcendence," the poet's "word is the making of the world, / The buzzing world and lisping firmament" (*CP*, 345). The poet's word succeeds the *Logos* and "official view" of philosophy and theological divination, so that, as in "The Final Soliloquy of the Interior Paramour" (*CP*, 524),

> We say God and the imagination are one ...
> How high that highest candle lights the dark.
>
> Out of this same light, out of the central mind,
> We make a dwelling in the evening air,
> In which being there together is enough.[38]
>
> (ellipsis is Stevens')

In the premise that "the world imagined is the ultimate good," the poet finds "the intensest rendezvous. / It is in that thought that we collect ourselves."[39] Within the "single shawl" of the sufficing idea, the persona and his "paramour"—his sense of the world—wrap themselves; and in the "light" of that idea, they "feel the obscurity of an order, a whole, / A knowledge, that which arranged the rendezvous." The integration becomes a means of elevation for the persona of the poem, and the perception of that integration defines a world in which he (and we) can live. Stevens writes: "The relation of art to life is of the first importance especially in a skeptical age since, in the absence of a belief in God, the mind turns to its own creations and examines them, not alone from the aesthetic point of view, but for what they reveal, for what they validate and invalidate, for the support that they give" (*OP*, 159). Like the idea of God, "Poetry is a purging of the world's poverty" (*OP*, 167); but a metaphysical view detaches abstraction and sublimity (male aspects of the Stevensian world) from earthliness and the sensible aspect of the "heavenly" (female figures). Stevens' cycles of decreation and aesthetic reimaginings heal this rift: "The central poem is the poem of the whole / ... the roundness that pulls tight the final ring" (*CP*, 442).[40]

Unlike traditional male/female dichotomies advanced by metaphysical thinking and theologies,[41] Stevens' configurations are not reductively divisive. Male and female have most often been thought in terms of dualities that mutually repel, or as halves of wholes that tend to fall apart: reason/emotion; imagination/reality; or, interestingly, reason/imagination. But for the most part, Stevens' rethinking of the male/female produces, as we have seen, affinitive figurations: there is no constructive imagination without an imaginative sense of things, no aesthetic appropriation without an accompanying appreciation; these are, we could say, experientially connate couplings. It might seem that this reciprocity excludes universality/particularity, but that difficulty, Stevens indicates, belongs to the "official view." Stevens' "unofficial view" sees the "general" as always localized and "particulars" contextually encountered—both held in the "icon" of the poem.[42]

The "fat girl, terrestrial" intonates, substantiates the words provided by the male figure as concept; her speech is the fluency of the poet's world:

> On her lips familiar words become the words
> Of an elevation, an elixir of the whole.
>
> (*OP*, 83)

In this rejuvenating, "alchemicanic" fiction of the whole the imaginative person discovers "meanings . . . of such mixed motion and such imagery"—the significative coalescence of the decreative/creative "new romantic." This reality, which is at the same time a transcendence, arises out of

> . . . the edgings and inchings of final form,
> The swarming activities of the formulae
> Of statement, directly and indirectly getting at.
> (CP, 488)

And this "final form" (rock; fluent mundo; huge, high harmony) is not the earth itself, but more the "good air" of earth.

The abstraction of the abstraction of male/female finds its "dwelling"—the "marriage-place"—in the various complexities of an "exterior made interior"; the "genius of poetry" chooses "as her only apt locale in a final sense the love and thought of the poet" (OP, 243). Through the poet's integration we "realize that we are creatures, not of a part, which is our everyday limitation, but of a whole for which, for the most part, we have as yet no language. This sudden change of a lesser life for a greater one is like a change of winter for spring" (OP, 189). As in "The Rock," a lesser simple seeing is transformed: the fecund leaves "bud the whitest eye" and, blossoming,

> They bear their fruit so that the year is known,
>
> As if its understanding was brown skin,
> The honey in its pulp, the final found,
> The plenty of the year and of the world.
> (CP, 527)

The fictional/seasonal fruit of the leaves transposes the mythical/paradisal fruit of the trees of Knowledge and of Life.[43] "In this plenty, the poem makes meanings of the rock," in which our powers' "precious portents" are revealed.

Stevens' male figure establishes categories of refraction—"in the intricate evasions of as"—provides the "blue area" within which the green world revolves. Female world finds its voice when combined with male belief, but the female is the resonant voice that speaks, the sense and "presence" of "reality." In their union poetry becomes "a present perfecting [the round/roundness of the "merely going round"], a satisfaction in the irremediable poverty of life" (*OP*, 167), and our mute sense of things becomes articulate: a fluent mundo. This is the fiction of the whole—the complicate fiction of beginnings and ends, the alpha and omega.

Notes

Chapter I. A New Knowledge of Reality

1. Within a Kantian framework these portents may well point to the "noumenal," but as it adheres to the subject, not the "objective."

2. In a 1949 letter to Victor Hammer, Stevens explains: "The simplest personification of the angel of reality would be the good man" (*Letters*, 656)—who would, we can safely assume, transcend egocentricism. (Stevens adds: "On the other hand, the angel of reality might not take human shape since, after all, angels are not human beings plus feathers"—extending the trope of Plato's "featherless biped.")

3. Here Stevens uses *belief* in its narrow application with reference to specifically religious belief, and not in the broader sense in which he advocates "belief in a fiction"—an advocacy which, for example, in 1942 led him to refer to the present era as one in which "we had reached a point at which we could no longer really believe in anything unless we recognized that it was a fiction" (*Letters*, 430).

4. In this respect (that decreation unveils the schema of an "uncreated" world), Cook's misreading of Stevens-on-decreation is close to Pearce's.

5. The Reverend Arthur Hanley recalls at least one conversation in which Stevens referred to God as the "uncreated" (Brazeau, *Parts of a World*, 294).

6. Cf. Stevens' "I think that the history of belief will show that it has always been in a fiction" (*Letters*, 370). This view of the "fictional" nature of belief will be discussed extensively in chapters 5 and 6.

7. In keeping with his unusual sense of the "real" and "fictional," Stevens' view of the more usual understanding includes this Decem-

ber 1948 comment: "These are the two poles of feeling over here now: fantasy on one hand and realism on the other: evasion and evasion" (*Letters*, 626).

8. As with paintings by Magritte, for example, the poetry raises the question of its relation to non-art. Unlike Magritte, however, Stevens' "unpainted" form is discontinuous with the art object in the poem. Magritte is drawn to his own work within his work; Stevens produces a work by another which is less expansive than his own poetic musings.

9. B. J. Leggett mentions the following passage from I. A. Richards: "The choice between the doctrine that we project values into nature and the doctrine that we discover them in her should be noticed as likely to show itself in *our* interpretations of several accounts of Imagination" (*Coleridge on Imagination*, 26)—relating the passage to "Stevens's 'imagination/reality complex'" (*Wallace Stevens and Poetic Theory*, 29). It can be added that the language of Richards' two "doctrines" interestingly parallels Stevens' "impose" and "discover"—though it is important to note that Richards wants to demonstrate that both halves of his dichotomy are simultaneously true, while Stevens chooses *discover*, rejecting *impose*. Stevens' heavily annotated copy of *Coleridge on Imagination* is now in the Stevens Collection at the Huntington Library.

10. Cassirer's "definite shape," which participates in the "revelation" of the "inexhaustibility of the aspects of things" is commensurate with Stevens' "definition with an illustration, not too exactly labelled."

11. Impacted in Stevens' phrase "things as they are" is also, unavoidably, his rejection of a metaphysical atemporality according to which the essentially real would not change. Appropriately, the way reality, in Stevens' usage, changes parallels the way Stevens' usage of the word *reality* changes: from decreative or decreated "reality" to a more fully inclusive (or inclusively full) "fluent reality." See, for instance, our discussion later in this chapter of (and following) Stevens' "Alpha" and "Omega."

12. Cf. "An Ordinary Evening in New Haven," where Stevens' suppositions turn to "colors whether of the sun / Or mind, . . . / / Confused illuminations and sonorities / So much ourselves, we cannot tell apart / The idea and the bearer-being of the idea" (*CP*, 466).

13. It is of some tangential interest that the Stevens Collection at the Huntington Library includes a copy of George B. Hill's two-

volume edition of *Selected Essays of Dr. Johnson* (London: Dent, 1889) bearing Stevens' signature and the date March 10, 1899.

14. While it is the case that "black reds" is an accepted description for the color of, for example, the "Mr. Lincoln" and "Europeana" varieties of rose and that "pink yellows" and "orange whites" are possible descriptions of the colorings of various other roses, the complexity of this terminology serves to underscore the complexity of effect the poem captures.

15. Stevens, as often, complicates the view with its seeming opposite—another adagium by which "there is nothing in the world greater than reality. In this predicament we have to accept reality itself as the only genius" (*OP*, 177). But the overlapping language (regarding imagination/reality) suits Stevens' interest in reality's complication. See our following discussion of the "hierophant" experience in "An Ordinary Evening" (and elsewhere).

16. We should note a probable allusion to Revelation (1:8): "I am Alpha and Omega, the beginning and the ending."

17. See Brazeau's *Parts of a World*.

18. A letter of September 23, 1922 (to Harriet Monroe) indicates that Stevens had just received from Paris photographs of the Poussins in the Louvre (*Letters*, 229); and a Parke-Bernet catalogue for March 10, 1959 (afternoon; p. 8, item 46) advertises the sale of Stevens' copy of "*Lettres de Poussin* (Poussin) Paris, 1929." A copy of the Parke-Bernet catalogue can be found in the Stevens Collection of the Watkinson Library at Trinity College.

19. And we might add, as Stevens so carefully constructs worlds within a world in, for example, "So-and-So."

20. "Metaphor" becomes, as Marie Borroff has seen, "a perception of relationship which is a valid step toward piecing the world together" ("Wallace Stevens," 10).

21. Hines, introducing a phenomenological turn, reads the section by way of Husserlian philosophy: "The formula or slogan of Husserl's phenomenology was *zu den Sachen selbst* (or, in Stevens' terms, 'Let's see the very thing and nothing else' [*CP*, 373])" (*Later Poetry*, 31). Macksey, though with another point in mind, notices the same parallel: "His cry of 'to the things themselves' and his insistence that all consciousness is intentional, that every *cogito* is an act, reveal fundamental aspects of Stevens' approach to writing poetry; the poems, ultimately, have to reveal themselves. In 'Credences of Summer' Ste-

vens echoes the watchword: 'Let's see the very thing and nothing else'" ("The Climates of Wallace Stevens," 192). But reference to two of Stevens' letters (from 1940 and 1942), in which he speaks of "poetry" as "the thing itself" and "a thing in itself," provides a different perspective on the line: (1) "For this purpose, poetry means not the language of poetry but the thing itself, wherever it may be found" (*Letters*, 377); (2) "It is simply a question of whether poetry is a thing in itself, or whether it is not. I think it is" (*Letters*, 403). Also of interest with respect to "thingness" in Stevens' poetry is Albert Gelpi's comment that the pervasively influential Ezra Pound "stated as the first and basic premise of Imagism the 'direct treatment of the "thing," whether subjective or objective,' thus admitting the rendering of a subjective 'thing' as a type of image" ("Stevens and Williams," 12). The quotation from Pound appears in *Literary Essays of Ezra Pound*, 3.

22. Typical of the way Stevens returns again to figurations, meanings, sounds which he has captured (or been captured by), the sound and sense of the full phrase "about the whitened sky" resonates, four years later, in "bud the whitest eye" of "The Rock."

23. Misguided metaphors are, in Stevens' language, like "leaves" that, unable to effect a "cure," would only "cover the rock" (*CP*, 526)—would only, as we suggest in chapter 6, "obscure" it. But Stevens proposes that more adequate figures can "Fix [the sun/summer] in an eternal foliage // And fill the foliage with arrested peace" (*CP*, 373), effecting the desired "cure."

24. The inadequacy of the "world of white and snowy scents" recalls the similarly deficient "houses . . . haunted by white nightgowns" in "Disillusionment of Ten O'Clock" (*CP*, 66), twenty-three years earlier.

25. The "com[ing] back / To what had been so long composed" significantly parallels, in its sense and language, the "coming back / To the real" (in the light of Stevens usage of *real*) of "An Ordinary Evening."

26. A "thought revolved"—a circumferential version of the "coming back and coming back"—suggests the "mundo . . . revolving . . . in crystal" of "Notes" (*CP*, 407). And the passage from "An Ordinary Evening" itself provides an importantly relevant example of Stevens' tendency to return to what is remarkably the same: "it comes in the end to that: // The description that makes it divinity" remembers "This is the last day of a certain year / Beyond which there is nothing left of time. / It comes to this and the imagination's life," from "Credences."

27. The "lion" here, as a force of negation, is a relative of the lion of Nietzsche's "three metamorphoses of the spirit"—a figuration explored in some detail in chapter 5.

28. Richard Wilbur recalls Stevens' remark (by postcard) that "most art" (the imagination's summer) "is created out of a condition of winter" (Brazeau, *Parts of a World*, 170).

29. The "rock of summer," overcoming the division between earth and sky, separates the poem's affluent "central sky" from the troubled estrangement of "common earth"/"central sky" in "An Ordinary Evening" (*CP*, 468–69)—discussed in chapter 5. In relation to that discussion, it is interesting to note Stevens' demythologizing use of "*as if* twelve princes . . ."

30. La Guardia cites, as a possible source for these lines, James' contention that the sensations of nonconceptual perceptions are "the mother-earth, the anchorage, the stable rock, the first and last limits, the *terminus a quo* and the *terminus ad quem* of the mind" (La Guardia, *Advance on Chaos*, 79). The quotation is from James' *The Meaning of Truth*, 151. We would suggest as more likely influences Revelation 1:8 (see note 16 above), and, contemporaneous with Stevens, Eliot's "In my beginning is my end" and "In my end is my beginning" (*Four Quartets*, 23 and 32).

Chapter II. The Vocabulary of Romanticism

1. Peterson attributes the "modernist elements" to the influence of Imagism, observing that "the references to sentimentality and the taint of obsolescent romanticism reflect the stylistic reforms of the Imagists" (*Stevens and the Idealist Tradition*, 13).

2. Stevens' "Originality is an escape from repetition" (*OP*, 177) explicates this subtlety. And Stevens' standard is radical: "As a man becomes familiar with his own poetry, it becomes as obsolete for himself as for anyone else. From this it follows that one of the motives in writing is renewal" (*OP*, 220). See the further discussion of "merely going round" ("Notes") in chapter 3.

3. "That slight transcendence . . . By light, the way one feels, sharp white" (belonging to the constellation of "the whitest eye" and "the whitened sky") again depends on the way the imagination "like light, . . . adds nothing, except itself."

4. See the discussion of poetry-as-transcendent-analogue in relation to Cassirerian philosophy in chapter 5.

5. Of course, this does not eliminate the chance that Bloom may be right in taking the denial itself as evidence of Stevens' anxiety over possible influence by "Wordsworth, Coleridge, etc." (*Anxiety of Influence*, 6–7).

6. See the discussion in chapter 6 of the transformation of categories with respect to male/female figuration in the poetry, which complements the more theoretical account in chapter 1 of reality's complication.

7. Stevens' remarks on Williams-as-romantic appear in his 1934 preface to Williams' *Collected Poems, 1921–1931*; his comments on Eliot-as-romantic occur in the 1935 essay "A Poet That Matters" (a review of Marianne Moore's *Selected Poems*). Both, in other words, are from the mid-1930s, the time when Stevens seems to have been most interested in the modern poet's relation to Romanticism. The poem "Sailing after Lunch," with its provisional "theory of poetry," was first published in 1935.

8. Gelpi, distinguishing between Williams and Stevens, identifies Stevens as Symbolist, Williams as Imagist (contrary to Peterson's identification of Imagist influence on Stevens; see note 1 above) and comments that "Imagism operates by projecting mind and medium to engage things, whereas Symbolisme absorbs things into mind and medium" ("Stevens and Williams," 13).

9. Stevens critics have often confused the Platonist form of the ideal/real dichotomy (both poles of which Stevens rejects) with that of imagination/reality, which, as we have tried to show, Stevens, on his own terms, accepts.

10. For discussions of other aspects of relatedness between Stevens and Keats, see Beckett's *Wallace Stevens* and Vendler's "Stevens and Keats' 'To Autumn.'"

11. Gelpi says that "the meticulous accuracy of the details confirms Williams' negative capability" ("Stevens and Williams," 18)—a remark which suggests that his understanding of Williams exceeds his grasp of Keats.

12. One can assume that the way Eliot "revives the past" is by "decreating" it (in Stevens' sense). Michael Beehler, pursuing Stevens' "vital element" with the rhetoric of "difference," extends this point: "The differential energy that characterizes both poetries . . . is readable not as an identity contained in both but as the procedure of dif-

ferentiation that deploys difference insistently and repeatedly" (*T.S. Eliot, Wallace Stevens, and the Discourses of Difference*, 176).

13. Bové makes an interesting observation about the privileged status often given to poems written by Stevens near the end of his life: "The Romantic desire both for synthesis by dialectic and for the developmental metaphor underlie the perspective which causes these critics to look for a 'final' position in Stevens" (*Destructive Poetics*, 183). Bové is referring specifically to Pearce and Bernard Heringman, but his remark applies equally well to a number of critics who posit a biographically "final position" for Stevens. See, for example, our discussion in chapter 3 of the critics' emphasis on "Of Mere Being."

14. Coleridge's delineation of primary and secondary is spelled out in chapter 13 of *Biographia Literaria* (1:202). For an extended discussion of Coleridge and Stevens (and a perspective different from ours), see chapters 2 and 3 of Peterson's *Wallace Stevens and the Idealist Tradition*.

15. The passage from Coleridge is an obvious predecessor for Stevens' "I have not but I am and as I am, I am" (*CP*, 405) of "Notes" and "He is, we are" of "Study of Images I" (*CP*, 463).

16. Interestingly, Beehler levels the difference in these lines, reading a "more harassing master" as a negative, offering: "Stevens sets his poem apart from that of the 'more harassing master' whose proof would . . . [repeat] the classical theory of metaphor as the communicating vehicle for a literal tenor that checks its evasions" (*Discourses of Difference*, 175)—i.e., for life-as-it-is. But in Stevens' evasions the "more harassing" is the "subtler," and "life as it is" is "as it is in the intricate evasions of as."

17. As Vendler notes (*Words Chosen Out of Desire*, 29), this passage should be read in relation to Shakespeare's "The lunatic, the lover, and the poet / Are of imagination all compact" (*A Midsummer Night's Dream*, V.i. 7–8).

18. This is the thesis of Stevens' essay "A Collect of Philosophy" (*OP*, 183–202).

19. Again, a musical analogy/metaphor which Stevens' language associates with the "hugh, high harmony" of "A Primitive Like an Orb."

20. A redescription of the "going round // And round and round" of "Notes" (*CP*, 405).

21. Stevens' generalization secures Charles Berger's conclusion about the poem's figurations: "When the mariners insist on the similarity between lemon and elm countries, they are really insisting on the likeness between the earthly paradise and our native climate" (*Forms of Farewell*, 104). And, interestingly, Stevens' formulation broadly reiterates both: "it comes in the end to that: // The description that makes it divinity" ("An Ordinary Evening"; *CP*, 475) and "It comes to this and the imagination's life" ("Credences"; *CP*, 372).

22. Berger points out that the nouns in Stevens' poem participate in the change along with the adjectives: "By folding over and turning around *e-l-m*, one gets close enough to *l-e-m-o-n* to see one reason why the mariners claim that the countries are reversible" (*Forms of Farewell*, 104).

23. See the discussion in chapter 6 of Stevens' spring and autumn as "minor" seasons, summer as the "major."

24. We could say that "X" is, amusingly, a "zenith" in the alphabetic A–Z, sharing with "the hierophant omega" a vertical symmetry that contrasts with the somewhat "stooping" "Z."

25. Bloom's *The Poems of Our Climate* also gives considerable attention to Stevens/Emerson.

26. On this, La Guardia associates Stevens with James, while distinguishing him from Emerson: "Emerson's 'unifying instinct' echoes Stevens' 'blessed rage for order,' but the point remains that, while for all three writers the unifying of contrary and remote things occurs through acts of the mind, for Emerson the unity exists whether the mind discovers it or not; for James and Stevens, it exists solely because the mind created it" (*Advance on Chaos*, 20). The general lines of La Guardia's distinction are sound, but the word *solely* makes Stevens (given his emphasis on imagination's relation to "reality") out to be more solipsistic than he is.

27. As we have indicated, Stevens is interested in "self-transcendence," or, as Sartre puts it, a "transcendence of the ego."

28. The ideal as "the actual become anaemic" provides a significant counterpoint to the "abstraction blooded" of "Notes."

Chapter III. The ABC of Being

1. Sidney's *Defence of Poesie*, for example, compares the two.

2. On this point, Beehler, using the disparity for entry into his discussion of "difference," offers: "Stevens forces us to think of the differ-

ence between philosophers and poets as irreducible, and thus of truth and knowledge as incessantly plural" (*Discourses of Difference*, 5).

3. While "Wallace Stevens' Poetry of Being" (and its Heideggerian language) continues to be influential more than two decades after its publication, Miller has offered an alternate (more deconstructive) view of Stevens in his subsequent essays "Stevens' Rock and Criticism as Cure" (discussed later in this chapter) and "Theoretical and Atheoretical in Stevens."

4. Cf. *Sein und Zeit*, 6.

5. It is not irrelevant that, as noted in chapter 2, Shelley's supposition is overturned in "Peter Quince at the Clavier" by the notion that the physical is beauty's source and not the superficial manifestation of a disembodied force.

6. For example, "tigers / In red weather" ("Disillusionment of Ten O'Clock"; *CP*, 66).

7. Miller, in fact, asserts that in Stevens' poetry, "only *The Rock* suggests something final and stable, but that title was affixed after Stevens had attained the ultimate immobility of death" ("Wallace Stevens' Poetry of Being," 149). But *The Rock* was published under Stevens' supervision in *The Collected Poems of Wallace Stevens* on October 1, 1954, nearly a year before his death on August 2, 1955. Or, if Miller intends the poem "The Rock" rather than the volume, it was published in the Summer 1950 issue of *Inventario* (Edelstein, *Wallace Stevens*, 228).

8. Stevens describes his own variation on these oscillations of interest in a letter of March 1951: "I have no wish to arrive at a conclusion. Sometimes I believe most in the imagination for a long time and then, without reasoning about it, turn to reality and believe in that and that alone. But both of these things project themselves endlessly and I want them to do just that" (*Letters*, 710)—a "conclusion" much like Cassirer's. Stevens' indication is that these oscillations are leisurely, but, of course, this shifting emphasis does not omit either pole from any given poem, nor does it speak to the speed of oscillation within any poem. For that we must look to the poems themselves.

9. We should note that Miller's later essay "Stevens' Rock and Criticism as Cure" gives an absorbing account of "The Rock" which leaves the earlier "luminous flitterings" well behind and is, in aspects, not incompatible with our view, here, of the effects of Stevens' hypotheticals.

10. The appearance of "the rock" in this earlier poem (1937) again shows that the significance Miller attaches to the title of Stevens' last volume is misplaced.

11. Though generally faithful to Hegel, this cannot account for a supposed "confrontation" of "pure being" since, as Hegel tells us, pure being "is pure indeterminateness and emptiness. There is *nothing* to be intuited in it, if one can speak here of intuiting. . . . Being, the indeterminate immediate, is in fact *nothing*, and neither more nor less than *nothing*" (*Science of Logic*, 82). In other words, there is essentially nothing to confront.

12. Bové suggests a variation on this theme when he tells us that "the truth of 'The Snow Man' " is that "all of what-is shares in nothingness, which is the originless origin" (*Destructive Poetics*, 206).

13. We should note that this explanation provides no more support for the Sartrean variation of the being/nothingness motif, described by Frye as the "confrontation of being and nothingness . . . in 'The Snow Man' " ("Stevens and the Variation Form," 401), than the Heideggerian or Hegelian.

14. See the discussion of Litz' poem-as-"ars poetica" in chapter 2.

15. For whatever reason Bové has capitalized "being" in his phrase "revealing their Being as a fiction," it seems to bear no relation to Heidegger's understanding of Being, which is the non-fictional "Being of beings." See our further discussion of Heidegger/Being in chapter 4.

16. While Bové emphasizes "actuality" within the Heideggerian context, Heidegger tends to place his emphasis on "possibility," which "as an *existentiale* is the most primordial and ultimate positive way in which Dasein is characterized ontologically" (*Being and Time*, 183), and at times uses "actuality" in a negative sense, for example: "The average everydayness of concern becomes blind to its possibilities, and tranquillizes itself with that which is merely 'actual' " (239). For Heidegger, "possibility" as an "existentiale" seen through understanding projection preserves the character of possibility *as possibility*, this special usage indicating the ontological condition of Dasein in its privileged relation to Being—a relation, however, which is at odds with Stevens' "possible fictions." Cf. *Being and Time*, 183–85; also *The Basic Problems of Phenomenology*, 274, 294, 308ff.

17. While it is fair to say that "the distinction between literal and figurative is . . . [a] bifurcation from [a] primal misnaming" (though it

is more amenably thought of as a primal naming which may miss a questionable mark), the "alogical" better belongs to the "primal misnaming" rather than the deduction from literal to figurative; once the literal is assumed, it is not alogical to interpret departures as figurative.

18. Though Miller is careful to say "the abyss of truth" (rather than the more substantiating "truth of the abyss") in his theoretical articulation, he goes on to specify that "truth is, for Stevens too, evasive, veiled, feminine, and dwells at the bottom of a well. The revelation or unveiling of what has been hidden brings the truth momentarily into the open" (20). With these particulars, one could say, Miller, like Thales stargazing, falls into a well of a different sort.

19. We could see this as another variation on "the theory / Of poetry is the theory of life" ("An Ordinary Evening").

20. Stevens' play on "this invisible activity, this sense" joins with the adagium "Weather is a sense of nature. Poetry is a sense" (*OP*, 161).

21. It could be objected that these two references to "validity" are in conflict since, on one hand, imagination exposes "its incapacity to validly create" and, on the other, the "imaginative act . . . undercuts its own validity." The second observation is, in effect, "invalidated" by the first since, by the first, there is no "validity" which could be undercut.

22. Giving new meaning, one might say, to the phrase "Miller Analogies."

23. As printed in *Opus Posthumous*, the third line of the poem ends with the word *distance*. Regueiro substitutes *decor* in accordance with the reprinting of the poem in *The Palm at the End of the Mind* (*Palm*, 398).

24. A remark (cited by Peterson in *Stevens and the Idealist Tradition*, 25) from Coleridge's *Biographia Literaria* provides an interesting gloss to both poem and essay: "The transcendental philosopher does not inquire, what ultimate ground of our knowledge there may lie out of our knowing, but what is the last in our knowing itself, beyond which *we* cannot pass" (1:186; emphasis is Coleridge's). Accordingly, we could say that Stevens sees the imagination as transcending transcendentalism. On the other hand, that notorious rationalist Canon Aspirin (in "Notes") shares the limitation of the "transcendentalist," since he reaches a "point, // Beyond which fact could not progress as

fact" (*CP*, 402) and another "point" (or is it the same one?) "Beyond which thought could not progress as thought" (*CP*, 403).

25. Compare, for example, "The wind moves slowly in the branches. / The bird's fire-fangled feathers dangle down" to "The white cock's tail / Tosses in the wind. / The turkey-cock's tail / Glitters in the sun" ("Ploughing on Sunday"; *CP*, 20).

26. Regarding myth, language, and art, Cassirer explains: "Instead of measuring the content, meaning, and truth of intellectual forms by something extraneous which is supposed to be reproduced in them, we must find in these forms themselves the measure and criterion for their truth and intrinsic meaning. Instead of taking them as mere copies of something else, we must see in each of these spiritual forms a spontaneous law of generation; an original way and tendency of expression" (*Language and Myth*, 8)—as with Stevens' "sudden rightnesses" of sound or, on a resonant note from "Notes," "the luminous melody of proper sound."

27. See further discussion of these lines in chapter 5.

28. The next line's "In which nothing solid is its solid self" is, by both possible readings, itself a commonness with "It is possible that to seem—it is to be."

Chapter IV. The Phenomena of Perception

1. Regarding the evolution of Husserl's thinking (and of interest in relation to Cassirer's philosophy) Suzanne Bachelard argues that, at least for the later Husserl, phenomenology "is not precisely a question of a dialectic between subjectivity and its 'objective' products, its 'contents'; one should rather speak of a duality between subjectivity and the forms in which it necessarily manifests itself" (*A Study of Husserl's Logic*, 223).

2. It is notable that Heidegger, on the other hand, thinks of his phenomenology as a fundamental ontology.

3. Subjectivity as the transcendentally subjective is established beyond the psychologically limiting egocentrism of ordinary experience. As chapter 1 indicates, the "angel of reality" in Stevens' "Angel Surrounded by Paysans" is an instrument of what is in this respect a similar transcendence.

4. According to Husserl, "it belongs to the meaning of everything contingent that it should have essential being and therewith an *Eidos*

to be apprehended in all its purity" (*Ideas*, 53). And he explains that "the essence (*Eidos*) is an object of a new type. Just as the datum of individual or empirical intuition is an individual object, so the datum of essential intuition is a pure essence" (*Ideas*, 55).

5. Husserl cultivates the "absolute '*essential universality*'" of the "pure '*eidos*' perception" such that "eidetic phenomenology, accordingly, explores the universal Apriori without which neither I nor any transcendental Ego whatever is 'imaginable'" (*Cartesian Meditations*, 70–72).

6. Ironically, Nietzsche's passage offers a poetical complement for Stevens' more analytical "Does not philosophy carry us to a point at which there is nothing left except the imagination? If we rely on the imagination (or, say, intuition), to carry us beyond that point . . . then the imagination is supreme." Cf. the discussion of this passage in chapter 3.

7. The pun is extended in "Poetry as an imaginative thing consists of more than lies on the surface" ("Adagia"; *OP*, 161).

8. Among the necessary consequences of this view is that, as Peter Koestenbaum notes, "the transcendental Ego is mostly passive, as is Kant's transcendental unity of apperception. Both emphasize the spectatorial and unifying or synthesizing characteristics of the Ego. One would expect to find the passive trait emphasized, since the context in which it occurs is epistemological" (Introduction to *Paris Lectures*, li).

9. The passage is also a conceivable source for the previously cited (chapter 1) reference in "The Bed of Old John Zeller" to "the structure / Of things as the structure of ideas." The poem appeared in *Accent* in Autumn 1944, the year in which *An Essay on Man* was published; "Three Academic Pieces" was given as a lecture at Harvard in February 1947.

10. Heidegger's "unconcealedness of what is, and this means, of Being" (*Poetry, Language, Thought*, 72), emphasizing the overcoming of concealment, separates itself from Stevens' "what has no / Concealed creator" (*CP*, 296), which from the outset denies "the concealed."

11. We should note that for Heidegger it is specifically Being (not the shepherd) which is housed in language.

12. To say that "self and world are unified" oversimplifies Heidegger's thought by overemphasizing "Being-in-the-world" at the expense

of the notions of "ekstasis," "Being-towards-death," etc. Cf. Richardson's careful articulation of the relation between Dasein and world in note 15.

13. While Hines seems to intend to distinguish "Being" from two different senses of "being" (i.e., "being" and "beings"), "something that exists" and "things that exist" constitute an unexplained (or inexplicable) overlap.

14. Macksey's elaboration includes: "Man lives in *ecstatic* identities (where the adjective has much of the weight with which Heidegger invests it)—man 'stands out' in the changing elements" ("The Climates of Wallace Stevens," 187). Despite a recognition of Heidegger's usage ("stands out"), Macksey forces the conjunction of terms by overlooking the direct opposition to Heidegger's "ekstasis" in Stevens' lines: "Ecstatic identities / Between one's self and the weather and the things / Of the weather" (*CP*, 258). Heidegger promotes the singularized difference of the individual. Stevens' phrase "ecstatic identities" should be an unmistakable clue that his usage encourages an imaginative stroke of identification; and the poem continues: "it is enough / To believe in the weather and in the things and men / Of the weather and in one's self, as part of that / And nothing more" (*CP*, 258)—in which case one "stands out" in the weather only via punning equivocation.

15. In Heidegger's subtler account of man and world, as Richardson notes, "the Being of the World is an existential component of Therebeing as finite transcendence" (*Heidegger*, 56); that is, the "disclosedness of the World pertains to the very Being of There-being. In fact, the term 'There' expresses this disclosedness of the World. The 'There' of Being and the disclosedness of the World are but one" (58). This is not to say, as Hines does, that Dasein and World are simply "unified."

16. Heidegger is explicit on this point: "*But the state-of-mind which can hold open the utter and constant threat to itself arising from Dasein's ownmost individualized Being, is anxiety.* In this state-of-mind, Dasein finds itself *face to face* with the 'nothing' of the possible impossibility of its existence" (*Being and Time*, 310).

17. Whatever Hines may intend by his claim that "Heidegger's 'ontological difference' is alluded to in these lines," Stevens had almost certainly read nothing by Heidegger at the time he wrote "The Countryman" (published in *The Auroras of Autumn* in 1950). But while, in a curious turn, Hines himself finds no evidence that Stevens

read Heidegger at all (*Later Poetry*, 24), an unpublished letter (now in the Stevens Collection [as WAS 2865] at the Huntington Library) from Stevens' French bookseller Paule Vidal, dated "7 Aout 1952," records the shipment (on August 4) of Heidegger's *Qu'est-ce que la Metaphysique?*—containing Heidegger's essay on Hölderlein (the apparent cause of Stevens' interest in the book) and excerpts from *Sein und Zeit*.

18. This, in yet another way, distinguishes the "difference" from Stevens' "interdependence of imagination and reality"—and his interest in mixing the categories of subjective, objective, intersubjective.

19. Richardson makes the point differently: "The process by which There-being transcends beings to Being is also a coming-to-pass of truth" (*Heidegger*, 94).

20. Heidegger says in *Being and Time* (269–70): "Dasein, as constituted by disclosedness, is essentially in the truth. Disclosedness is a kind of Being which is essential to Dasein. *'There is' truth only in so far as Dasein is and so long as Dasein is.* . . . *Because the kind of Being that is essential to truth is of the character of Dasein, all truth is relative to Dasein's Being.* Does this relativity signify that all truth is 'subjective'? If one Interprets 'subjective' as 'left to the subject's discretion,' then it certainly does not. For uncovering, in the sense which is most its own, takes asserting out of the province of 'subjective' discretion, and brings the uncovering Dasein face to face with the entities themselves." While Stevens (in company with Cassirer) is not an advocate of subjective arbitrariness, he is (unlike Heidegger) interested in the ways an artist's individual eccentricities produce eccentric "rightnesses of sound."

21. Notice how again and again Stevens' "sense" defies "empirical sensibility" as his descriptions unfold: "by means of a separate sense"; "this invisible activity, this sense"; "our sense of these things changes and they change"; etc.

22. Regarding poetry-as-freedom, Hines (though skewing the terms) concurs not with Heidegger but with Stevens' "The imagination is the liberty of the mind and hence the liberty of reality" (*OP*, 179).

23. Though if Hines means to indicate that philosophy (its successes or failures aside) is generally unconcerned with fulfillment, he neglects its history: from Socratic meditation, and Aristotle's notion of the contemplative life, to the anti-metaphysical dance of Nietzschean aphorisms.

Chapter V. Sun and Symbol

1. Baird, warning of related dangers, offers: "Impressive as its achievements have been thus far, [philosophical approach] seems to me more an imposition of the critic's will than an exposition of the poet at hand" (*The Dome and the Rock*, xiii).

2. On this point, Nietzsche's asystematic (anti-systematic) interests are infamous. And for Cassirer, symbolic forms—and art among them—are irreducibly plural and not interchangeable; that is, philosophical theory must "resist the temptation to compress the totality of forms . . . into an *ultimate* metaphysical unity, into the unity and simplicity of an absolute 'world ground' " (*Einstein's Theory of Relativity*, 446).

3. See, for instance, Doggett on Stevens/Vaihinger and La Guardia on Stevens/James. Discussions of Stevens/Santayana are too numerous to mention.

4. For Bates, though Stevens and Nietzsche "appealed to different models of human history, they agreed that men create heroes—as well as gods and poems—in order to dominate reality" (*Wallace Stevens*, 261). But, stressing Nietzsche's interest in the hero as war-hero, he does not attend to the breadth of qualities projected for the *übermensch*, who would experience "the happiness of a god full of power and love, full of tears and laughter, a happiness that, like the sun in the evening, continually bestows its inexhaustible riches, pouring them into the sea, feeling richest, as the sun does, only when even the poorest fisherman [rows] with golden oars" (*Gay Science*, 268–69). Regarding "will to power," Bates' view could be said to be a simplified version of Heidegger's reading—which sees Nietzsche's "will" as will-to-mastery (of self/earth/Being), the "eternal return" as metaphysical doctrine, and Nietzschean philosophy generally as the culmination of Western metaphysical thinking. But it has been well argued by, among others, Bernd Magnus (in *Heidegger's Metahistory of Philosophy* and *Nietzsche's Existential Imperative*) that this is a willful misreading. At the least, Nietzschean "will-to-power," in its highest form, must be distinguished from "will-to-domination" (over others or the earth); it is the sort of self-overcoming exemplified by the artist.

5. Bates says that "Merely to gloss Stevens' poems with passages from Nietzsche would of course be an exercise in futility" (*Wallace Stevens*, 248); and (the questionable conclusion aside) in keeping with

his rhetoric, he offers few examples of the Nietzschean in Stevens' poems.

6. The similarity of the Nietzschean metamorphoses to Carlyle's everlasting nay and yea in *Sartor Resartus* is obvious. But the tone, imagery, and philosophical orientation of the Nietzschean version are more relevant to Stevens.

7. The expression "God is dead" can be traced from Martin Luther (as a dramatic declaration of Christ's crucifixion [Dupré, *Transcendant Selfhood*, 13]) through Hegel (addressing the "loss of self") and Marx (who perceives the "death" as a humanistic opportunity). For Marx as for Nietzsche, "the criticism of religion disillusions man so that he will think, act and fashion his reality as a man who has lost his illusions and regained his reason; so that he will revolve about himself as his own true sun" (Marx, *Early Writings*, 44). But with Nietzsche the idea comes into its full philosophical flowering. Embracing Hegel's sense of loss, he also sees, more profoundly than Marx, the dawn of an era of new human possibility.

8. This declaration, rather than contradicting the notion of art-as-perfection, is necessary to it: by the "death of God" man is reunited with his native creativity.

9. O'Connor cites this passage (Fadiman translation) in *The Shaping Spirit* (77–78)—noting its similarity to Stevens' "Crude Foyer."

10. "Humanity's bleak crown," associating with Christ's crown of thorns and the crowning achievements of metaphysical thinking, matches with Nietzsche's ascetic, "adorned" with thorns but with "no rose." The third and fourth stanzas show the "foyer" as the cognitive and spiritual locus "In which we read the critique of paradise / And say it is the work / Of a comedian, this critique; / In which we sit and breathe / / An innocence of an absolute." Here, again, "intellectual" and "spiritual" are associates, in the rarefied atmosphere of their sterile "absolute": "the critique of paradise" suggests both Kant's *Critique of Pure Reason* and, coupled with "comedian," Dante's *Divine Comedy*.

11. This line offers another instance of the disparity between Stevens' usage of "there" (indicating a place which is not "here") and Heidegger's term "There-being" (which, in the Stevensian sense of the terms, is neither "here" nor "there"); Stevens, as usual, advocates "being here."

12. This coalescence self-consistently associates with the much

later formulation in "Credences": "The trumpet cries / This is the successor of the invisible."

13. As Bloom says, "The sun-worship of stanza VII [of 'Sunday Morning'] represents a different idea of order, one that is yet to be and that relates itself to the image of Zarathustra's solar trajectory in Nietzsche" (*Poems of Our Climate*, 34).

14. As Bloom notices, the phrase also occurs in the "*Incipit tragoedia*" which heads Aphorism 342 (p. 274), "the final section of *The Gay Science* in its first edition" (*Poems of Our Climate*, 228).

15. Here the "imagination's new beginning" repeats Zarathustra's "the child is innocence and forgetting, a new beginning [*ein Neubeginnen*]." Stevens' "realist" briefly intersects Nietzsche's "realists," whose obsession with sobriety is, beneath the surface, a passionate, primitive, "intoxication": though believing themselves dispassionate rationalists, they passionately fasion the ideal of objectivity (*Gay Science*, 121).

16. Compare to Stevens' "God is a postulate of the ego" (*OP*, 171), and, of course, "the idea of God is the ultimate poetic idea" (*OP*, 193).

17. Remembering Nietzsche's "Creation—that is the great redemption from suffering, and life's growing light."

18. A phrase well synchronized with Stevens' earlier "The sky will be much friendlier then than now."

19. See, for example, *Thus Spoke Zarathustra*, part 4 ("On Science"), in which "the conscientious in spirit . . . took the harp away from the magician and cried: 'Air! Let in good air! Let in Zarathustra!'" (413).

20. Here the "barbarous chanting of what is strong, this blare" brings together the orgiastic chanting of the "ring of men" in "Sunday Morning" with Remus' horn-blowing in "Ploughing on Sunday."

21. This prefigures Sartre's dialectic of the "in-itself"/"for-itself."

22. This is an often-misread passage. Peterson, for instance, finds a "requital to the human desire to share in divinity" (*Stevens and the Idealist Tradition*, 93); but Stevens, taking (as usual) the unusual route, implies that God/Jove envied human imperfection and so participated in the human by mating with a human woman (or in the case of Jove, many women). "Cy Est Pourtraicte, Madame Ste Ursule, et Les Unze Mille Vierges" ends on a similar note: "the Lord," in response to Ursule's prayer, "felt a subtle quiver, / That was not heavenly love, / Or pity" (*CP*, 22). The generally blasphemous nature of both passages invites willful misunderstanding.

23. Bates notes that "four months after telling Church he had read

Notes to Chapter V

Human, All-Too-Human, Stevens had completed 'Esthétique du Mal'" (*Wallace Stevens*, 254).

24. Bates sees the description as negative: "Section IV [of "Description without Place"] places Nietzsche's distorting mind with Lenin's; each sees his peculiar obsessions reflected in a pool of water" (*Wallace Stevens*, 254). But Bates has mistakenly coupled the figure of Nietzsche with the tattered, depreciated form of Lenin; Stevens clearly intends their juxtaposition as a contrast. The terms surrounding "Nietzsche" in the poem—"deepness," "mastering," "total affluence," "first," "final," "gildering," "innate grandiose," "innate light"—are anything but negative.

25. Stevens renders it, not quite accurately, as "*Ewiges Wiederkehr*."

26. Bates mentions this passage as a "rhythmic equivalent" of the eternal return (*Wallace Stevens*, 259).

27. See the discussion of Heideggerian "ekstasis" in chapter 4.

28. A re-turn of lines from the much earlier "Farewell to Florida": "the snake has shed its skin upon / The floor" (*CP*, 117).

29. Stevens' usage (of "ignorance") is similar to that in Thoreau's "Walking": "Methinks there is . . . need of a Society for the Diffusion of Useful Ignorance, what we will call Beautiful Knowledge, a knowledge useful in a higher sense: for what is most of our boasted so-called knowledge but a conceit that we know something, which robs us of the advantage of our actual ignorance? What we call knowledge is often our positive ignorance; ignorance our negative knowledge" (622).

30. Peterson, taking a different approach to Stevens' phraseology, proposes that "Coleridge's 'repetition in the finite mind of the eternal act of creation in the infinite I AM' becomes the projection of 'the idea of God into the idea of man'" (*Stevens and the Idealist Tradition*, 38–39). Although recognizing that "the idea of God" does not have the same meaning for Coleridge (a devout believer) as for Stevens (and Nietzsche), Peterson discusses the inadequacy of what she sees as Stevens' conversion of Coleridge, concluding that "the romantic faith in the poet's unique power to pierce the veil, to have, as it is now euphemistically phrased, 'imaginative insights into reality,' becomes a meaningless anachronism, a literary husk deprived of its metaphysical core" (39). This is a substantial objection, but one answered by Stevens' Nietzschean reliance on art as a means of overcoming the metaphysical, and, more generally, by Stevens' Cassirerian grasp of the progression from mythic forms to religious to aesthetic.

31. Although Stevens frequently (and understandably) protested to

Church against Nietzsche during the years of World War II, he wrote to Church in August 1946: "If you go to Switzerland and pass through Basel, take a good look at it for me. Somehow I am more and more constantly interested in Basel than in Jerusalem. Then, too, you can walk there in Nietzsche's footsteps" (*Letters*, 532). This somewhat reverential curiosity (underscored by the comparison of Basel to Jerusalem) strikes a note of deep empathy for Nietzsche—evident in Stevens' frequent references to Nietzsche and allusions to his work.

32. Stevens owned a copy of *An Essay on Man* (written in English by Cassirer and published just before his death in April 1945) and quoted from it in "Imagination as Value" (*NA*, 136). The copy is now at the Huntington Library in the Stevens Collection.

33. "Abstract concept" here is philosophical/scientific/historical abstraction, not Stevens' "abstraction blooded."

34. See discussion in chapter 3 of Stevens' "reality is a vacuum" (*OP*, 168).

35. John Michael Krois' recent book on Cassirer discusses Cassirer as "phenomenologist": "For Hegel, phemonology studies and recalls the way that mind 'appears' [*als erscheinend*], that is, objectifies itself in things so as to appear for itself in these as something opposite to itself. Cassirer follows Hegel here: the philosophy of symbolic forms studies the objectification of life in the works of culture and 'recollects' it" (*Cassirer*, 78). Krois also addresses the question of Cassirer's complex relation to the "Life-philosophers," including Nietzsche and Heidegger: on one hand, Cassirer disavows their disinterest in the sciences and believes that their "break with the idealist tradition limited the concept of transcendence in a way that made it impossible to conceive of generally valid ideals, be they ethical or theoretical" (67); and, on the other hand, he shares (as Stevens does) their "dissatisfaction with the idealists' claim to comprehend logically reality as a whole" and their assumption that "lived experience [cannot] be reduced to scientific knowledge" (215). Again, what Cassirer intends by "generally valid ideals," modified by his view of symbolic formings, diverges from metaphysics' demand for universal validity. See note 2.

36. Though this criticism is directed first against Spengler, Cassirer continues, "The same holds, although in a different sense, for Martin Heidegger's philosophy" (229).

37. In parallel, Beehler's interest in difference draws him to "Stevens' suggestion that phenomenology is only another name for semiology" (*Discourses of Difference*, 44).

38. Cf. Stevens' "our revelations are not the revelations of belief, but the precious portents of our own powers"—discussed in chapter 1.

39. With respect to Cassirer, Krois points out that despite the sense in which *The Myth of the State* "remains the last word of Cassirer's philosophy . . . it would be wrong to ascribe too great a concern for the political to Cassirer even at this stage of his career. He believed that politics was shaped by something more fundamental, the cultural forces—intellectual, ethical, and artistic. These cultural forces determine the political" (*Cassirer*, 213–14).

40. As we have seen, Cassirer does not intend that these "forms" are unrelated to "reality"—only that the specific pleasure of aesthetic apprehension depends on formal qualities.

41. See note 35 for a Cassirerian parallel.

42. Remembering "Poetry is a sense" (*OP*, 161).

43. Though printed as "lacqued" in both *The Necessary Angel* and *The Palm at the End of the Mind* (300), it seems likely that Stevens intended the word to be "lacquered."

44. Here again we find a way in which Stevens aligns himself with Cassirer as opposed to Heidegger. According to Cassirer's own distinction, "the Philosophy of Symbolic Forms does not question [the] temporality which Heidegger discloses as the ultimate foundation of existentiality and attempts to explain in its diverse factors. But our inquiry begins *beyond* this sphere, at precisely the point where a transition is effected from this existential temporality to the *form* of time. It aspires to show the conditions under which this form is possible, the conditions for the postulation of a 'being' which goes beyond the existentiality of 'being-there.' In regard to time as to space, this μετάβασις from the meaning of existence to the objective meaning of the 'logos' constitutes its proper theme and problem" (*Phenomenology of Knowledge*, 163n).

45. Here the lines merge with the language of "Two or Three Ideas," in which we are no longer "the observer, the nonparticipant, the delinquent"; and the thought converges with "the partaker partakes of that which changes him" (*CP*, 392).

46. As we have seen in other contexts, Stevens differentiates "emotion" and "personality" from "sentimentality" or "egocentrism" (the personal)—these last being the targets of Eliot's contention that poetry escapes emotion/personality.

Chapter VI. The Marriage of the Rest

1. Stevens' language associates the pensive connoisseur (and eagle) with Nietzsche, who "walked in the Alps in the caresses of reality."

2. It seems likely that this usage of "supreme fiction" is related to what Stevens identifies as Richards' view that "poetry is the supreme use of language" (*NA*, 19).

3. Stevens, prefacing this remark with "the major poetic idea in the world is and always has been the idea of God" (placing "major" in relation to the "idea"), reveals something of the relatedness between "major man" and the "idea of God." It is also of interest, concerning the way constructions and phrases linger and resurface for Stevens even over a span of decades, to read "a part of philosophy, and a part of science" (1940) in relation to "A part of labor and a part of pain" (*CP*, 68) from "Sunday Morning" (1915).

4. The object of belief in Stevens' poem "A Primitive Like an Orb" is, by the title, "primitive," but with the wholly positive connotation of cleared (of past fictions), "clairvoyant" sight (*CP*, 441).

5. La Guardia declares, simply, that "Stevens' concept of fictions derives from William James" (*Advance on Chaos*, 17). Both La Guardia and Peterson demonstrate considerable compatibility between Stevens and James, but Stevens' "concept of fictions" is assuredly of complex derivation, with both Nietzsche and Santayana overshadowing James' influence. Although Cassirer's view of fictionality is more like Stevens' than any of these, it is (as indicated in chapter 5) doubtful that Cassirer's work exerted substantial direct influence before the publication of *An Essay on Man* (1944).

6. Remembering Stevens' "the best definition of true imagination is that it is the sum of our faculties" (*NA*, 61).

7. See, for instance, *The Republic*, bk. 6, 511d–e. It should be noted that Plato sees "imagination" (*eikasia*) as the lowest conceptual form on the "divided line." Holly Stevens indicates that her father owned a copy of Jowett's translation of Plato (*Souvenirs*, 19).

8. Another version of "this landscape of the mind // Is a landscape only of the eye."

9. Stevens' distinction between "essential imagination" and "a thing created by the imagination" can be read in terms of our distinction between poetry as "axis for all imaginative integrations" and a particular "central complex of poetic imagery."

10. While these categories, as they stand, may be repugnant to contemporary rethinking of gender roles, the abstract content in their integrations is for the sake of a fully human and, one could say, androgynous awareness.

11. Our reading of the male figure as concept does not depend on the possible Freudian implications of this passage.

12. La Guardia connects the first division of "Notes" to William James' contention that "a system of classification 'must always be abstract'" (*Advance on Chaos*, 37). The James quotation is from *The Will to Believe and Other Essays in Popular Philosophy*, 320.

13. Here, again, Stevens seems drawn to the Freudian double-entendre.

14. Appropriate to the "male figure," Stevens' play on Descartes' *Regulae* shows the "captain," as "apprentice," perceiving the *Rules for the Direction of the Mind* as "rules of the world."

15. Here as elsewhere Stevens uses "alphabet" in relation to a way of making sense of (or formulating) the world: the "thoughts, . . . dreams / Of inaccessible Utopia." In this particular instance it is a negative usage, but to believe this is a rejection of language structures themselves (or the structure of language) misses the point: it is not every alphabet which is "murderous," but specifically the evasive alphabet of Utopia.

16. There is an interestingly similar emphasis on the relation between form and the unformed in "form gulping after formlessness" and "the form / Of a generation that does not know itself."

17. Riddel cites this passage from Cassirer in *The Clairvoyant Eye* (152).

18. The thematic relation of these lines to *Paradise Lost* is obvious; more obscure is the likely source of Stevens' title: "Of thoughts revolv'd, his final sentence chose" (*Paradise Lost*, 9.88).

19. This negative scenario, in which everything is always already "red," "an unending red"—"red-emerald," "red-slitted-blue," "red-rose-red," "ruby-water-worn"—is the "ancient cycle" (*CP*, 382), the what-is-no-longer, of the vitally positive "rubies reddened by rubies reddening."

20. The title "Phosphor Reading by His Own Light" is unmistakably a Stevensian transmutation of Rembrandt's "The Philosopher Reading." The poem's dark page reverses the Rembrandt's bright white, but as in the Rembrandt, the night is green.

21. Moore uses the phrase in the poem titled "Poetry."
22. The fictive man, conceived as a specific reflection of that which sustains "reality," is that image greater than which, in the moment of imagining, nothing greater can be conceived; and such an image is persuasively real (in Stevens' terms) for us. For a further discussion of Stevens/Anselm, see our article "Stevens' Conversion of Anselm: 'The Utmost Must Be Good and Is.'"
23. If we accept Anselm's premises (including the meaningfulness of such predication), thought finds itself powerless to deny God's existence without contradiction.
24. As with the Heraclitean "[Listen] not to me but to the Logos" (Kirk and Raven, *The Presocratic Philosophers*, 188 [Fragment 199]) or, as in the contemporary distinction between speech and language, major man (as "Logos" and "form to speak the word") is distinct from the voice that speaks. In the poem's complications, it is the poet's "world" which is "fluent" (in the generative integration of male and female) and the "fat girl, terrestrial" who is its voice; the poet/persona (himself an integration of the male and female), by his naming, embraces that "world."
25. While we have generally left the issue of the relation between Nietzsche's *übermensch* and Stevens' male figures to the side, Bates discusses similarities—and there are some, despite Stevens' disclaimer. But Stevens' claim is ambiguous. He may mean to convey only that "major man" is not Nietzsche's "*übermensch*" (who is a distant possibility, and not what Stevens desires here: an "abstraction blooded"); but the same would not apply to Zarathustra, who is not a "shadow," and, as Nietzsche says, is not the *übermensch*. On a "lighter" note, we can be confident that Stevens' "sun" (which casts no shadows) is "the sun of Nietzsche gildering the pool" (*CP*, 342).
26. The Stevens Collection at the Huntington Library includes a two-volume set of Arnold's *Essays in Criticism*. The volumes are signed by Stevens and dated October 1898.
27. The song at Key West resonates with the much later "As if the innocent mother sang in the dark / Of the room and on an accordion, half-heard, / Created the time and place in which we breathed . . ." ("Auroras"; *CP*, 419; ellipsis is Stevens').
28. Stevens no doubt intends us to read these lines with a sidelong glance at Shakespeare's "of imagination all compact" (*A Midsummer*

Night's Dream, V.i.8), noting that major man comes not from "imagination" but from "reason."

29. Marjorie Perloff comments about this image: "One thinks of the Steuben glass in the windows of Fifth Avenue, the crystal globe containing the figures inside it—arrested motion, a beautiful stasis" ("Revolving in Crystal," 60).

30. Bates remarks in this regard that "one cannot love abstract concepts or logical categories" (*Wallace Stevens*, 210); though the general point is debatable, it fits well with Stevens' persona's relation to male/female figurations.

31. While the title of the poem seems to be the empiricist's "what we see is what we think" (i.e., the senses determine our cognition), the last line, as Stevens' last lines often do, poses the significant contrary: "Since what we think is never what we see," which forces a reinterpretation of the title.

32. Berger aptly identifies the "fat girl" of "Notes" as "both an object of desire and the principle of desire itself" (*Forms of Farewell*, 23). But the female as "principle of desire" should be differentiated from the male principle-as-such.

33. Compare "Poetry is a cure of the mind" (*OP*, 176).

34. In parallel, Merleau-Ponty raises the question not for metaphor but for vision: "How does it happen that my look, enveloping them [the visibles], does not hide them, and, finally, that, veiling them, it unveils them?" ("Eye and Mind," 131).

35. This returns to "On the Road Home": "It was when I said, / 'There is no such thing as the truth,' / That the grapes seemed fatter . . ."

36. As we have seen, Stevens' view on the matter of reality-as-such is like Cassirer's, for whom "the naked core of mere sensation, which merely *is* (without representing anything), never exists in the actual consciousness" (*Phenomenology of Knowledge*, 141).

37. It is notable that in this instance "sense" (as the "poet's sense") produces the "major."

38. This is perhaps Stevens' most eloquent explanation of the "unofficial" hypothesis that "the theory of poetry is the theory of life."

39. On this point, Bates says that Stevens' "God and the imagination are one" is indicated (by the "We say") to be "myth rather than empirical fact or logical deduction; but it is a myth to live by, one that

identifies the world imagined with the Goodness Personified of religion" (*Wallace Stevens*, 299–300). But without reference to the "we say," the offering that "God and the imagination are one" is a self-evidently "fictional" hypothesis. And while the "Goodness Personified of religion," in its particulars, was once sufficient, it is, in Stevens' view, no longer so. In other words, "we say" more likely signals the heuristic strategy of imprecise identification which attends to a difference as well as a resemblance.

40. The "ring" here can be seen as both a bell tone (note), which brings sky in touch with earth, and a circumference which bands the "blue" and "green" (as if by a marriage band—associating with Zarathustra's "nuptial ring of rings, the ring of recurrence" [340]).

41. Here we mean particularly Western theologies.

42. As we have seen, this "unofficial view," while incompatible with traditional metaphysics, is in concert with certain recent trends in philosophical thinking.

43. "Final found" signals the re-turning of the fruit of the Tree of (Eternal) Life, within Stevens' variations on the seasonal.

Works Cited

Arnold, Matthew. *Essays in Criticism, Second Series*. New York: Macmillan, 1903.
Bachelard, Suzanne. *A Study of Husserl's Formal and Transcendental Logic*. Translated by Lester E. Embree. Evanston, Ill.: Northwestern University Press, 1968.
Baird, James. *The Dome and the Rock: Structure in the Poetry of Wallace Stevens*. Baltimore: Johns Hopkins University Press, 1968.
Bates, Milton J. *Wallace Stevens: A Mythology of Self*. Berkeley: University of California Press, 1985.
Beach, Joseph Warren. *A Romantic View of Poetry*. Minneapolis: University of Minnesota Press, 1944.
Beckett, Lucy. *Wallace Stevens*. Cambridge: Cambridge University Press, 1977.
Beehler, Michael. *T. S. Eliot, Wallace Stevens, and the Discourses of Difference*. Baton Rouge: Louisiana State University Press, 1987.
Benamou, Michel. *Wallace Stevens and the Symbolist Imagination*. Princeton, N.J.: Princeton University Press, 1972.
———. "Wallace Stevens and the Symbolist Imagination." In *The Act of the Mind: Essays on the Poetry of Wallace Stevens*, edited by Roy Harvey Pearce and J. Hillis Miller. Baltimore: Johns Hopkins University Press, 1965.
Berger, Charles. *Forms of Farewell: The Late Poetry of Wallace Stevens*. Madison: University of Wisconsin Press, 1985.
Bewley, Marius. *The Complex Fate: Hawthorne, Henry James and Some Other American Writers*. New York: Gordian, 1967.
Biemel, Walter. "Poetry and Language in Heidegger." In *On Heidegger and Language*, edited and translated by Joseph J. Kockelmans. Evanston, Ill.: Northwestern University Press, 1972.

Bloom, Harold. *The Anxiety of Influence: A Theory of Poetry.* New York: Oxford University Press, 1973.

———. "*Notes toward a Supreme Fiction*: A Commentary." In *Wallace Stevens: A Collection of Critical Essays,* edited by Marie Borroff. Englewood Cliffs, N.J.: Prentice-Hall, 1963.

———. *Wallace Stevens: The Poems of Our Climate.* Ithaca, N.Y.: Cornell University Press, 1977.

Borroff, Marie. "Wallace Stevens: The World and the Poet." In *Wallace Stevens: A Collection of Critical Essays,* edited by Marie Borroff. Englewood Cliffs, N.J.: Prentice-Hall, 1963.

Bové, Paul A. *Destructive Poetics: Heidegger and Modern American Poetry.* New York: Columbia University Press, 1980.

Brazeau, Peter. *Parts of a World: Wallace Stevens Remembered.* New York: Random House, 1983.

Cambon, Glauco. *The Inclusive Flame: Studies in American Poetry.* Bloomington: Indiana University Press, 1963.

Cassirer, Ernst. *Einstein's Theory of Relativity.* In *Substance and Function and Einstein's Theory of Relativity.* Translated by William Curtis Swabey and Marie Collins Swabey. New York: Dover, 1953.

———. *An Essay on Man: An Introduction to a Philosophy of Human Culture.* New Haven, Conn.: Yale University Press, 1944.

———. *Language and Myth.* Translated by Susanne K. Langer. New York: Dover, 1953.

———. *The Logic of the Humanities.* Translated by Clarence Smith Howe. New Haven, Conn.: Yale University Press, 1961.

———. *Mythical Thought.* Vol. 2 of *The Philosophy of Symbolic Forms.* 3 vols. Translated by Ralph Manheim. New Haven, Conn.: Yale University Press, 1955.

———. *The Phenomenology of Knowledge.* Vol. 3 of *The Philosophy of Symbolic Forms.* 3 vols. Translated by Ralph Manheim. New Haven, Conn.: Yale University Press, 1957.

———. *Symbol, Myth, and Culture: Essays and Lectures of Ernst Cassirer, 1935–45.* Edited by Donald Phillip Verene. New Haven, Conn.: Yale University Press, 1979.

Coleridge, S. T. *Biographia Literaria.* 2 vols. Edited by J. Shawcross. London: Oxford University Press, 1907.

Cook, Eleanor. "The Decreations of Wallace Stevens." *Wallace Stevens Journal* 4 (1980): 46–57.

Works Cited

Doggett, Frank. *Stevens' Poetry of Thought*. Baltimore: Johns Hopkins University Press, 1966.

Dupré, Louis. *Transcendent Selfhood: The Loss and Rediscovery of the Inner Life*. New York: Seabury, 1976.

Eberhart, Richard. "Emerson and Wallace Stevens." *Literary Review* 7 (1963): 51–71.

Eco, Umberto. *Semiotics and the Philosophy of Language*. Bloomington: Indiana University Press, 1984.

Edelstein, J. M. *Wallace Stevens: A Descriptive Bibliography*. Pittsburgh: University of Pittsburgh Press, 1973.

Eliot, T. S. *Four Quartets*. New York: Harvest/Harcourt, 1971.

———. *The Sacred Wood: Essays on Poetry and Criticism*. London: Methuen, 1928.

Emerson, Ralph Waldo. *Nature*. In *Selections from Ralph Waldo Emerson: An Organic Anthology*, edited by Stephen E. Whicher. Boston: Houghton Mifflin, 1957.

Frye, Northrop. "The Realistic Oriole: A Study of Wallace Stevens." In *Wallace Stevens: A Collection of Critical Essays*, edited by Marie Borroff. Englewood Cliffs, N.J.: Prentice-Hall, 1963.

———. "Wallace Stevens and the Variation Form." In *Literary Theory and Structure: Essays in Honor of William K. Wimsatt*, edited by Frank Brady, John Palmer, and Martin Price. New Haven, Conn.: Yale University Press, 1973.

Gelven, Michael. *A Commentary on Heidegger's "Being and Time."* New York: Harper and Row, 1970.

Gelpi, Albert. "Stevens and Williams: The Epistemology of Modernism." In *Wallace Stevens: The Poetics of Modernism*, edited by Albert Gelpi. New York: Cambridge University Press, 1985.

Hegel, G. W. F. *The Phenomenology of Mind*. Translated by J. B. Baillie. New York: Harper and Row, 1967.

———. *Hegel's Science of Logic*. Translated by A. V. Miller. London: Allen and Unwin, 1969.

Heidegger, Martin. *The Basic Problems of Phenomenology*. Translated by Albert Hofstadter. Bloomington: Indiana University Press, 1982.

———. *Being and Time*. Translated by John Macquarrie and Edward Robinson. New York: Harper and Row, 1962.

———. *On Time and Being*. Translated by Joan Stambaugh. New York: Harper and Row, 1972.

———. *Poetry, Language, Thought*. Translated by Albert Hofstadter. New York: Harper and Row, 1971.
———. *Sein und Zeit*. Tübingen: Max Niemeyer, 1972.
———. *Wegmarken*. Frankfurt am Main: Vittorio Klostermann, 1967.
———. *What Is Called Thinking?* Translated by J. Glenn Gray. New York: Harper and Row, 1968.
———. "The Word of Nietzsche: 'God Is Dead.'" In *The Question Concerning Technology and Other Essays*, translated by William Lovitt. New York: Harper and Row, 1977.
Hines, Thomas J. *The Later Poetry of Wallace Stevens: Phenomenological Parallels with Husserl and Heidegger*. Lewisburg, Pa.: Bucknell University Press, 1976.
Husserl, Edmund. *Cartesian Meditations: An Introduction to Phenomenology*. Translated by Dorion Cairns. The Hague: Martinus Nijhoff, 1973.
———. *Ideas: General Introduction to Pure Phenomenology*. Translated by W. R. Boyce Gibson. London: Allen and Unwin, 1931.
James, Henry. *Theory of Fiction: Henry James*. Edited by James E. Miller, Jr. Lincoln: University of Nebraska Press, 1972.
James, William. *The Meaning of Truth*. New York: Longmans, 1932.
———. *The Will to Believe and Other Essays in Popular Philosophy*. New York: Henry Holt, 1912.
Johnson, Samuel. "Preface to Shakespeare, 1765." In vol. 7 of *The Yale Edition of the Works of Samuel Johnson*, edited by Arthur Sherbo. 9 vols. New Haven, Conn.: Yale University Press, 1968.
Keats, John. *Selected Poems and Letters*. Edited by Douglas Bush. Boston: Houghton Mifflin, 1959.
Kermode, Frank. *Continuities*. London: Routledge and Kegan Paul, 1968.
———. *Wallace Stevens*. Edinburgh: Oliver and Boyd, 1960.
Kirk, G. S., and J. E. Raven. *The Presocratic Philosophers: A Critical History with a Selection of Texts*. Cambridge: Cambridge University Press, 1957.
Koestenbaum, Peter. Introduction to *The Paris Lectures*, by Edmund Husserl, translated by Peter Koestenbaum. The Hague: Martinus Nijhoff, 1975.
Krois, John Michael. *Cassirer: Symbolic Forms and History*. New Haven, Conn.: Yale University Press, 1987.
La Guardia, David. *Advance on Chaos: The Sanctifying Imagination*

of *Wallace Stevens*. Hanover, N.H.: University Press of New England/Brown University Press, 1983.

Leggett, B. J. *Wallace Stevens and Poetic Theory: Conceiving the Supreme Fiction*. Chapel Hill: University of North Carolina Press, 1987.

Leonard, J. S., and C. E. Wharton. "Stevens' Conversion of Anselm: 'The Utmost Must Be Good and Is.'" *South Atlantic Review* 52 (1987): 85–94.

Litz, A. Walton. *Introspective Voyager: The Poetic Development of Wallace Stevens*. New York: Oxford University Press, 1972.

Macksey, Richard A. "The Climates of Wallace Stevens." In *The Act of the Mind: Essays on the Poetry of Wallace Stevens*, edited by Roy Harvey Pearce and J. Hillis Miller. Baltimore: Johns Hopkins University Press, 1965.

MacLeod, Glen G. *Wallace Stevens and Company: The Harmonium Years, 1913–1923*. Ann Arbor, Mich.: UMI Research Press, 1983.

Magnus, Bernd. *Heidegger's Metahistory of Philosophy: Amor Fati, Being and Truth*. The Hague: Martinus Nijhoff, 1970.

———. *Nietzsche's Existential Imperative*. Bloomington: Indiana University Press, 1978.

Martz, Louis L. "Wallace Stevens: The World as Meditation." In *The Achievement of Wallace Stevens*, edited by Ashley Brown and Robert S. Haller. Philadelphia: Lippincott, 1962.

Marx, Karl. *Early Writings*. Edited and translated by T. B. Bottomore. New York: McGraw-Hill, 1964.

Melville, Herman. *Moby-Dick*. Norton Critical Edition. Edited by Harrison Hayford and Herschel Parker. New York: Norton, 1967.

Merleau-Ponty, Maurice. "Eye and Mind." Translated by Carleton Dallery. In *The Essential Writings of Merleau-Ponty*, edited by Alden L. Fisher. New York: Harcourt, 1969.

Miller, J. Hillis. "Stevens' Rock and Criticism as Cure." *Georgia Review* 30 (1976): 5–31.

———. "Theoretical and Atheoretical in Stevens." In *Wallace Stevens: A Celebration*, edited by Frank Doggett and Robert Buttel. Princeton, N.J.: Princeton University Press, 1980.

———. "Wallace Stevens' Poetry of Being." In *The Act of the Mind: Essays on the Poetry of Wallace Stevens*, edited by Roy Harvey Pearce and J. Hillis Miller. Baltimore: Johns Hopkins University Press, 1965.

Morse, Samuel French. *Wallace Stevens: Poetry as Life*. New York: Pegasus, 1970.

Nietzsche, Friedrich. *The Birth of Tragedy and The Case of Wagner*. Translated by Walter Kaufmann. New York: Vintage, 1967.

———. *The Gay Science*. Translated by Walter Kaufmann. New York: Vintage, 1974.

———. *Thus Spoke Zarathustra*. In *The Portable Nietzsche*, edited and translated by Walter Kaufmann. New York: Viking, 1954.

O'Connor, William Van. *The Shaping Spirit: A Study of Wallace Stevens*. Chicago: Henry Regnery, 1950.

Pack, Robert. *Wallace Stevens: An Approach to His Poetry and Thought*. New Brunswick, N.J.: Rutgers University Press, 1958.

Pearce, Roy Harvey. *The Continuity of American Poetry*. Princeton, N.J.: Princeton University Press, 1961.

———. "Toward Decreation: Stevens and the 'Theory of Poetry.'" In *Wallace Stevens: A Celebration*, edited by Frank Doggett and Robert Buttel. Princeton, N.J.: Princeton University Press, 1980.

Perlis, Alan. *Wallace Stevens: A World of Transforming Shapes*. Lewisburg, Pa.: Bucknell University Press, 1976.

Perloff, Marjorie. "Revolving in Crystal: The Supreme Fiction and the Impasse of the Modernist Lyric." In *Wallace Stevens: The Poetics of Modernism*, edited by Albert Gelpi. New York: Cambridge University Press, 1985.

Peterson, Margaret. *Wallace Stevens and the Idealist Tradition*. Ann Arbor, Mich.: UMI Research Press, 1983.

Plato. *The Republic*. Translated by Paul Shorey. Vol. 6 of the Loeb Classical Library edition of *Plato*, edited by E. H. Warmington. Cambridge, Mass.: Harvard University Press, 1935.

Pound, Ezra. *Literary Essays of Ezra Pound*. Edited by T. S. Eliot. New York: New Directions, 1954.

Regueiro, Helen. *The Limits of Imagination: Wordsworth, Yeats, and Stevens*. Ithaca, N.Y.: Cornell University Press, 1976.

Richards, I. A. *Coleridge on Imagination*. London: Kegan Paul, 1934.

———. *Practical Criticism: A Study of Literary Judgment*. New York: Harcourt, 1929.

Richardson, William J. *Heidegger: Through Phenomenology to Thought*. The Hague: Martinus Nijhoff, 1974.

Riddel, Joseph N. *The Clairvoyant Eye: The Poetry and Poetics of Wallace Stevens*. Baton Rouge: Louisiana State University Press, 1965.

---. "The Contours of Stevens Criticism." In *The Act of the Mind: Essays on the Poetry of Wallace Stevens*, edited by Roy Harvey Pearce and J. Hillis Miller. Baltimore: Johns Hopkins University Press, 1965.

---. "Metaphoric Staging: Stevens' Beginning Again at the 'End of the Book.'" In *Wallace Stevens: A Celebration*, edited by Frank Doggett and Robert Buttel. Princeton, N.J.: Princeton University Press, 1980.

---. "Walt Whitman and Wallace Stevens: Functions of a 'Literatus.'" In *Wallace Stevens: A Collection of Critical Essays*, edited by Marie Borroff. Englewood Cliffs, N.J.: Prentice-Hall, 1963.

Shelley, Percy Bysshe. *The Poetical Works of Shelley*. Edited by Newell F. Ford. Boston: Houghton Mifflin, 1975.

---. *Shelley's Critical Prose*. Edited by Bruce R. McElderry, Jr. Lincoln: University of Nebraska Press, 1967.

Sukenick, Ronald. *Wallace Stevens: Musing the Obscure*. New York: New York University Press, 1967.

Thoreau, Henry David. "Walking." In *The Portable Thoreau*, edited by Carl Bode. New York: Penguin, 1977.

Vendler, Helen Hennessy. *On Extended Wings: Wallace Stevens' Longer Poems*. Cambridge, Mass.: Harvard University Press, 1969.

---. "The Qualified Assertions of Wallace Stevens." In *The Act of the Mind: Essays on the Poetry of Wallace Stevens*, edited by Roy Harvey Pearce and J. Hillis Miller. Baltimore: Johns Hopkins University Press, 1965.

---. "Stevens and Keats' 'To Autumn.'" In *Wallace Stevens: A Celebration*, edited by Frank Doggett and Robert Buttel. Princeton, N.J.: Princeton University Press, 1980.

---. *Wallace Stevens: Words Chosen Out of Desire*. Knoxville: University of Tennessee Press, 1984.

Verene, D. P. "Cassirer's Concept of Symbolic Form and Creativity." *Idealistic Studies* 8 (1978): 14–32.

Waggoner, Hyatt H. *American Poets: From the Puritans to the Present*. New York: Dell, 1968.

Whitman, Walt. *Leaves of Grass*. Comprehensive Reader's Edition. Edited by Harold W. Blodgett and Sculley Bradley. New York: New York University Press, 1965.

Williams, William Carlos. *Paterson*. New York: New Directions, n.d.

---. "Wallace Stevens." *Poetry* 87 (1956): 234–39.

Wordsworth, William. *Selected Poems and Prefaces*. Edited by Jack Stillinger. Boston: Houghton Mifflin, 1965.

Yeats, William Butler. *The Collected Poems of W. B. Yeats*. New York: Macmillan, 1956.

Young, Edward. "Conjectures on Original Composition." In *Criticism: The Major Statements*, edited by Charles Kaplan. New York: St. Martin's, 1975.

Index

Anselm, 150
Aristotle, 181 (n. 23)
Arnold, Matthew, 151–52

Bachelard, Suzanne: *A Study of Husserl's Formal and Transcendental Logic*, 178 (n. 1)
Baird, James, x; *The Dome and the Rock*, 42, 45, 46, 182 (n. 1)
Bates, Milton J.: *Wallace Stevens: A Mythology of Self*, x, 46, 103, 182 (nn. 4, 5), 184–85 (n. 23), 185 (nn. 24, 26), 190 (n. 25), 191 (n. 30), 191–92 (n. 39)
Beach, Joseph Warren: *A Romantic View of Poetry*, 61–62
Beckett, Lucy: *Wallace Stevens*, 49
Beehler, Michael: *T. S. Eliot, Wallace Stevens, and the Discourses of Difference*, 172–73 (n. 12), 173 (n. 16), 174–75 (n. 2), 186 (n. 37)
Benamou, Michel, 18; *Wallace Stevens and the Symbolist Imagination*, 17, 39, 42, 74–75

Berger, Charles: *Forms of Farewell*, 174 (nn. 21, 22), 191 (n. 32)
Bewley, Marius: *The Complex Fate*, 48–49
Biemel, Walter, 94
Bloom, Harold, x, 39; *Wallace Stevens: The Poems of Our Climate*, 47, 48, 103, 174 (n. 25), 184 (nn. 13, 14); *The Anxiety of Influence*, 172 (n. 5)
Borroff, Marie, 32, 170 (n. 20)
Bové, Paul A., x, 96; *Destructive Poetics*, 42–43, 65–68, 74, 173 (n. 13), 176 (n. 12)
Brazeau, Peter: *Parts of a World*, x, 10, 169 (n. 17)
Burnshaw, Stanley, 131

Cambon, Glauco, 10; *The Inclusive Flame*, 33, 85, 89, 94
Carlyle, Thomas: *Sartor Resartus*, 183 (n. 6)
Cassirer, Ernst, x–xi, 36, 103, 127–39, 161, 185 (n. 30), 186 (n. 35), 188 (n. 5); *An Essay on Man*, 10–11, 57, 61, 92–93, 127–28, 134, 135, 138, 139, 179 (n. 9); *Language and Myth*, 33, 78, 130, 178 (n. 26),

201

Index

Cassirer, Ernst (cont'd)
186 (n. 32); *The Phenomenology of Knowledge*, 81, 128–29, 131, 133, 137, 158, 159, 187 (n. 44), 191 (n. 36); *The Logic of the Humanities*, 127; *Symbol, Myth, and Culture*, 128; *Mythical Thought*, 129–30, 147; *Einstein's Theory of Relativity*, 182 (n. 2); *The Myth of the State*, 187 (n. 39)
Cézanne, Paul, 12
Church, Henry, 14, 127, 140, 142, 153, 186 (n. 31)
Coleridge, S. T., 42, 43, 48–49, 142; *Biographia Literaria*, 49, 177 (n. 24), 185 (n. 30)
Communism, 131–32
Cook, Eleanor, 6

Dante: *The Divine Comedy*, 183 (n. 10)
Descartes, René: *Regulae ad Directionem Ingenii*, 145
Doggett, Frank, 1; *Stevens' Poetry of Thought*, xii, 78, 81, 146, 182 (n. 13)

Eberhart, Richard, 57
Eco, Umberto: *Semiotics and the Philosophy of Language*, 129
Eliot, T. S., 27, 44, 45–47, 56, 187 (n. 46); *The Sacred Wood*, 46, 47; *Four Quartets*, 171 (n. 30)
Emerson, Ralph Waldo, 3, 56–57, 103, 174 (n. 26)
Epicurus, 121

Frye, Northrop, 10, 42, 48, 76, 176 (n. 13)

Gelpi, Albert, 170 (n. 21), 172 (nn. 7, 11); *Wallace Stevens: The Poetics of Modernism*, x
Gelven, Michael: *A Commentary on Heidegger's "Being and Time,"* 97

Hanley, Rev. Arthur, 167 (n. 5)
Harris, Joel Chandler, 115
Harvard University, xiii
Hegel, G. W. F., 3, 183 (n. 7), 186 (n. 35); *Hegel's Science of Logic*, 63, 176 (n. 11); *The Phenomenology of Mind*, 107
Heidegger, Martin, 59, 63, 66, 75, 83, 94–102, 128, 178 (n. 2), 182 (n. 4), 183 (n. 11), 186 (n. 35), 187 (n. 44); *Being and Time*, 83, 98–99, 100–101, 176 (n. 16), 180 (n. 16), 181 (n. 20); *Poetry, Language, Thought*, 94, 95, 101–2, 128, 129, 179 (n. 10); *Wegmarken*, 94; *What Is Called Thinking?*, 99–100; *Sein und Zeit*, 181 (n. 17); *Qu'est que la Metaphysique?*, 181 (n. 17)
Heraclitus, 190 (n. 24)
Heringman, Bernard, 173 (n. 13)
Hines, Thomas J., x, xii; *The Later Poetry of Wallace Stevens*, 19, 61, 81, 86, 90, 96–97, 99–100, 101–2, 123, 169 (n. 21), 180–81 (n. 17)
Hölderlin, Friedrich, 181 (n. 17)
Husserl, Edmund, x, xi, 83–92, 96, 128; *Cartesian Meditations*, 84, 86, 90, 179 (n. 5); *Ideas*, 85–86, 90, 92, 178–79 (n. 4)

James, Henry, 10
James, William, xii–xiii, 142,

171 (n. 30), 174 (n. 26), 188 (n. 5), 189 (n. 12)
Johnson, Samuel, ix, 14

Kant, Immanuel, 3, 128–29; *Critique of Pure Reason*, 183 (n. 10)
Keats, John, 43, 45–46, 156
Kermode, Frank: *Continuities*, 4
Koestenbaum, Peter, 179 (n. 8)
Krois, John Michael: *Cassirer*, 128, 186 (n. 35), 187 (n. 39)

La Guardia, David: *Advance on Chaos*, xiii, 171 (n. 30), 174 (n. 26), 182 (n. 3), 188 (n. 5), 189 (n. 12)
Leggett, B. J.: *Wallace Stevens and Poetic Theory*, 168 (n. 9)
Lenin, Nikolai, 13, 132, 185 (n. 24)
Litz, A. Walton: *Introspective Voyager*, 47, 48
Luther, Martin, 183 (n. 7)

Macksey, Richard A., 63–64, 65, 84, 98, 169–70 (n. 21), 180 (n. 14)
MacLeod, Glen G.: *Wallace Stevens and Company*, x
Magnus, Bernd: *Heidegger's Metahistory of Philosophy*, 182 (n. 4); *Nietzsche's Existential Imperative*, 182 (n. 4)
Magritte, René, 168 (n. 8)
Mallarmé, Stéphane, 17–18
Marx, Karl, 183 (n. 7)
Melville, Herman, 140
Merleau-Ponty, Maurice, 12, 191 (n. 34)
Miller, J. Hillis, x, xii, 60–62, 63, 64, 65, 69–71, 74, 77, 81, 96, 106, 175 (nn. 3, 7, 9), 176 (n. 10); *The Act of the Mind*, 1
Milton, John: *Paradise Lost*, 189 (n. 18)
Moore, Marianne, 149

Nietzsche, Friedrich, x, xi, 13, 95, 103–27, 132, 140, 151, 171 (n. 27), 181–90 passim; *Thus Spoke Zarathustra*, xi, 23, 104–6, 107, 108, 109–20, 123, 126–27, 184 (nn. 15, 19); *The Gay Science*, xi, 50–51, 91, 94, 104, 107–8, 117, 119, 121, 123, 144, 182 (n. 4), 184 (nn. 14, 15); *The Birth of Tragedy*, 110, 117; *Twilight of the Idols*, 116; *Human, All-Too-Human*, 120

O'Connor, William Van: *The Shaping Spirit*, 1, 183 (n. 9)

Pack, Robert: *Wallace Stevens*, 1, 25
Pearce, Roy Harvey, xii, 7–8, 173 (n. 13); *The Continuity of American Poetry*, x, 1, 2–4, 47, 54–56; *The Act of the Mind*, 1
Perlis, Alan: *Wallace Stevens: A World of Transforming Shapes*, 34
Perloff, Marjorie, 191 (n. 28)
Peterson, Margaret: *Wallace Stevens and the Idealist Tradition*, xiii, 39, 171 (n. 1), 173 (n. 14), 184 (n. 22), 185 (n. 30)
Phenomenology, xi, 83–93, 137
Plato, 10, 115, 143, 167 (n. 2), 172 (n. 9); *The Republic*, 188 (n. 7)
Pound, Ezra, 170 (n. 21)
Poussin, Nicolas, 21

Regueiro, Helen, x, xii; *The Limits of Imagination*, 2, 8, 19, 20–21, 26–27, 58, 74–76, 106
Rembrandt, 189 (n. 20)
Richards, I. A., 188 (n. 2); *Practical Criticism*, 44, 58, 141–42; *Coleridge on Imagination*, 168 (n. 9)
Richardson, William J.: *Heidegger*, 94, 101, 180 (n. 15), 181 (n. 19)
Riddel, Joseph N., x, 1, 7, 42, 46, 54; *The Clairvoyant Eye*, 39, 78, 83–84, 189 (n. 17)
Rodríguez-Feo, José, 149, 151

Santayana, George, xii–xiii
Sartre, Jean-Paul, 174 (n. 27)
Shakespeare, William: *As You Like It*, 156; *A Midsummer Night's Dream*, 173 (n. 17), 190–91 (n. 28)
Shelley, Percy Bysshe, 43, 53, 56, 60, 175 (n. 5)
Sidney, Sir Philip: *Defence of Poesie*, 174 (n. 1), 176 (n. 13)
Simons, Hi, 65, 141–42
Socrates, 181 (n. 23)
Spengler, Oswald, 186 (n. 36)
Stevens, Elsie, 148
Stevens, Holly, 188 (n. 7)
Stevens, Wallace: supreme fiction, xi, xiii, 13, 14, 69–71, 77, 90, 92, 95, 102, 129, 135, 140–45, 146, 151; decreation, 2–8, 25, 30, 61, 64, 66, 74, 83, 87; the giant, 145–47; the hero, 145, 147–48; major man, 145, 148–52; female figures, 145, 153–65

WORKS:
—"About One of Marianne Moore's Poems," 11
—"Adagia," 8, 10, 14, 15–16, 37, 46, 47, 48, 58, 68, 73, 76, 82, 87, 94, 102, 107, 117, 118, 126, 130, 133, 144, 163, 165, 169 (n. 15), 171 (n. 2), 177 (n. 20), 179 (n. 7), 181 (n. 22), 184 (n. 16), 186 (n. 42), 191 (n. 33)
—"Anecdote of the Jar," 25
—"Angel Surrounded by Paysans," 4–6, 178 (n. 3)
—"Another Weeping Woman," 80–81, 94
—"As at a Theatre," 143
—"Asides on the Oboe," 50–51, 101, 131, 140, 143
—"As You Leave the Room," xii, 93–94, 148
—"Auroras of Autumn, The," 31–32, 125, 146, 189 (n. 16), 190 (n. 27)
—*Auroras of Autumn, The*, 2, 180 (n. 17)
—"Bed of Old John Zeller, The," 12, 179 (n. 9)
—"Beginning, The," 126
—"Bouquet of Roses in Sunlight," 15, 90–92, 101, 155, 159
—"Bouquet, The," 158–59
—"Clear Day and No Memories, A," 71–72
—"Collect of Philosophy, A," xi, 76, 77, 79, 87, 89, 122, 141, 164, 173 (n. 18), 179 (n. 6), 184 (n. 16)
—"Comedian as the Letter C, The," 88
—"Connoisseur of Chaos, The," 65–66, 140

—"Conversation with Three Women of New England," 72–73, 101
—"Countryman, The," 97
—"Creations of Sound, The," 47, 154
—"Credences of Summer," 22–25, 29, 30, 35–36, 53, 56, 60, 64, 66, 77, 85, 88–89, 91, 135, 159, 170 (nn. 23, 26), 174 (n. 21), 184 (n. 12)
—"Crude Foyer," 112–13, 188 (n. 8)
—"Cy Est Pourtraicte, Madame Ste Ursule, et Les Unze Mille Vierge," 184 (n. 22)
—"Description without Place," xiii, 13, 30, 52, 77–78, 82, 121–22, 123, 132, 143, 144, 162, 190 (n. 25)
—"Dezembrum," 107, 158
—"Discovery of Thought, A," 124–25
—"Disillusionment of Ten O'Clock," 170 (n. 24), 175 (n. 6)
—"Doctor of Geneva, The," 110
—"Domination of Black," 72
—"Dutch Graves in Bucks County," 119
—"Effects of Analogy," 42, 84, 88, 135–36
—"Esthétique du Mal," 26, 47, 52, 73, 79, 86–87, 116, 117, 119–20, 124, 137–38, 148–49, 151
—"Evening without Angels," 108
—"Examination of the Hero in a Time of War," 51, 148
—"Extracts from Addresses to the Academy of Fine Ideas," 98, 144–45, 180 (n. 14)
—"Farewell to Florida," 185 (n. 28)
—"Farewell without a Guitar," 154
—"Figure of the Youth as Virile Poet, The," 11, 12–13, 15, 32, 51, 57, 59, 79, 82, 91, 96, 103, 138, 152–53, 188 (n. 6)
—"Final Soliloquy of the Interior Paramour," 162–63
—"Good Man Has No Shape, The," 143
—*Harmonium*, 63, 77
—"High-Toned Old Christian Woman, A," xiii, 70, 77, 140
—"Holiday in Reality," 155
—"Honors and Acts," 54, 162, 164
—"Idea of Order at Key West, The," 43–44, 152
—*Ideas of Order*, 38, 40, 96, 129, 131
—"Imagination as Value," 46–47, 57, 88, 127, 130, 131–32, 152, 186 (n. 32)
—"Irrational Element in Poetry, The," 52, 171 (n. 2)
—"Landscape with Boat," 111, 150–51
—"Latest Freed Man, The," 70, 113–14, 115, 123
—"Less and Less Human, O Savage Spirit," 80, 120–21
—*Letters of Wallace Stevens*, 5, 7, 12, 14, 28, 29, 36, 40, 41, 42, 49–50, 54, 57–58, 65, 70, 79–80, 84, 87, 88, 90, 95, 100, 126, 133, 134, 140, 141, 142, 143, 146, 148, 149, 151, 153–54, 156, 167–92 passim

Stevens, Works (cont'd.)
— "Life on a Battleship," 145–46
— "Like Decorations in a Nigger Cemetery," 54, 68, 108, 112
— "Man and Bottle," 25
— "Man on the Dump, The," 56–57
— *Man with the Blue Guitar and Other Poems, The*, 96, 132–33
— "Man with the Blue Guitar, The," 5, 36, 47, 63, 87–88, 94, 95, 100, 118, 133, 146, 148
— "Men Made out of Words," 162
— "Metaphor as Degeneration," 19–20
— "Metaphors of a Magnifico," 90
— "Motive for Metaphor, The," 56, 148
— "Mountains Covered with Cats," 121
— "Mrs. Alfred Uruguay," 95–96, 151
— "Mud Master," 129
— "Mythology Reflects Its Region, A," 143, 157
— *Necessary Angel, The*, 38, 48, 80
— "News and the Weather, The," 55
— "Noble Rider and the Sound of Words, The," 6, 7, 8, 12, 13, 53, 95, 100, 133, 188 (n. 2)
— "Note on Samuel French Morse, A," 84
— "Notes toward a Supreme Fiction," xiii, 10–11, 14–15, 18, 28, 31, 33–34, 40, 43, 44, 45–46, 53, 56, 62, 70, 80, 81, 89–90, 92, 110, 113, 119, 121, 122–23, 124, 132, 134–35, 137, 138, 141, 145, 146, 148, 150–57, 161–62, 170 (n. 26), 174 (n. 28), 177–78 (n. 24), 187 (n. 45), 189 (n. 19)
— "Not Ideas about the Thing but the Thing Itself," 92, 127
— "Nuances of a Theme by Williams," 119–20
— "Of Bright and Blue Birds & the Gala Sun," 22, 123
— "Of Heaven Considered as a Tomb," 90
— "Of Mere Being," xiii, 61, 74–80, 112, 120
— "Of Modern Poetry," 6–7, 70, 73, 100, 133
— "On the Road Home," 57, 70, 95, 116, 123, 191 (n. 35)
— "Ordinary Evening in New Haven, An," 1, 2, 16–18, 28–31, 33, 44, 45, 48, 49, 51–52, 69, 82, 83, 91, 107, 124, 125, 126, 136, 143, 158, 164, 168 (n. 12), 170 (n. 25), 171 (n. 29), 173 (n. 20), 174 (n. 21), 177 (n. 19)
— *Owl's Clover*, 131, 146, 155, 189 (n. 16)
— "Paisant Chronicle," 149–50
— "Parochial Theme," 118–19
— *Parts of a World*, 96, 132–33
— "Pastor Caballero, The," 71
— "Pediment of Appearance, The," 137
— "Peter Quince at the Clavier," 42, 138, 175 (n. 5)

- "Phosphor Reading by His Own Light," 148
- "Plain Sense of Things, The," 26–28, 32, 35, 64, 65
- "Ploughing on Sunday," 114–15, 178 (n. 25)
- "Poems of Our Climate, The," 25–26, 107
- "Poem with Rhythms," 157–58
- "Poem Written at Morning," 21–22, 24
- "Poetry Is a Destructive Force," 32, 64
- "Poet That Matters, A," 39, 47, 52, 149
- "Primitive Like an Orb, A," 10–11, 44, 47–48, 50, 66, 99–100, 146–47, 163, 173 (n. 19), 188 (n. 4)
- "Pure Good of Theory, The," 133–34
- "Rabbit as King of the Ghosts, A," 114
- "Reality Is an Activity of the Most August Imagination," 101
- "Relations between Poetry and Painting, The," 2, 80, 87
- "Reply to Papini," 66
- "River of Rivers in Connecticut, The," 81–82
- "Rock, The," 2, 23, 36–37, 63, 67–71, 149, 160–61, 164, 170 (nn. 22, 23), 175 (n. 7)
- *Rock, The*, 175 (n. 7)
- "Rubbings of Reality," 45
- "Sailing after Lunch," 40–42
- "Sail of Ulysses, The," 126
- "St. Armorer's Church from the Outside," 118
- "Sea Surface Full of Clouds," 90, 131
- "Sense of the Sleight-of-Hand Man," 126, 132, 155, 162
- "Snow Man, The," 63–66, 68, 88
- "So-and-So Reclining on Her Couch," 6, 8–10, 13, 179 (n. 10)
- "Souls of Women at Night, The," 125–26
- *Souvenirs and Prophecies*, 20, 145
- "Study of Images I," 138–39, 145, 173 (n. 15)
- "Sunday Morning," 43, 53, 55, 56, 63, 106, 108–9, 115, 119, 121, 184 (nn. 18, 20), 188 (n. 3)
- "Surprises of the Superhuman, The," 108
- "Things of August," 147, 155
- "Thirteen Ways of Looking at a Blackbird," 90, 131
- "Thought Revolved, A," 29, 147
- "Three Academic Pieces," 20, 21, 92, 93, 113, 136, 179 (n. 9)
- "Two Illustrations That the World Is What You Make of It," 68, 101
- "Two or Three Ideas," 12, 40–41, 105–6, 108, 187 (n. 45)
- "Variations on a Summer Day," 121
- "Waving Adieu, Adieu, Adieu," 109
- "Well Dressed Man with a Beard, The," 61, 145

Stevens, Works (cont'd.)
— "What We See Is What We Think," 153
— "Whole Man: Perspectives, Horizons, The," 144
— "Williams," 44
— "Woman That Had More Babies than That, The," 142, 152, 163
— "World Is Larger in Summer, The," 93
Sukenick, Ronald: *Wallace Stevens: Musing the Obscure*, 77

Thoreau, Henry David, 185 (n. 29)
Transcendentalism, 3, 56–57
Trompe-l'oeil, 9

Vendler, Helen Hennessy, x, 26–27; *On Extended Wings*, 18–19, 28, 54, 124; *Wallace Stevens: Words Chosen Out of Desire*, 173 (n. 17)
Verene, D. P., 127
Vidal, Paule, 181 (n. 17)

Waggoner, Hyatt H.: *American Poets*, 19
Weil, Simone: *La Pesanteur et la Grâce*, 2–6
Whitman, Walt, 53–56
Wilbur, Richard, 171 (n. 28)
Williams, William Carlos, 44–45; *Paterson*, 45
Wordsworth, William, 42, 43, 45–46

Yeats, William Butler, 79
Young, Edward, 38

www.ingramcontent.com/pod-product-compliance
Lightning Source LLC
Chambersburg PA
CBHW010833230426
43671CB00018BA/2949